The Activist Leader

THE ACTIVIST LEADER

A New Mindset for Doing Business

Jon Miller and Lucy Parker

WILLIAM COLLINS

William Collins
An imprint of HarperCollins*Publishers*
1 London Bridge Street
London SE1 9GF

WilliamCollinsBooks.com

HarperCollins*Publishers*
Macken House,
39/40 Mayor Street Upper,
Dublin 1, D01 C9W8
Ireland

First published in Great Britain in 2023 by William Collins

1

Copyright © Lucy Parker and Jon Miller 2023

A catalogue record for this book is available from the British Library

ISBN 978-0-00-856751-4 (Hardback)
ISBN 978-0-00-856752-1 (Trade paperback)

Typeset in Sabon MT by Palimpsest Book Production Ltd,
Falkirk, Stirlingshire

Printed and Bound in the UK using
100% Renewable Electricity at CPI Group (UK) Ltd

This book is produced from independently certified FSC™ paper
to ensure responsible forest management.

For more information visit: www.harpercollins.co.uk/green

The Activist Leader

Contents

PROLOGUE

We are writing about a new kind of leadership in business. The urgency with which that's needed is plain for everyone to see and is probably why you're reading this book right now.

Our proposition is simple: to be a successful business leader in today's world you are expected to deliver societal value alongside financial value. Not one at the expense of the other.

And doing that takes a new mindset: the ability to think like an activist about the role your business plays in the world. We live in a time of growing crises, and we need business leaders who are capable of recognising these new realities, who understand where they fit in and what they need to do to help.

But most business leaders still don't think like this. They have grown up through their careers in a different paradigm. They are confident and capable in delivering financial value. Delivering social value as well feels an alien idea; antithetical almost.

That's a problem for the world, and a problem for business, too: the critical issues facing society are becoming critical business issues. They come from all angles and they keep coming. Companies are expected to have a credible response on these challenges and the consequences of getting it wrong can be fierce. That's created a new kind of jeopardy for business leaders and demands a whole new set of capabilities.

For more than a decade now, we've worked with leaders in many types of business, in many sectors and all over the world – helping them to make this mindset shift. We've seen how it redefines their leadership.

Harnessing the problem-solving power of your business to tackle the issues in society is energising. It strengthens your sense of purpose. And it can bring you closer to being the kind of leader you hoped to be.

That's what this book is about. We will focus on *how*: *how to think about it* and *how to go about doing it*. It's not theoretical. This is happening already, and we'll introduce you to some businesses and business leaders who are doing pioneering work.

Most people when they look at the problems facing the world feel powerless – but if you're a leader in a big business today, you're *not* powerless. This new mindset can animate your leadership, and have a transformative impact – for you, for your business and for broader society.

I.

Why We Need a New
Kind of Business Leader

1.

The Activist Mindset

Corporations know all about activism – usually because they're in the firing line of activist campaigns. Few companies these days haven't been targeted by climate protestors or environmental groups, and many have faced consumer campaigns on everything from animal welfare to LGBTQ+ equality. It doesn't stop there: more and more companies are finding themselves the target of *employee activism* on societal issues – walkouts, leaks, petitions and public statements. And in recent years the phenomenon of *shareholder activism* has become the stuff of CEO nightmares. If you're a business leader today, you're more likely to be the target of activism rather than an activist. This book is an invitation to switch that around. What if business leaders were the activists?

For many people, the phrase 'activist leader' might conjure heroic images of historical figures – perhaps from the American civil rights movement, such as Martin Luther King; some may think of an LGBTQ+ activist such as Harvey Milk, who became mayor of San Francisco; or an environmental activist such as Rachel Carson, whose book *Silent Spring* prompted the green movement of the 1960s. It may even bring to mind political activists such as Václav Havel of the Czech Republic, or Nelson Mandela of South Africa – both of whom became presidents after freeing their countries from the grip of oppressive regimes. These individuals became icons of modern history – indeed, many would describe them as history-makers. They are dramatic examples of the power of activism to change the world and in these archetypes are some clues about the activist mindset.

You may be wondering, what does all this have to do with running a business? After all, corporate leaders aren't generally hired to change the world, but to build a successful and growing business. Here, we're not talking about giving up the day job and devoting your life to social causes; we're talking about approaching your day job with a different mindset. And these archetypes of activism give us useful clues about this mindset: these are people who see vividly what needs to change, they believe they can do something about it, and they mobilise others around them to make that happen.

The elision of *business* and *activism* runs counter to the usual state of play, bringing together two worlds that are usually taken to be at odds with each other. Indeed, targeting businesses has become the mainstay of many *NGO activist* groups. For example, environmental activists have long aimed their campaigns at brands: Apple on e-waste, Shell on climate, Unilever on palm oil, Primark on toxic emissions – all are examples of brands that have been the subject of such activism. The architect of many of these campaigns is Greenpeace – which itself has become an archetypal activist organisation. Their modus operandi is to pinpoint the problematic question and force attention onto it as a mechanism to catalyse change. In our work with companies we've seen how effective NGO campaigns like this can be to influence the actions of business on societal issues.

Another flavour of activism which has preoccupied many leadership teams in recent years is *shareholder activism*. These are investors who want change in the boardroom: they think a company can be run better and they intend to rattle the cage until that happens. Some shareholder activists have become feared names in the boardroom, such as Elliott Advisers and Jana Partners; they may be hedge funds, but their approach is straight out of the activists' playbook. This starts with a really clear point of view on what needs to change, and why – as *The Economist* puts it, they come armed with 'the slide deck, enumerating all the failings'[1] – and then they orchestrate sophisticated campaigns, mobilising the resources at their disposal (in their case, huge financial muscle power), aimed squarely at destabilising the status quo.

But you don't have to be an international NGO or a billion-dollar hedge fund to be an activist. Not many of us are Martin Luther King or Václav Havel. People in any walk of life may find themselves in a situation that demands action, and they rise to the moment. When you meet these stories, they are inspiring and they have a lot to teach us about the nature of activism. Take Candy Lightner, who campaigned for tougher laws after her thirteen-year-old daughter was killed by a drunk driver. But as recently as the 1980s many people drove while intoxicated, with little legal consequence. In the US, the organisation formed by Lightner, Mothers Against Drunk Driving (MADD), has dramatically changed attitudes towards drunk driving. Today, thanks in some great part to their work, most people in most countries regard drunk driving as reckless and socially irresponsible – and likely to get you thrown in jail.

Stories like this catch the public imagination because of their David and Goliath quality: the plucky underdogs who set out to challenge the status quo, to take on an issue that seems much bigger than them. Anyone who's seen the movie *Erin Brockovich* can't fail to be moved by the courage of the junior legal clerk who takes on a large gas company found to be contaminating the drinking water of a local town, pushing through a settlement for $333 million.[2] Lightner and Brockovich are both famous stories of activism – more often, individuals like this remain unsung heroes.

What emerges from stories like these is that it seems always to start when someone is struck by something that calls out for change – and the critical juncture comes when you flip from thinking '*Somebody* should do something about this' to saying '*I'm* going to do something about this'. It's a decision point, the moment you become a protagonist – one who drives forth the action. We've seen this happen with business leaders, too: something clicks, a penny drops, and they make a personal commitment to *do something* – not just discussing it but making it a part of their leadership agenda. In movies, a moment like this this is known as 'crossing the threshold'. As screenwriter Christopher Vogler puts it: 'This is the moment that the balloon goes up, the ship sails, the romance begins, the wagon gets rolling.'[3] That's when the story starts.

There are business leaders today with an activist mindset and we feature some of them in this book. In businesses big and small, in all sectors, and in different parts of the world. They're upending the usual dynamic, where corporations are always seen as the bad guys, the perpetrators, the problem in the great issues facing the world. Instead, they've set about demonstrating that it's possible to run a successful business at the same time as actively engaging with the societal issues that surround them. They're showing what it looks like when delivering financial value is brought into alignment with creating value for society. As we'll see, they provide a radical new picture of leadership in business.

People in business approach the term activism with caution. It comes loaded with connotations of implacability or unreasonableness that makes them draw back initially. And, for certain, they don't want to be seen as crusaders, distracted from delivering commercial performance. Yet even leaders of some of the biggest companies on the planet are recognising the spirit of activism that is needed in business today. 'An activist; yes. A zealot; no,' Mark Schneider, CEO of the food giant Nestlé, told us. He is acting foremost as a business leader: for him, the success of the business and the impact on the big issues are in synthesis: 'I have chosen to work in business and I have to do this *within the business.*' For Ajay Banga, former CEO of Mastercard, the phrase *activist leader* is something of a tautology. He told us:

> I think every leader ought to be an activist leader. I mean, passive leadership is a very peculiar form of leadership. Active leadership requires you to demonstrate the desire to make change happen, to make an impact on the things that matter – whether that's what matters for your employees and consumers, or on issues like inequity or climate change – or whatever you, as a leader, see are the issues for your business.

Jamie Dimon, CEO of JPMorgan Chase, America's largest bank, echoes Banga when he reflects on what the activist mindset means to him: 'Being engaged, thoughtful, willing to take on the issues.' He puts his finger on the attitude that unlocks everything else: a willingness to walk towards the challenging issues, and to engage with those who bring those challenges to the door of business. Dimon tells us:

> To me, the activist part is being prepared to say: 'you make a good point; you're right and we're going to give it some serious thought.' Then do your homework on the issue – study it. Find where the real problem is and organise around it. Once you have the right people around it, it's amazing what you can get done.

Lars Fruergaard Jørgensen, CEO of the global pharma company Novo Nordisk, talks about *pragmatic activism*:

'Activism sometimes, in its purist sense, can become too political, or get blocked by its own idealism. Corporations can bring
a pragmatism that means they are probably the organisations
that can drive most change in today's society,' he says.

Take a look at how Greenpeace spells out its approach to
driving change in a way that captures what it means to be
an activist:

> We intervene where our action is most likely to spark positive
> change . . . targeting those who have the power to make a
> difference, engaging people and communities who can
> leverage change, or working for the adoption of environmen-
> tally responsible and socially just solutions.[4]

This book is about business leaders who have something of
this impulse to 'leverage change'. Leaders who look at the societal issues around them and ask where their intervention is most
likely to spark positive change. They start by getting to grips
with the situation, understanding what's really going on. They
form a clear point of view on why change is needed and how
it might happen. They do what they can do with great imagination and also huge practicality. But they know they cannot
be the whole answer, so they mobilise others. Their clarity
creates a kind of magnetism: others are drawn to get involved,
to become part of the effort. And the strength of their commitment becomes a source of great inner resilience: they're not
easily deterred but take the inevitable setbacks as part of the
journey – and they keep going. Taken together, we call these
traits *the activist mindset*.

These may sound like extraordinary qualities – and many
activists achieve extraordinary things – but these instincts are
in us all. More and more, we meet people in business who
exhibit these qualities. They look at where their business fits in

the context of big societal issues and trends in the world, and not only through the lens of corporate interests. They look at a longer time horizon, not only through the narrow focus on near-term outcomes – quarterly results, seasonal sales figures, next week's headlines. They shift from the 'winner-takes-all' mentality – where shareholder value comes at the expense of other stakeholders – and think about how creating shareholder value can also create value for society. And instead of seeing social issues only as potential threats to the business, they seek them out as opportunities to create value. Simply put, it's a longer, broader view of business leadership.

A few years ago, businesses began speaking out on hot issues in the public arena, on topics such as racial justice, or gun control, or immigration, making statements, signing pledges, using their voice. It prompted a rash of articles in the business media about what was dubbed 'CEO activism'. The Harvard Business Review published a thoughtful article called 'The New CEO Activists', placing this trend in a US political context.[5] Many companies began asking us for guidance on what they should speak up on, and how. As politics has become more polarised and the public information space ever more noisy, the trend has intensified.

From war in Ukraine to Roe vs Wade in the US, the pressure to have something to say about some of the most fractious fault lines in society is growing. Of course, using your voice on an issue can be a powerful contribution. But, as numerous businesses have found, the risk is being seen as performative, merely posturing – unless the words are backed up with substantive action. People, and especially employees, are asking where the business stands: they're not looking for words, or even policy, they want to understand what the company is doing on these issues. Business leaders today need to anticipate the challenge and to get onto the front foot, to be ready to meet what's coming.

If you've spent much time on the inside of a corporation, you'll appreciate that this is a stark contrast from the default mentality in traditional businesses – what we call the *corporate mindset*, which we describe in more detail later on. The distinction is redolent of the difference between a *growth mindset* and a *fixed mindset*, identified by education psychologist Dr Carol Dweck of Stanford University in her investigation of why some people fail and others succeed at school. The fixed mindset is averse to the possibility of failure, hides flaws or mistakes and responds to criticism as an attack. On the other hand, the growth mindset, associated with greater success, is more likely to embrace challenges and possible failures, and accepts setbacks as part of the learning process.[6] These mindsets show up in business, too: the former is like a description of much that's frustrating about corporate life – especially for people in it. It's also what makes companies reluctant to engage seriously with difficult societal issues. The growth mindset describes businesses at their best – adaptive, innovative and capable of seeing things in new ways. It makes it possible for them to look at societal challenges and think, *we can do something here* – for the issue, and for the business.

The corporate mindset says: let's stay with the pack. Let's wait and see – wait for the regulators, wait for public pressure, wait for our competitors to move. Let's not stick our neck out. The idea of becoming an activist can seem like an anathema – absurd, even. But things have changed: given the scale and intensity of the crises facing the world – and the central role of business in many of them – the risk of *not* getting involved outweighs the risk of getting involved.

We're now at a point where the greatest enemy of change isn't doing nothing, it's doing simply the minimum. The climatologist Michael E. Mann uses the term *inactivism* to capture the growing sense that *not* being active on these issues is equivalent to positively holding things back.[7] On the climate crisis, he argues, the real blockers to driving change are no longer the shady practitioners of climate denial and disinformation – the science has largely prevailed. Inactivism is the real blocker: checking the boxes with an attitude of compliance, or finding reasons to do something but stopping short of doing enough. When the Organisation for Economic Co-operation and Development (OECD) spelt out the 'consequences of inaction' on climate change, they warned that 'the severity of these impacts will depend on how much we act now'.[8] Almost every corporate has some form of plan to make progress on environmental and social issues but it's the activist leaders among them who ask, *what will it take to make the change that's needed?*

There's a new cultural force behind the idea of activism. Everywhere you look, the idea is alive in the popular imagination. And business is on the receiving end of much of that intense energy. But there are many people in businesses who feel that force as well and who see the opportunity to own that spirit of activism for themselves. And working in the massive organising force that business represents, they see that they're not powerless in this situation.

Maybe you're in the early stages of your working life, or maybe you're the CEO – either way the invitation in this book is the same: can you become the type of leader in business that the world needs now? That question is relevant wherever you sit in a business: you may be on the executive team or the board, but maybe you're in R&D or procurement, a data analyst or a strategy director, you may head up the operations or manage the people in the business, maybe you talk to consumers or investors – all those roles play their part in this story.

This isn't a question of deciding whether or not the business should be involved in these issues, but about *how*. Businesses are intrinsically involved in the climate crisis, the collapse of biodiversity, the growing mountains of waste and soaring levels of inequality – issues for society which have become critical issues for business. In this book, we will see examples of companies that are trying to break out of the fixed, corporate mindset and find new ways to act on these issues that help to drive the growth mindset. We will meet some of the leaders in these businesses – at all levels in business, in all corners of corporations – who are bringing dimensions of the activist mindset into their leadership.

There are different styles of activism and we thought it might be informative to explore what kinds of activist there are out there. Drawing on the classic personality types of Keirsey, Eysenck and Myers-Briggs, and researching the lives of activists we admire, we've identified five archetypes, each capturing different aspects of the activist character, presented below. We're not proposing a scientific model here but offering it as stimulus to your own thinking. You might feel that more than one applies to you; and different archetypes may apply at different points in your career. Activists tap into their own strengths, whatever those may be. They're not thrusting themselves forward for the sake of being in the limelight; their power is drawn from the fact that they are working in the service of something bigger than themselves. And most of them didn't think of themselves as activists; they simply set out to create change because they saw the need for change.

What kind of activist leader are you?

The Fixer

Many activists are natural problem-solvers: they apply practical and organisational skills to an issue in a direct 'hands-on' way. They see what needs doing, and just get on and do it. A great example of The Fixer in action is Jean-Henri Dunant: in 1859, he was on a business trip and witnessed the carnage following the Battle of Solferino. He took the initiative, organised people from the local town to provide assistance to the injured, purchased supplies and organised a makeshift hospital. He went on to be the co-founder of the Red Cross.

If you're the kind of person who cannot simply 'walk by' but will roll up your sleeves and get involved, you're probably a Fixer. You'll likely have a practical, fact-based, data-driven style, with fast and effective organisational skills. However, your get-stuff-done approach may come at the expense of new thinking, and you may have trouble dealing with chaos and uncertainty.

The Mobiliser

For some, activism is about mobilising available resources, connecting with others, creating a sense of a movement. They have a strong and creative understanding of what levers they can pull, of how they can make one plus one equal more than two. Peter Benenson brings The Mobiliser archetype to life: in 1960, the pinstriped lawyer was on his daily commute when he read a story of two Portuguese students jailed for raising a toast to 'liberty'. He set up a campaign to show the world was watching. He went on to found Amnesty International.

If you have the ability to get things moving, to effectively harness resources, you might be a Mobiliser. This means you'll probably have strong interpersonal skills to rally support, excellent 'organisational intelligence' and an ability to 'make things happen'. But you may be easily bored by routine tasks and administration and you may sometimes find it hard to stay focused.

📢 The Campaigner

This is many people's idea of an activist: out there advocating for change, putting it on the agenda and directing attention to it. Take Margaret Sanger, for example: she was a nurse in the slums of New York's Lower East Side. She saw families kept in poverty by the lack of birth control, and became a campaigner for change. She opened the first birth control clinic, but was arrested for distributing 'obscene' information. The subsequent trial ignited a public debate, and her efforts led eventually to the legalisation of contraception in the US.

If you're drawn to speaking up for what needs to change, you may be a Campaigner. A typical Campaigner is charismatic and persuasive, with a strong sense of justice. They have high 'cognitive empathy' scores – a natural sense for the perspectives of others. But watch out: Campaigners can sometimes come across as naïve or unrealistic, and they're prone to burn-out.

The Pathfinder

Pathfinders redefine what's possible: they find a way – or make one. Where others might get stuck in old paradigms, Pathfinders dream up new ones – reframing old problems, challenging the status quo, making new things possible. Mohammad Yunus is a great example: a young economist in Bangladesh, he was convinced that access to credit could alleviate the poverty that surrounded him – but the banks would do nothing to help. He resolved to find a way, and pioneered the concept of *microcredit* – for which he was awarded the Nobel Peace Prize.

If you're the kind of person who believes *there-just-has-to-be-a-way*, you're a Pathfinder. Bold, practical and innovative, Pathfinders are sharp-minded original thinkers, self-confident individuals drawn to difficult challenges. However, you can be impatient with those who easily accept limits and your intense focus can become 'tunnel vision'. Watch out that your self-belief doesn't look like arrogance.

🌉 The Bridge-builder

Some activists create change by bringing people together: mediating between the conflicting agendas of multiple stakeholders, finding common goals and facilitating shared solutions. An example of a Bridge-builder is Scilla Elworthy: in the 1980s, during the height of the Cold War, she regularly brought together nuclear policymakers from both sides, creating a 'safe space' for them to get to know each other and explore the possible terms of treaties. It is a recognised contribution to averting conflict, and Elworthy was nominated three times for a Nobel Prize.

If you're a natural Bridge-builder, you're probably a good listener and natural negotiator, with strong 'cognitive empathy'. You're idealistic and optimistic – which gives you great resilience and perseverance. Bridge-builders may sometimes be very 'big picture' at the expense of detail; they can be too quick to trust and often too conflict-avoidant.

2.

A Time of Multiple Crises

Most of us are acutely aware of the issues facing the world. Our task in this book isn't to put the case for activism – the *why* – but to look at what it takes to make a difference – the *how*. But in this chapter we pause to look at the *why*.

We're talking about issues where businesses play an inherent role – through their manufacturing processes, through their workforces, their supply chains, through the products or the services they take to market, their footprint in the world. The emphasis varies from sector to sector, but for all businesses this is about the climate crisis, and about acute levels of inequality. If you're a leader in a healthcare company, it's likely also to be about affordability of medicines; if you're in a consumer goods company, it might be plastic waste in the ocean, or the sourcing of an ingredient such as palm oil. Businesses in the tech sector are dealing with the issue of online harms; food companies, the nutritional quality of their products; mining companies, their treatment of toxins in the natural environment around their sites. These are issues in which businesses are implicated as being more often part of the problem rather than the solution. They are the impact of the collective actions of business – and the world is looking to businesses to get on the case and do their part.

There are other kinds of issues, too. As the world was rocked by the Russian invasion of Ukraine in 2022, it quickly became clear that companies wouldn't be able to sit on the sidelines: people expected them to take a clear position. And not just the oil and gas companies that were most entwined with the Russian economy – even consumer goods companies felt the pressure. Pretty soon, companies of all kinds were pulling out of Russia and having to deal with the knock-on consequences and complexities of that on their operations. Some proactively provided support to Ukraine, finding practical ways of applying their core capabilities to the situation on the ground – such as food companies working on emergency supply logistics, or agricultural companies supporting the planting season for Ukraine's crops. Twitter released a service to help Russian users evade censorship.[1] Hilton provided a million room nights to Ukrainian refugees across Europe.[2] And many businesses made philanthropic contributions to humanitarian relief efforts. Such a stark situation demands an unequivocal response. But this isn't the kind of issue that we have in mind when we talk about activism in business: it didn't result from the actions of business and isn't likely to be resolved by the actions of business.

When covid took hold, a similar pattern played out in the business world. Companies had much to do to cope with the operational hit, some had know-how and resources that were particularly relevant and turned them to the public good. Many, many businesses offered humanitarian support. As companies and as individuals, people wanted to find ways to respond and help. As the Ukraine war has done, the pandemic highlighted how important a part businesses play in society and the communities where they operate. But these situations are not a consequence of business operations and, ultimately, cannot be solved by it.

The proposition here is that companies in today's world must deliver social value alongside financial value and, therefore, the issues that we concern ourselves with in this book are those where the operations of the business play an intrinsic part in that issue. And it's a two-way street because, at some point, these issues become a problem for the business. This is the concept of *double materiality*, which is at the front edge of the conversation about ESG (see p. 250) and which looks not only at the impact of the issue on the business – the traditional concern of ESG – but also the impact of the business on the issue. Many of these are urgent issues for the world, and will become existential threats to business.

So we begin with a clear, shared view of the challenges – their urgency, scale and interconnectedness. Few people reading this will be unaware of them – most likely they're the reason they picked up the book in the first place. Each is the focus of multiple NGO reports, of academic studies, major conference platforms, and a constant stream of data and news flow. They are not remote, future scenarios, or threats that will manifest themselves at some point over the horizon. These issues aren't 'out there' beyond the business; they go right to the heart of a company's ability to operate. Below, we share a brief snapshot of the statistics and scenarios that are driving the debate – the hard facts pushing these issues up the global agenda.

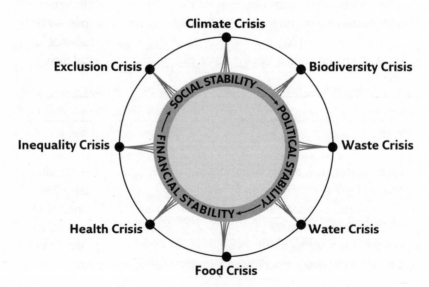

Figure 1: A time of multiple crises

Climate Crisis

First and foremost, there is the *Climate Crisis*. We know that climate change is accelerating: the planet has warmed by just over 1°C since the industrial revolution, and most of that warming has taken place since 1975.[3] The impacts are already evident: the ice caps are melting, the sea is rising – getting warmer and more acidic. The frequency and intensity of extreme weather events is increasing: hotter heatwaves, stronger storms, longer droughts, more floods. In 2021, rainfall was recorded for the first time ever at the highest point on Greenland's ice sheet,[4] and in 2022 temperatures in Antarctica jumped more than 40°C above normal.[5] We are becoming worryingly used to climate change smashing meteorological records.

Biodiversity Crisis

Then there is the associated *Biodiversity Crisis*. 28% of all species are threatened with imminent extinction – including 41% of all amphibians and 26% of mammals.[6] 40% of all insects species are declining globally and a third of them are endangered.[7] Scientists call it 'the Sixth Extinction': species are going extinct 1,000 times faster than background rates typical of Earth's past.[8] The doomsday scenario here is global ecosystem collapse – and scientists are warning that we are pushing past the resilience of ecosystems towards a 'tipping point' of sudden and radical disruption.

Waste Crisis

Food waste, e-waste, chemical waste, plastic waste – growing levels of global consumption are leading to a growing *Waste Crisis*. The volume of plastic entering the ocean annually is forecast to triple in the next twenty years.[9] By 2050 this would mean that, by weight, there will be more plastic in the planet's waters than fish.[10] We are all walking around with microplastics in our organs: some people may be ingesting a credit card's worth of microplastics each year.[11] About 53 million tonnes of apparel gets produced every year – more than 70 per cent of that ends up in landfills or on bonfires.[12] Aside from the sheer *waste* of all this waste (a huge inefficiency on a resource-constrained planet), scientists are warning that the associated ecotoxicity represents a 'potentially catastrophic risk to humanity' through effects on fertility, cognition and food safety.[13]

Water Crisis

Changes in climate and in land use are driving a *Water Crisis*. Already two billion people live in countries experiencing water stress.[14] Melting glaciers in the Himalayas and the Andes threaten the water supplies for hundreds of millions of people.[15] Lake Chad – recently the sixth largest lake in the world, and a primary source of water for Chad, Nigeria, Niger and Cameroon – has shrunk by 90%.[16] And water security is expected to become a serious challenge even in temperate climates: globally, the gap between water supply and demand is projected to reach 40% by 2030.[17]

Food Crisis

An effect of climate change, biodiversity loss and water scarcity is the *Food Crisis*. In 2020, nearly one in three people in the world (2.37 billion) did not have access to adequate food.[18] Rising sea temperatures, ocean acidification and overfishing are pushing global fish stocks towards collapse. Soil acidification and temperature rises are leading to reduced crop yields for the major global food staples – maize, soybeans, rice and wheat. More than half of the world's topsoil has been lost.[19] And, of course, there are bees: 75% of our food supply relies on pollinators,[20] and yet more than 40% of bee species is at risk of extinction, and the mysterious Colony Collapse Disorder is being reported around the world; in the US, annual rates of colony loss hit 45.5% in 2021.[21]

Health Crisis

The global *Health Crisis* has multiple facets, alongside the covid pandemic and the threat of other novel viruses. Levels of both chronic undernutrition[22] and chronic diseases associated with obesity and unhealthy diets are increasing.[23] Mental health – anxiety and depression, as well as dementia – are at record levels.[24] Health systems globally are struggling under these pressures, even in advanced economies: for example, in Europe. hospitals are reporting severe staffing shortages,[25] and in the US, twenty-seven million people lack health insurance.[26] Pollution is now a leading cause of death – responsible for one in five deaths in 2018.[27] Then there is the growing spectre of antibiotic resistance, which the WHO refers to as 'one of the biggest threats to global health'.[28]

Inequality Crisis

Cutting across all these challenges is the growing global *Inequality Crisis*. Although inequality between countries has fallen, it's well documented that inequality *within countries* is on a steep upward trajectory.[29] In most countries, the gap between rich and poor is at record levels in terms of distribution of income and wealth. We've become used to dramatic headlines about inequality – telling us, for example, that the world's 2,153 billionaires have more wealth than 4.6 billion people,[30] or that just three people – Bill Gates, Jeff Bezos and Warren Buffett – own as much wealth as the entire bottom half of the US population.[31] Meanwhile, extreme poverty is getting worse across the globe – exacerbated by the pandemic. Even in advanced economies, poverty is a growing concern: in the UK, for example, more than half of people living in poverty are in a working family,[32] and 43% of people using foodbanks in the US are from working households.[33] According to the OECD, inequality is now an issue at a 'tipping point'.[34]

Exclusion Crisis

As economic inequalities grow, a deep-rooted *Exclusion Crisis* is becoming more exposed. There is increasing evidence of the systematic exclusion of large populations based upon their race, ethnicity or gender, as well as characteristics such as sexual orientation, gender identity, religion, disability or socio-economic status. Deep social inequities show up as reduced access to healthcare, to education, to financial services, to digital services and even to food and clean water. Often this is compounded by lack of access to justice and basic human rights. The killing of George Floyd in 2020 ignited a global wave of *Black Lives Matter* protests demanding immediate action on racism. His tragic last words, 'I can't breathe', seemed to speak for millions who feel there's no room for them in our current system.

It doesn't require a huge imaginative leap to see the implications of these multiple crises on social, political and financial stability. Climate-related shortages of food and water, and resultant mass population displacement, are examples of destabilising effects – and are already happening. Inequality can also lead to devastating consequences: so often in history we've seen that acute inequalities lead to demagogue leaders, and to wars. Russia today is a case in point, the most unequal of all the world's major economies,[35] and around the world we're seeing how the rise of inequality is driving the rise of populist authoritarian politicians.

The global agenda is dominated by these issues. The World Economic Forum's *Global Risks* report sets out the top threats that business leaders should have on their radarscreens. And the emergence of ESG as an investor priority grows out of an awareness that many of these critical societal issues are already critical business issues. The UN's *Sustainable Development Goals* aim to create a consensus on what needs to happen and to mobilise action. The concept of *Planetary Boundaries* sets out the environmental limits within which we need to keep if we're to have a sustainable future.

None of this is likely to be new information. The point of outlining these multiple crises is not to present a catalogue of catastrophe, but to invoke a shared sense of the scale and urgency of global challenges.

A new reality for business leaders

The concept of 'wicked problems' was described in the 1970s by a pair of urban planners, Horst Rittel and Melvin Webber, who contrasted them with 'tame' problems: fixing a broken traffic light is a tame problem; urban regeneration is a wicked problem.[36] Tame problems are like a maths equation or a crossword puzzle – there's a right and wrong answer; you win or you lose. Wicked problems are difficult even to define precisely.

The crises described here are all wicked problems. As we write, the world is having to deal with the conflict in Ukraine – war is perhaps the ultimate example of a wicked problem. Not only are the variables complex and the uncertainty extreme, but the stakes couldn't be higher. And just as times of war call forth leaders who can rise to meet the moment – as we've seen with Volodymyr Zelenskyy, the actor and comedian turned President – so this age of global crises demands a new kind of leadership, from each of us.

Often on the inside of a company, the rationale for stepping up to tackle these issues is expressed in terms of a new level of expectation coming from all stakeholders – and that new demand is in itself a reality. Yet the question that lies behind that is: what's driving those stakeholders? For a leader with an activist view, the impetus comes from the issues themselves. Together these issues are entirely reshaping the context in which businesses will operate, and it means that today's business leaders face a different reality from their predecessors. Running a large company today is a very different experience and requires a new kind of mindset.

The default perspective in business has been to see these crises as *somebody else's job*. If you're a leader with an activist mindset, you'll look at these issues and see perhaps they're part of *your* job. You see the reality of these crises, that some things need to change. You grasp that your business is intrinsically connected to many of these issues – and therefore you can be part of creating real change.

3.

A New Business Imperative

Companies keep getting bigger and more profitable while the issues keep getting more urgent and intractable. This level of misalignment is, literally, unsustainable: so the pressure from stakeholders will continue to grow and with it the demand for real and visible action from business. The business world is realising it needs leaders who can grasp that challenge and turn what is a threat into an opportunity.

We often get asked, simply, *what's going on?* By boards, who are registering new expectations from investors and want to understand what's driving this. By leadership teams, who are facing new pressures from employees and consumers and want to understand these changing dynamics. By operational teams, who seek to understand the nature of the change they need to deliver. By CEOs, who sense that fundamental shifts are happening, and want to understand how to get ahead of them. These are all seasoned players in the business world, they know how to play the game – but they're all picking up on a continuous stream of signals that the rules have changed.

The sacking of Rio Tinto CEO Jean-Sébastien Jacques in 2020 was a sure signal that new rules apply:[1] the boss of one of the world's most powerful companies was ousted by an outcry from indigenous groups in Australia, following the destruction of sacred Aboriginal sites. He left the company by 'mutual agreement' with the board, following intense pressure from groups of investors – who sided with the traditional First Nation landowners. A decade ago, it would have been difficult to imagine such a captain of industry brought down by an issue like this. But these days it cannot be treated as the marginal concern of a marginal community. Things are changing.

Many were surprised to see Carl Icahn, a man with a reputation as one of Wall Street's most ruthless investors, launch a campaign to change the way McDonald's treats pigs. It was a coming together of shareholder activism and social activism – a potent combination. Interestingly, it's reported to be at the behest of his daughter, Michelle, that he took up the cause.[2] We regularly hear business leaders tell us they are assailed at their kitchen table by younger members of their family on societal issues. Younger consumers, in particular, are quick to punish companies that are perceived to be causing social or environmental harm. And you're just as likely to be cancelled for something you *don't* say or do. A new generation is demanding new things of business.

The phenomenon of employee activism is another signal of the shift underway. In a number of companies it's risen to become externally visible, and on a broad range of issues – including racial justice, gender equality, recycling and child labour. When employees at Amazon took to the streets to protest the company's climate change position, their banners didn't suggest an incremental improvement in the reduction of carbon emissions; they called for 'Climate Leadership'.[3] A particularly striking moment was when more than 7,500 Amazon employees backed a shareholder resolution requesting the company to put forward a comprehensive climate action plan.[4] The resolution was voted down, but even so it marked a new wave of increasingly sophisticated employee action on societal issues.

Find yourself on the wrong side of the story and the fallout can be brutal. You become the clickbait of the day, a political football, pulled into polarised agendas. Consumers may abandon you – or even organise boycotts. Employees become disaffected, and top talent looks elsewhere. Your reputation is shredded and the share price plummets. Almost overnight, a respectable CEO becomes a social pariah. All of this may sound extreme, but such are the times in which we live. And business leaders are waking up to this.

Power dynamics have changed. The very structure of a corporation has changed: a modern company runs through a series of complex networks, with multifaceted connections to the outside world. Running a successful business today means working with a vast web of inter-relationships. The notion that there's a clearly delineated 'inside' and 'outside' of a company has become less relevant, and leadership teams are no longer 'in control' in the way they once were. Meanwhile, those who once had little power can find themselves with considerable clout. In their bestseller *New Power*, Jeremy Heimans and Henry Timms describe the shift from 'old power', which can be accumulated like capital, to 'new power', which is more like a current: 'Like water or electricity, it's most forceful when it surges. The goal with new power is not to hoard it but to channel it.'[5]

Businesses are increasingly finding themselves on the receiving end of these new power surges. Often, this is met by an old corporate instinct to try and retain a sense of neutrality – but that's not effective in the face of global movements like #MeToo or Black Lives Matter, or on contentious issues like immigration or transgender rights. When rioters stormed the Capitol, people wanted to know whether corporates would pull their donations to politicians who inflamed the situation by denying the election results. When Russia invaded Ukraine, the world watched as some companies were quick to withdraw from Russia and others appeared to vacillate. When the Supreme Court overturned Roe vs Wade, employees wanted to know how companies would support workers who needed an abortion. In this hyperconnected world, as Heimans and Timms call it, they identify what they call a 'new expectation: an inalienable right to participate'. They explain new power as 'more flash mob than United Nations', contrasting it to 'the twentieth-century belief in managerialism and institutionalism as the way to get things done'. More than ever before, business leaders are expected to have a swift response to developments that burst onto the public stage – but more than that, they have to learn to take on these topics in new and, to them, counterintuitive ways.

There's a wholly new level of energy in the corporate stakeholder base, driven by the intensity of societal issues. And leadership teams are asking themselves what they should do about it. They know their response can't be performative: nobody wants to be accused of green-washing, pink-washing, purpose-washing, woke-washing. How to take credible action on the issues that concern the world, steering a path through the competing demands of multiple stakeholders, while keeping the business on track, is a new imperative.

All this comes on top of the challenges that their predecessors faced, which are still around: market disruption, digital transformation, the race for innovation, the war for talent. While handling all that, leaders now also face the urgent demand to respond to the crises facing the world. This is universal, it applies to all business, of all kinds, in all sectors, and in all geographies. Many business leaders we speak to intuitively grasp this. They know they have to act. As one board chair recently told us, 'Businesses are very simple – we only do things when we have to. And these days, we have to!'

The case for action

Sometimes we're asked for the business case for acting – to which we are sometimes tempted to reply, 'show us the business case for *not* acting'. Nevertheless, taking on these issues in a meaningful way is a significant commitment for a company and so there must be a comprehensive commercial basis for acting. In the broadest sense, that rationale is clear: ultimately, the viability of business depends upon the stability of the systems that enable its operations. In plain-speak, businesses can't function in societies and systems that are broken. As the protestors' placards remind us, there are no profits on a dead planet. At the macro-level, this is the commercial argument for action – you could even call it an existential imperative.

Businesses need to make money; otherwise they go under. So the question here is not whether businesses should take on societal issues *instead of making profits*; it's how to think about taking greater action, faster, on societal issues *in order to sustain profitability* for the long term. So any business will want to understand the costs and benefits of a specific course of action, as for any other strategic move they might make.

Fortunately, the case for businesses to engage with environmental and social issues is now a well-researched topic, which wasn't the case when we started advising companies in this area a decade ago. The major business schools, the big consultancies, the management thinkers and the business media all regularly look at this. Whether they're coming at it as an ESG question, or sustainability, or CSR, or purpose, lots of individuals and organisations are investigating links between social value and financial value.

Some common themes emerge: everyone agrees it helps to engage and motivate employees, and it attracts and retains talent. It resonates with consumers – especially next-generation consumers. It can help control costs, lower cost of capital and underpin return on equity. This may sound like a sort of corporate utopia, too good to be true. But evidence is mounting of the commercial benefits along all these dimensions. There are dozens of studies in this area, with new ones coming out all the time. Here's a snapshot of typical findings:

- 65 per cent of employees want to work for an organisation with a strong social conscience.[6]
- 87 per cent of employees say that the business they work for should take a public position on societal issues relevant to their business.[7]
- 54 per cent of consumers have reduced or stopped purchasing from organisations they believe have acted inappropriately on environmental and social issues.[8]
- Gen Z consumers say environmental and social performance is the top factor in whether they say good things about a company or trust it.[9]
- 85 per cent of investors now factor ESG criteria into their decisions.[10]
- A strong ESG score translates into a 9 per cent lower cost of capital.[11]
- Effective ESG execution can help combat rising operating expenses with the potential to affect operating profits by as much as 60 per cent.[12]

This last datapoint comes from McKinsey, who looked at the increase of regulatory pressure on a whole raft of societal issues and they estimated that 'the value at stake may be higher than you think': by their analysis, typically one-third of corporate profits are at risk from state intervention. Overall, McKinsey's meta-analysis of research in this area concludes that companies that pay attention to environmental, social and governance concerns 'do not experience a drag on value creation – in fact, quite the opposite': 63 per cent of studies showed positive findings, against only 8 per cent of negative findings.[13] Historically, for many business leaders the assumption has been that a company's sustainability initiatives are a cost on the company's performance, so the new proliferation of data that point towards business benefits has been a big shift in recent years. Every company and each situation will have its own distinct rationale, and it's likely to include some mix of those risks and benefits.

Some would say, however, that the data is not completely persuasive: believers talking up their own book. Though new studies come through all the time, they are scattered, not comparable and not yet comprehensive. In *Reimagining Capitalism*, Harvard's Professor Rebecca Henderson has an interesting angle on that, turning the logic on its head. She observes that, taken as a whole, the evidence that performance against ESG criteria can be correlated with financial performance is not conclusive – yet, she says it is 'hugely encouraging, since it suggests that, at the very least, firms trying to do the right thing are not underperforming their competitors'.[14] In today's context in which many shy away from ESG, fearing it represents a direct trade off against financial performance, she argues that the evidence provides, at minimum, reassurance that ESG is not a drag on competitiveness. And the way forward is not to pull back from ESG, generically, but rather to drill down into the specific and material different aspects of ESG as relevant for different businesses and generate new data on those.

And these days every business is a talent business. So the 'Great Resignation' (or the 'Big Quit') has put employee relationships at the top of the agenda for leadership teams: loss of talent is the No. 1 threat facing business, according to a survey of 500 CEOs.[15] While the stresses of covid have exacerbated the problem, this didn't start with the pandemic; it's been a trend for over a decade[16] and a global study by Gallup showed that growing employee disengagement is already having a substantial impact on productivity.[17] *Fortune*'s CEO study highlights that the great majority of employers have set about countering the trend with financial incentives which, while surely gladly accepted, turns out not to win loyalty long term because employees are looking for different things as well. For themselves personally, they want flexibility, autonomy and development opportunities. And, on a broader canvas, the culture, values and the purpose of the organisation matter to them. Companies will find it much harder to staunch this disaffection unless they get serious about their role in society. Nobody is likely to feel much pride in or loyalty to a corporation that continues with business as usual while the global crises intensify around them. Yet, turning that around, more and more companies are discovering that to be able to demonstrate in tangible terms how they're working to contribute solutions to major societal challenges is a strong differentiator in acquiring and retaining talent.

It's also a matter of business resilience. Investors are looking for evidence that companies have a sustainable operating model for the future. The questions they ask of leadership teams have a different slant: what are their plans for mitigating operational risk, for ensuring secure raw material supply and robust supply chain capability? Are they equipped to step up to new regulatory standards coming through? Ensuring the preparedness of the business to handle the shocks emerging from climate change and other environmental challenges has become a priority – and failure to do so is from where so much reputational risk as well as operational risk springs. Increasingly, the dialogue with investors is turning towards the opportunities to be created from the way the world is changing: is there enough investment in innovation, is there a fast enough response to new consumer and customer demands, is the business positioned to take advantage of the new markets opening up from the disruptions underway?

Being able to make the business case serves to get things moving inside the business. But this isn't to pretend that there aren't costs involved and investments needed in the short and medium term; it's seldom that there's a clear line of sight to a sales uplift – much though people wish there were. And often, taking up these issues in a meaningful way leads to significant transformations in a company's operations or even an evolution of the business model. These aren't easy, quick-fix issues: they often require coming to terms with intractable trade offs, working with incomplete information, being prepared to re-base assumptions – and taking tough decisions. That's why it's a question of leadership.

Stakeholders are making new demands

Earning the trust of all the different constituencies of interest on social performance is a critical success factor for leadership in business today. Getting that right in itself forms part of the commercial imperative for action. At its best it can reinforce brand value and open up opportunities – just as failing to get it right can significantly increase risk. For many years, 'licence to operate' was a comfortable phrase in corporate conversation, usually accompanied by a tick in the box to suggest that, as a well-run business, everything was well bedded down and running smoothly. But as environmental and social crises intensify, what it takes to establish a licence to operate is changing shape. Expectations are much greater. When you look at stakeholder groups involved today, you can see new demands coming from three domains: financial, social and political.

*Figure 2: Corporate stakeholders demanding
more of business on societal issues*

Stakeholders in each of these arenas are looking to business to
become part of the solution to societal challenges:

  – In the **financial** arena, the rise of ESG reflects investor
    concerns about how societal issues can impact
    financial value. There has been a surge in investor
    expectations on ESG – and a quantum shift in
    support for ESG among the biggest investors – asking
    companies to disclose data, set targets and provide
    plans to tackle the environmental and societal issues
    that are material to their business. New international
    sustainability standards making their way through the
    system are set to change fundamentally what
    businesses measure and how they report. We look at
    the activist leader's perspective on this in The New
    Realities of ESG (p. 239).

– In the **political** arena, regulators are become
  increasingly active in response to the accelerating
  impacts of climate change and biodiversity loss, as
  well as growing levels of inequality and social
  exclusion. We're seeing a 'third wave of regulation' on
  these social issues, similar in scale to those which
  accompanied the industrial revolution and then the
  post-Second World War years. And innovative models
  of collaboration are emerging to build bridges
  between the public and private sector response to the
  big issues. Meanwhile, businesses are now under
  continual pressure to speak up on hot topics in an
  increasingly politicised and contentious public debate.
  We explore this through the lens of activist leadership
  in A Shared Agenda with Government (p. 280) and
  Politics and the Corporate Voice (p. 290).

– In the **social** arena, public pressure is channelled
  through the increasingly sophisticated work of NGOs
  and civil society organisations. From action at the
  on-the-ground at community level right through to
  the agendas of the major multi-lateral institutions,
  there's a strong impetus around tackling these issues
  and keeping them front of mind. And a new issue-
  focused, data-led breed of NGO is emerging to
  challenge the status quo by driving transparency into
  some of the most opaque areas of corporate practice.
  Meanwhile, the search for more sustainable,
  responsible options is starting to influence the
  attitudes and behaviours of consumers. But the
  concerns of stakeholders in the social sphere are no
  longer only coming from the external world. Closer
  to home for companies, employees – acting as citizens

in the workplace – are raising concerns about societal
issues and pushing their employers for a response.

It's not just the breadth of different stakeholder groups
getting involved or the energy with which they're taking on the
issues that's new; it's the intersections between different stakeholder groups: local communities alongside shareholder groups,
global NGOs working with employees, activist investors taking
up societal issues, regulatory pressure influencing investor
concerns. Most significantly, what this tells you is that the
concerns and priorities of the major constituencies of interest
are converging – new kinds of multistakeholder alignments are
forming, driven by the conviction that businesses can do something to create change.

Judy Samuelson, who at the Aspen Institute founded and
leads the Business and Society Program, like us, works closely
with business leaders as they first start to grapple with today's
big societal issues – and her observations resonate deeply with
our own experience:

> The wake-up call to the CEO comes with a swift kick in the
> rear from an aggressive campaign, or an encounter with an
> employee in the cafeteria or parking lot, or a provocative
> question at the all-hands or from his kid at the kitchen table.
> These personal experiences take executives to the heart of
> the matter. They enable change in how he or she perceives
> and calculates value – they have the power to change what
> one *believes*.[18]

Prompts and pressures to deal with these questions come
from lots of different angles. And we find that when leaders
begin to see this imperative, they quickly turn to how: 'How
do we go about doing this?'

Yet, the intensity of the issues themselves is only part of the reason that stakeholders are increasingly focused on the role of business; it's also that the nature of companies has changed. Big businesses are bigger than ever before, and with the increase in size comes an increase in their social and environmental impacts – their externalities.

Big business keeps getting bigger

To many, the phrase 'big business' sounds inherently pejorative, bringing to mind mighty industries using their power to bolster their profits at the expense of everyone and everything else. And we're not just talking about the huge corporations that dominate the headlines: their names may have become synonyms for runaway capitalism, but all business is implicated.

We've grown accustomed to the fact that many businesses today are enormous and have become an integral part of the way we live. But it hasn't always been quite like this: big businesses are getting bigger. Analysis by Barclays shows that, since 2000, market concentration has increased in three-quarters of non-financial sectors and is up by about 60 per cent.[19] Of course, if you're a leader of a business that's growing market share that's a clear picture of success. Scale is good, and more scale is better – and, as an executive who's been part of achieving that, you're probably expecting a bonus. But for the world, it's a little more complicated.

In his book *The Curse of Bigness*, law professor Tim Wu describes a range of negative impacts that arise from the growing scale of corporations – everything from reduced levels of innovation and consumer value to the undermining of democracy. His argument is that the major multinational corporations represent a 'power which is truly beyond the purview or control

of any individual nation'.[20] This is a new take on an enduring
theme: the phrase 'curse of bigness' comes from Louis Brandeis,
the nineteenth-century reformer and Supreme Court Justice who
pointed out that oligopolies such as Standard Oil and U.S. Steel
were becoming so big they were more powerful than the government. *Scale*, once again, is the dominant theme in the public
discourse about business: *big* business – *Big* Tech, *Big* Pharma,
Big Agriculture, *Big* Soda, *Big* Oil, *Big* Banks.

Many corporations have become so big that it's difficult even
to meaningfully describe their scale. We've all probably seen
comparisons with national economies – setting company revenues against countries' GDPs; although this is not comparing
like for like (they are two very different economic measures), it
still gives pause for thought: Microsoft's revenues in 2017 were
$89 billion, exceeding Slovakia's GDP at $85 billion in the same
year; Volkswagen $276 billion revenues was on a par with Chile's
GDP at $277 billion.[21]

And these big companies keep getting bigger. A key measure
of that is market capitalisation: there has been an accelerating
long-term trend upwards in big corporate valuations, which was
turbo-charged by the covid pandemic. The top fifty companies
by value added $4.5 trillion of stock market capitalisation in
2020, taking their combined worth to about 28 per cent of
global gross domestic product. This is a big change: in 1990,
the equivalent figure was less than 5 per cent.[22] A cluster of tech
companies have taken corporate scale to new heights, becoming
emblematic of the concern about the risks inherent in such a
concentration of power in a few players and the ability of the
biggest to override the systems they are part of.

Bigger companies make bigger profits, and these also show
an accelerating long-term trend upwards. In 2018 Apple declared
record profits of $60 billion, about the same as the GDP of
Costa Rica.[23] Other eye-watering profits include Nestlé – $44

billion, Citigroup – $32 billion and JPMorgan Chase – $33 billion.[24] These kinds of numbers are relatively new: in 1980, Walmart surpassed $1 billion in annual sales for the first time; today, it has worldwide revenues approaching $600 billion.[25] The company first established an international division in 1993, and now has 2.3 million employees working in approximately 10,500 stores around the world. Off the back of that expansion, Walmart's brand value has nearly doubled in the past six years alone: estimated at $54 billion in 2016, it was $112 billion in 2022.[26]

The expanding reach of big businesses isn't just seen in the megacorps. Companies that in the 1990s were national heroes in their home markets have made unprecedented investments in their international footprint to become global leaders in their sectors. Engineering business Rolls-Royce, born in the UK's industrial heartland, grew its aerospace business by supporting its airline customers as air travel grew around the world; today it has 50,000 employees, an operating presence in more than forty countries[27] and a total supply chain spend of £7 billion.[28] Pharmaceutical business Novo Nordisk, one of Denmark's largest companies, marked a milestone in 2007 when for the first time more than half its workforce was employed outside Denmark's borders[29] – now it has 47,000 employees, sales in more than 160 markets around the world and produces half the world's insulin.[30] Tech services business Wipro established a leadership position in software and services in its home market of India in the nineties and played its part in 'taking India global' following the country's economic liberalisation – and these days earns 75 per cent of its revenues from global clients.[31]

The sheer scale and speed of this growth has shaped the public imagination about business. And this 'bigness' isn't just about the size of these businesses per se, it's about all businesses.

These companies shape the markets they operate in and determine industry practices; their supply chains and distribution networks spread out to envelop all kinds of businesses, from the large international companies to local small enterprises and even the tiniest economic entities who work as retailers, distributors and smallholder farmers in communities all over the world. Whoever you are, whatever size of business, you're in their orbit. The system itself is a big business system.

The impacts of business keep getting bigger

Take any of the multiple crises in the world that we looked at in the previous chapter and it's evident that business has a part to play. On climate, for example, just 100 companies have been the source of 71 per cent of the entire world's industrial greenhouse gas emissions since 1988.[32] On waste, just four major companies are responsible for six million tons of plastic waste every year.[33] The production of just a few commodities – beef, soy, palm oil and timber – is responsible for almost three-quarters of tropical deforestation – yet the products those commodities are used in span multiple industries and thousands of companies.[34] For economists, these are examples of negative *externalities* – where the harms caused by a product or service, either in its production or consumption, are not priced into its cost. For most people, these look like examples of businesses making profits at the expense of environmental impact.

The environmental impacts of business are often obvious; it can be harder to get a grip on negative social impacts – but here, too, they are intensifying. The challenge of in-work poverty worldwide helps to illustrate the challenge: zero-hours contracts are causing households to spiral into debt; front-line employees are missing out on health benefits; workers earning less than the living wage are struggling to make ends meet. The global supply chains of big businesses contain hundreds of millions of people whose basic human rights cannot be taken for granted. The picture highlights the degree to which business models are based on assumptions that society at large will pick up the tab on those impacts.

If you want to understand how a business can deliver societal value and financial value hand-in-hand, the concept of externalities is central. The underlying source of societal concerns about business is driven in great part by negative externalities, where the activities of a business impose harms or costs on wider society, thereby destroying societal value. Mostly, business models don't take account of these impacts. The clue is in the name – they are *external* to the value creation of the business. Kate Raworth in *Doughnut Economics*, her seminal book on reshaping the economic system, writes about externalities in usefully down-to-earth, practical terms as 'those incidental effects felt by people who were not involved in the transactions that produced them – such as toxic effluent that affects communities living downstream of a river-polluting factory, or the exhaust fumes inhaled by cyclists biking through city traffic'.[35]

As industries boom, so do their externalities. This is true for all businesses, even those in industries we might presume are somehow inherently positive. Even renewable energy – at first glance, a seemingly safe bet for an ESG portfolio – is throwing off externalities. As investment in renewables grows, so does demand for the metals and minerals required by these technologies. But mining cobalt in the Congo, for example, exposes companies to corruption and child labour risk in their supply chain. Rare earth extraction has also led to water pollution and forced population displacement.[36] And in the not too distant future, spent photovoltaic modules will need disposing of. By 2050, PV waste will be around 90 million metric tons annually – twice today's total e-waste, including computers, TVs and mobile phones.[37]

The soaring demand for alternative types of milk is another example of negative externalities that took people by surprise. Concerned by the environmental impact of dairy, millions have switched to alternatives such as soy, oat and almond. Almond milk seemed to have a particularly good story on climate change: a glass of dairy milk entails six times more carbon emissions than a glass of almond milk.[38] As a consequence, demand for almonds has gone through the roof. But over 80 per cent of the world's almonds are grown in California, which has been in severe drought for most of this decade. The almond boom led to farmers ripping up relatively biodiverse citrus groves, creating a monoculture fed by increasingly deep-water wells that threaten state-wide subsidence issues.[39] The media, which never misses an opportunity to burst a bubble – very often one it has helped to create – relished the headlines: 'The deadly truth behind your almond-milk obsession'[40] and 'Lay Off the Almond Milk, You Ignorant Hipsters'.[41]

Often, externalities are the unintended consequence of a successful product that answers a real need in society. Take the inconspicuous disposable soft contact lens, a hit with consumers who value the comfort and convenience. But they're an environmental nightmare: researchers in the UK found that 780 million contact lenses are discarded every year, with only 3 per cent being recycled. Many are flushed down the toilet, adding to the risk of plastic pollution in the ocean.[42] Use of soft contact lenses is predicted to grow – and so will the impact of plastic pollution. As in so many industries and company success stories, that was not the intention, but it is one consequence.

Activist leadership is about recognising those externalities associated with your operations and the implications of them for how you do business. Traditionally, society has looked to governments and lawmakers to control these externalities – regulating and taxing negative externalities, subsidising positive externalities. But as the scale of global business grows, so does the volume of negative externalities – and social pressure has grown for companies to get to grips with their impacts on the world, and not wait to be regulated.

Businesses are integral system players

Companies have become the focus of concern not just because they are big, but because they're critical players in global systems. This is a new dimension to business leadership: running a company today means thinking not only of the performance of your own operations, but of the health of the systems of which your business is a part. And the multiple global crises are clear threats to the health of these systems – and, therefore, risks to business.

Businesses shape and mobilise the systems they operate in: food systems, health systems, energy systems, infrastructure and transport systems, technology and information systems, communication systems, financial systems. Take food, for example. Just four major corporations produce, process, transport, finance and trade the world's food. Together they account for some 90 per cent of the global grain trade;[43] and just four corporations control more than 50 per cent of the global commercial seed market.[44] The $7.5 trillion global grocery market is now dominated by a small number of major retailers: data from 2014 shows that the top ten retailers controlled nearly 30 per cent of the global grocery retail market.[45] According to a study by Oxfam,[46] only ten companies own almost every food and beverage brand in the world – Nestlé, PepsiCo, Coca-Cola, Unilever, Danone, General Mills, Kellogg's, Mars, Associated British Foods and Mondelez. With such scale, these businesses are integral parts of the global food system, and by extension, of the global food crisis.

Over the years we've been working with businesses on these issues, the focus has shifted more and more onto the systemic nature of the issues – and the role of business in those systems. Accompanying this has been a shift from top-down government-led solutions to a cross-sector approach led by the key system players. And business is so often the linchpin of those efforts, connecting together many different players in the system, with direct touchpoints across their value chains and a global reach. It's a different way to think of what it means to run a business. 'You get to a point where you realise you're not just a player in a bigger system,' one senior executive recently told us. 'You *are* the system.'

Because of their scale and dominance, decisions taken by the leaders of big businesses have consequences that radiate far beyond their own balance sheets. These companies have the power to move markets, to set standards – indeed, to shape the future, for better or worse. For those with an activist mindset, this creates the opportunity to make a difference. It's a major step beyond conventional 'responsible business' thinking: not just taking steps to improve your own company's performance on an issue, but looking at how to improve the performance of the whole system.

* * *

The new imperative facing business is calling forth a new kind of leadership intelligence. It demands an alertness to how the operating context of the business is being radically altered by the changes in the world. That requires an awareness of how and why the urgency of issues facing society are fast becoming business issues; an ability to interpret the deeper patterns and interconnections between them and, crucially, to understand where their company fits in that landscape. It means recognising that the world simply can't afford externalities at this level, so the pressure on business will build. It asks leaders to rethink the scope of their influence and create change across their ecosystems. Businesses need leaders who can rise to the massively intensified demand that's coming from dramatically diverse stakeholder groups to engage on even the toughest societal issues – and who are capable of walking into those conversations in entirely new ways.

The new imperative is reshaping the leadership agenda in business. A decade ago, societal issues and ESG were peripheral in the thinking of most leadership teams. Today, they have captured the attention of corporate leadership and finance teams and put a wide range of societal issues on board agendas. Companies have long had sustainability departments and corporate social responsibility initiatives – and typically they were worthy but incremental. There is new and formidable talent in many sustainability teams now: people who've moved from senior operational roles, or have built up deep subject matter expertise. Together, ESG and sustainability have become two sides of the same coin: ESG raising the bar on targets and transparency, and sustainability shaping the plans to deliver on those. Working in concert, they're forging a new approach to social value.

The same inescapable logic that's driving ESG and sustainability into the core of business is driving them *upwards* as well. Increasingly, CEOs are making societal issues part of how they show up as leaders. The reality, of course, is that it's their commitment that creates impetus in the business. As one sustainability director put it to us recently: 'Nothing was going to get done, no target was going to fly and no ambition was going to get signed off, if we didn't have that leadership from the CEO.' At the same time, this new imperative affects all the leaders in a business, not just the CEO: operations teams set different parameters for performance; procurement asks different questions of suppliers, marketing talks differently to consumers; R&D spends its innovation budget differently; the investor relations team considers different risks. Wherever you sit in a business and whatever your sphere of influence, how to respond to this new imperative is your question and the choices you make influence its chances of success.

The stronger this new imperative becomes, the clearer it is that many leaders in business are still approaching social value as a tick-box exercise in the traditional incremental model. There are still many businesses that lack the impetus or ambition to shift the established paradigm. That's why business needs a new kind of leader, one whose definition of value creation brings financial and social value into harness for success. And inside the company itself it takes a spirit of activism to override the norms of business to make that happen and accelerate the change that's needed for the world and for the business.

II.

How to Think
Like an Activist

How to Think
Like an Activist

If you want to make change happen in today's business world, you need to think like an activist. This section captures what we've learned about how to go about doing that and we'll show what it looks like when companies take on societal challenges with a spirit of activism.

It starts with **focus**, being clear on what matters – to you and your business. Then we look at why you need **perspective**, the ability to step outside the corporate mindset and see the issues as the world sees them. And unless you turn and face into the challenge, nothing will change – we call this making a **pivot**. As with achievements of any significance, in business or in life, everything you do will need to be fuelled by a clear **ambition** to make an impact.

Activism demands **disruption**: you will want to do something different – ask yourself 'what if we had to make this possible?'. And then the work begins: taking action in the **core** of the business, as well as driving broader **system** change; and **advocacy** – speaking up on what you're doing, and why, to mobilise others. And, finally, we show why you need **momentum** to keep going, treating every challenge and setback as a spur to further action.

This is how you think like an activist. Nine steps, each

flowing from the last – although, once you start, you'll naturally find you're doing them all at once. If you aim to create change, in your business or in the world, it starts with a change of mindset.

This is a significant journey to start on. It isn't easy but it's doable. Many leaders in business are doing it. And, once you get going, we've seen how it unlocks energy and innovation in the business, and how it can animate and elevate your leadership.

How to Think Like an Activist

① • • • • • • • • **FOCUS**: be clear what matters and why   p.63

• **②** • • • • • • • **PERSPECTIVE**: see it as the world sees it   p.77

• • **③** • • • • • • **PIVOT**:   adopt the activist mindset   p.96

• • • **④** • • • • • **AMBITION**: aim to make a real impact   p.113

• • • • **⑤** • • • • **DISRUPTION**: do something different   p.124

• • • • • **⑥** • • • **CORE**: take action in the business   p.138

• • • • • • **⑦** • • **SYSTEM**:   drive for systemwide change   p.160

• • • • • • • **⑧** • **ADVOCACY**:   find your voice on the issue   p.189

• • • • • • • • **⑨** **MOMENTUM**: get going, keep going   p.213

Dramatis personae

Over the course of the chapters that follow, we'll see a few dozen examples of companies, each bringing to life different dimensions of activism in business. These are the protagonists in this story, and you'll meet them as we go through the nine steps of *How to Think Like an Activist*.

Below are snapshots of some of these stories; our hope is that they will inspire and inform. When we feature a company, we're not holding them up as a paragon of virtue. We've chosen them because we recognise a spark of activism in each of them.

When you're reading these stories, you could be asking: is this for real? Are these companies serious about tackling the issue, or are they just covering their backs? Are they acting with ambition, or just doing the bare minimum? We all know that lots of companies do a lot of greenwashing, and anything companies say or do is subject to scepticism. Ultimately, the only credible answer to that distrust is being able to demonstrate meaningful action. And in our experience, leaders with an activist spirit welcome this level of scrutiny; indeed, they ask these tough questions of themselves.

So we're not saying that the companies comprising our *dramatis personae* don't have difficult questions to answer – indeed, for many of them, that's why they're engaging with these big questions in the first place. Neither are we saying that they have 'done enough' on the issues they are tackling – and, probably, nor would they. These are complex issues and won't be fixed easily. We're not suggesting anyone has got it all sorted – as we'll see, one of the hallmarks of the activist mindset is using the inevitable challenges and setbacks along the way as a springboard.

The examples we'll share are in different sectors, focusing on different issues, and at varying stages of maturity – some are just getting started, others have well-established programmes facing the next challenge. What you can see in each of them is the emergence of a new leadership intelligence: the ability to see what matters, and why, and to get going – and keep going

– in the search for solutions. There are moments of courage
and creativity, as well as stamina and resourcefulness. All useful
characteristics for an activist leader.

Anglo American

Mining giant Anglo American has established the world's largest
workforce initiative tackling HIV/AIDS. It was a health issue that
became a critical issue for the company, ravaging their workforce.
Over three decades, they've been on the front lines of the issue,
working to find solutions to each new hurdle as they met it – and
have become trusted experts on the issue globally.

See Momentum, p. 213

Apple

In 2018, Apple announced the ambition 'to make products without
taking from the Earth'. It sounds impossible, especially given
Apple's reliance on a metal with a big environmental footprint –
aluminium. Their solution was bold: develop a new kind of
aluminium, reinventing the way it's been produced for over a
century. In 2018 Apple launched a new MacBook, made with a
100 per cent recycled aluminium shell.

See Disruption, p. 124

Aviva

Through its role as major insurer and as a large investor, Aviva is
aiming to catalyse action on climate change, as well as setting
the pace for the industry through its own net zero targets. CEO
Amanda Blanc has been challenging business as usual in the
industry. She told us: 'If *I* can be the activist then nobody needs
to say, "you need to do more!"'

See What Makes a Leader, p. 313

bp

When Bernard Looney became CEO of bp in 2020, he announced, *I get it*: 'I get the huge frustration, the anxiety – the anger.' It was a real pivot: the company set a net zero target – including emissions from cars, homes and factories, as well as across its operations – and began the transition to an integrated energy company, helping to drive the shift to net zero.

See Pivot, p. 96

Brambles

The global logistics company Brambles has launched a programme 'Pioneering Regenerative Supply Chains'. Brambles counts many of the world's biggest consumer goods companies as customers, and partners with them 'breakthrough challenges'. In recognition of this work, they topped the Dow Jones Barron's ranking as the most sustainable company globally.

See System, p. 160

Coca-Cola

Since having been identified as the world's number one source of plastic in the ocean, Coca-Cola has become a leader in the fight against plastic waste. They made the decision to shift gear, and have been working across the system to pioneer new solutions. CEO James Quincey is clear on what it takes: 'Make it an inherent part of the business vision.'

See Core, p. 138

CVS

When CVS rebranded as a health services company, it announced a new purpose: *Helping people on their path to better health*. Soon after came another announcement – one that would surprise the retail world: CVS would stop selling cigarettes, reportedly a $2 billion decision. Larry J. Merlo, their CEO, said: 'Put simply, the sale of tobacco products is inconsistent with our purpose.'

See Momentum, p. 213

Google

Through Earth Engine, Google has put a vast treasure trove of open-source satellite imagery at the disposal of climate researchers – together with analytics tools and scientists to help generate insights. 'It's a remarkable level of transparency and information that just wasn't available before,' says Mikaela Weisse of the NGO Global Forest Watch.

See Advocacy, p. 189

H&M

As one of the biggest players in the apparel industry, H&M has been an advocate of a living wage in its global supply chain. When Helena Helmersson – previously H&M's sustainability director – became CEO in 2020, she stepped up efforts on this: 'If you really want to drive systemic change, and raise the bar for the whole industry, you need to consistently work on different levels.'

See Pivot, p. 96

IBM

Commitment to diversity, equity and inclusion is nothing new for IBM. They enacted equal pay for equal work almost three decades before the US Equal Pay Act; they refused to comply with segregation laws in the US South; today, they are working to defend LGBT+ rights in countries where they are under threat.

See Politics and the Corporate Voice, p. 290

Intel

Microprocessors use minerals sourced from some of the most war-torn places on the planet. As one of the world's biggest chip-makers, Intel made a commitment to 'conflict-free' products – a daunting task, given the lack of transparency in the supply chain. 'The solution isn't easy,' said then CEO Brian Krzanich, 'but nothing worthwhile ever is.'

See Advocacy, p. 189

JPMorgan Chase

As racial equity became a burning issue during the Black Lives Matter protests, it brought to the surface hard questions about economic inequality. JPMorgan Chase published fresh data and analysis on the problem, and pointed to where new solutions might come from. It helped set the agenda for policymakers and civil society organisations, as well as to the corporate and finance sector.

See Advocacy, p. 189

LEGO

Each year, LEGO produces 110 billion plastic bricks. In 2015 the company decided to act on the challenge of plastic use. They set up a *Sustainable Materials Centre* to make LEGO fully sustainable by 2030. In 2021 they made a breakthrough and announced that they would begin retailing recycled plastic bricks: a recycled 1-litre PET bottle can make ten 2x4 LEGO bricks.

See Momentum, p. 213

Levi's

'Almost 100 billion pieces of clothing are now made each year . . . part of a wasteful cycle of overproduction and overconsumption,' according to Levi's. The company has launched a *Buy Better, Wear Longer* consumer campaign, while integrating sustainability criteria across its innovation and design processes.

See Pivot, p. 96

Maersk

Shipping company Maersk asked a 'disruptive question': what would it take to radically reduce the emissions from our ocean-going vessels, and how would we do it? This challenge unlocked the problem-solving passion of their engineering teams, according to Nils Andersen, CEO at the time: 'They've been bitten by the bug for making a better world,' he said. The result was a revolution in how ships are designed, built and even recycled.

See Disruption, p. 124

Mastercard

Currently, two billion people lack access to financial services. Mastercard founded the Lab for Financial Inclusion to tackle this – working with partners across the system. The company explicitly states that this is not CSR or philanthropy; it leverages their core digital payments technology, aligned with the long-term strategic vision of the business.

See System, p. 160

Microsoft

Satya Nadella, Microsoft's CEO, showed what a big ambition looks like when he announced their intention to be 'carbon negative' by 2030 – meaning that within the present decade the company aims to remove more carbon than it emits each year. He calls it a *Moonshot*, saying: 'We understand companies like ours that can do more, should do more.'

See Ambition, p. 113

MTN

Now Africa's largest mobile network operator, MTN was founded in post-apartheid South Africa on a promise of being an inclusive business. It pioneered pre-paid *pay-as-you-go* mobile to increase access to a service that has become, in effect, a social utility. Pre-paid has now become a global standard for lower-income customers in many industries.

See Core, p. 138

Nestlé

Nestlé CEO Mark Schneider persuaded investors to back a $3.6 billion package to tackle climate change and regeneration through a broad range of actions, including aiming to reach net zero in the supply chain. Schneider told us: 'Our industry stands for a quarter of all emissions – and we are the largest food company – so this is our calling.'

See What Makes a Leader, p. 313

Nike

Nike produced a *Materials Sustainability Index* tracking the impact of hundreds of raw materials. The data they needed didn't exist, so they developed it – and then open-sourced it. 'All footwear and apparel companies face similar issues regarding the lack of materials information,' they explained. 'Because we believe that there should be a system-wide approach to problem solving and innovation within our industry, we are making Nike MSI publicly available.'

See System, p. 160

Novo Nordisk

With diabetes rising calamitously, Novo Nordisk – the world's largest producer of insulin – decided to take an activist stance. Seeing how diabetes was rising fastest in cities, the company framed the concept of *urban diabetes*, the touchstone for a global programme: a network of more than forty cities around the world, sharing knowledge to tackle diabetes.

See Advocacy, p. 189

Olam

One of the world's largest agribusinesses, Singapore-based Olam aims to 'reimagine food systems to operate within nature's boundaries', setting out a five-point agenda for regenerative agriculture. They are working across the industry and beyond; as CEO Sunny Verghese says, 'system transformation requires surprising alliances'.

See Advocacy p. 189

P&G

As the world's largest consumer goods company, P&G has huge marketing muscle and influence. Marc Pritchard, P&G's Chief Brand Officer, sees this as advocacy power: 'Brands affect nearly every person on the planet, every day, and can be agents of change.' In 2019, P&G launched the 'We See Equal' campaign to advance gender equality, using the influence of their brands.

See Advocacy, p. 189

PepsiCo

When PepsiCo was challenged on wasteful use of water in water-stressed areas, they set tough targets for using water more efficiently, as well as ambitious goals to provide safe drinking water for people who currently don't have it. They began with a target to provide drinking water to three million people. As of writing, they've reached fifty-five million.

See Momentum, p. 213

Philips

Philips disrupted its own business model in lighting, embedding circular economy thinking into its proposition: *Lighting as a Service*. It required rethinking every aspect of the business. As Philips' CEO Frans Van Houten explained: 'We tore down the entire value proposition to see what we might change and how.'

See Disruption, p. 124

Rolls-Royce

Rolls-Royce produces aerospace engines and power systems designed to run on fossil fuels – and so is at the heart of energy transition. The company is determined to do more than simply adapt to the transition; it aims to help drive it forward: Warren East, then CEO said, "This is a fantastic opportunity and it's great to work for a company that can do something about it.'

See Focus, p. 63

Solvay

Closing the loop in EV batteries is a major opportunity for the chemicals company Solvay – and keeping essential materials in the value chain is a significant challenge for the world. CEO Ilham Kadri describes the challenge of simultaneously running the business and disrupting the industry: 'We need to keep one eye on the microscope, and one eye on the telescope.'

See Systems and Circular Transformation, p. 263

Standard Chartered

Standard Chartered set themselves a bold ambition: to make the financial system a hostile place for criminals. CEO Bill Winters committed to applying the bank's expertise to de-risk the global banking system – which had become a facilitator of criminal activity, from modern slavery to the trade in illegal wildlife – by working with law enforcement and multi-lateral agencies around the world.

See Pivot, p. 96

Tesco

As one of the world's largest food retailers, Tesco made a 'pivot' on the issue of food waste – from focusing on reducing waste in its own stores, to working towards eliminating waste from the global food system. The problem is at crisis point – with around 35 per cent of all food wasted – and Tesco has become recognised as a global leader in the search for solutions.

See Pivot, p. 96

Tetra Pak

Tetra Pak is the leading producer of cartons globally, and so intrinsically part of the global challenge on plastic waste. The main job of a carton is to keep the contents safe and fresh, and this is achieved through layers of polymer and aluminium. Creating a fully recyclable carton requires nothing short of a revolution in the product – and the system of recycling.

See System, p. 160

Unilever

In 2010 Unilever announced its ambition to double sales and halve environmental impacts. Ten years later it had achieved 80 per cent of its goals – and its most sustainable brands had grown 46 per cent faster and delivered 70 per cent of turnover growth. And when covid showed up the issue of inequality worldwide, Unilever stepped up with a commitment that everyone in its supply chain would earn a living wage by 2030.

See Advocacy, p. 189

Walmart

Walmart is mobilising its supply chain on the urgent issue of biodiversity loss, setting new standards on regenerative agriculture. 'We're losing critical landscapes and biodiversity at an alarming rate,' said Doug McMillon, CEO. Walmart's actions will ripple out to thousands, even hundreds of thousands, of companies, helping to shift the entire system.

See System, p. 160

1.

FOCUS: be clear
what matters and why

Thinking like an activist . . .	• Decide what matters – to you, and to your business
	• Identify the high-impact opportunities to change the game
	• The most contentious areas may be your biggest chance for leadership

Decide what matters – to you, and to your business

The sheer velocity – and ferocity – of the societal challenges coming at businesses can be overwhelming. Business leaders can feel besieged by the demands of multiple stakeholders, often with competing priorities. And every day seems to bring fresh issues, an ongoing onslaught of worrying headlines. It can be hard to keep your bearings. To make it worse, any issue gets more complex the closer you look. Everything connects with everything; pick up one thread and you soon find you're drawn into everything else.

Deciding where to focus is the starting point for an activist leader. It's impossible to ignore the issues clamouring for attention – but you can't lead on all of them. There may be many, many important topics to respond to, and indeed you may need to find ways to do that. But if everything is a priority, nothing is a priority. If you're serious about making an impact, you need to decide where the opportunities are to really make a difference.

Focus is hardwired into business leadership already. Whenever you see a successful business, it's because someone has decided what the business should focus on and has galvanised activity to achieve it. When businesses fail, it's often because they've lost the sharpness of that focus. Much of what it means to be a good leader in business is about focus: deciding what matters, and going for it. This is what unlocks many of the personal qualities we most associate with leadership. Steve Jobs described it like this: 'You have to be burning with an idea, or a problem, or a wrong that you want to right. If you're not passionate enough from the start, you'll never stick it out.'[1]

This capability to hold in the mind's eye what you aim to achieve and then home in on where action is required couldn't be more relevant for activist leaders in business. Societal issues are messy: complex, fluid, interconnected and urgent – it can be hard to distinguish the signal from the noise. This is often why companies want to talk to us in the first place: to help them make sense of it all, to help them prioritise and focus. The first step is to understand: where do you have a responsibility to act, and where do you have an opportunity to lead?

Identify the high-impact opportunities to change the game

A scan of the sustainability or ESG report from any big business will tell you that there is a broad array of issues on which a company might need a credible position and a plan. Figure 3 offers an impressionistic view of the keywords that you might expect to hear discussed under the banner of ESG. It's a snapshot of issues covered by rating agencies, investors, the major consultancies and accountancy firms, business media and organ-isations such as the UN Principles for Responsible Investment (PRI), as well as campaigning civil society groups. In recent years, these terms have become more familiar in the boardroom and among leadership teams in all sectors.

Figure 3: ESG keywords
A snapshot of the broad spectrum of issues that surround businesses

For the most part, companies realise they've got to have a cred-ible position on many of these topics. As a responsible business today, you need these issues covered to be in the game, and you need to show you have a plan that you're continually improving performance. Getting it wrong may be a reputational risk. Getting it right just means you're hitting a baseline of societal and regulatory expectations – which is important. It's table stakes – but it's not leadership.

We find that talking about the difference between 'playing the game' and 'changing the game' can help to think through where to focus, since you can probably only change the game on very few issues. Mark Schneider, CEO of Nestlé, gave us a clear picture of this:

> Since you can't solve all the world's problems, you have to pick your battles; you have to pick your priorities. There are lots of other things you could do, of course. But you can't lead the charge on all of them, at the end of the day, you're unlikely to get the traction you need.

Nestlé, one of the world's largest agricultural businesses, has identified their 'big four' priorities: climate and regenerative agriculture, plastic pollution, water stewardship and responsible sourcing. Mastercard, a global digital payments player, is a different kind of business with different priorities. As their CEO Michael Miebach explained to us, climate is a huge issue for every company, and they want to meet the rising expectations of corporate practice but 'it's not for us to be the leader on that'. They're clear where they aim to change the game:

> We made choices: where could we have a real impact? Where's our comparative advantage? So, the conclusion for us was financial inclusion, financial resilience and sustainable growth. That's our sweet spot. We want to be number one there. That's why we set big goals – because we believe we can contribute and we can help pull others along. Then on data and responsible AI issues, they're in the same category for us: we want to be a leader.

It's in the nature of businesses to be competitive, so leading companies tackling societal issues with an activist spirit often bring a competitive spirit to it as well. As they do on products and services, they aim to set the pace in a fast-moving world and show what's possible once you decide to focus. It's not taking on the issue per se that's distinctive or earns you the leadership position, it's *how* you go about it.

It's worth asking yourself, 'What do we want to be famous for?' It's difficult to be famous for ten things. If you're serious about making an impact, it's best to pick a small number and really go for it. We've heard business leaders voice concern that being publicly committed to making a real impact might be interpreted as grandstanding. But becoming famous for delivering societal value isn't about grandiose-sounding claims. It's rooted in challenging yourself to make a demonstrable difference on something that matters to the company and the world, and then setting about earning the trust and respect of stakeholders – including, and maybe especially, sceptical stakeholders – for the work you're doing.

Leading companies today have highly sophisticated sustainability departments working on how to respond credibly to the full spectrum of relevant issues – gathering data, setting targets, developing plans, reporting transparently – playing the game with commitment. That forms the bedrock of responsible business practice today. In itself, this is often impressive work and without it nothing else is possible. But leadership in social value starts by thinking like an activist about those issues where the business has the opportunity to change the game

The most contentious areas may be your biggest chance for leadership

It can seem obvious to everyone outside a company what issues the business should be focused on; at the same time, businesses themselves often can't see where their real opportunities to lead are. There's a blind spot: the issues that are high-impact opportunities are so often also highly contentious for the business.

This is what we call the *yes-but syndrome*, because we often hear leaders saying exactly that: '*Yes, but* . . .' It goes like this: '*Yes*, we'd like to help change the game on sustainable packaging . . . *but* we're one of the biggest sources of plastic pollution and it's too contentious.' Or, '*Yes*, we would take on the issue of sustainable beef . . . *but* we're one of the world's biggest meat retailers and we really get attacked on this.' That *but* can trip you up; it can stop the organisation in its tracks, preventing it from taking even the first step on the very issues that the world is most concerned about.

The key is to turn that around – from *yes-but* to *yes-because*. It's *because* you play a role in this issue that you have the possibility to take it on. Who has more sway over the packaging ecosystem than one of the world's major plastic producers? Who is better placed to help tackle the question of how to make the production of beef more sustainable than a major meat retailer? These are the high-impact opportunities. That switch in mindset is what starts you thinking like an activist: it's *because* the business is influential in the system that you have the wherewithal to make a difference. It's because it is complex that figuring out a new way to tackle it can be a genuine source of value to society and to the business.

In the chapters ahead, we'll look at how some businesses have become leaders in tackling the issues they decide to focus on. In setting themselves up to do that, they make it clear that they aim to take this on *because* it's difficult – including issues where the company has historically been under attack. For example, PepsiCo had been heavily criticised for being a 'water hog'; many companies would have seen this as a reason to keep their heads down on the issue, but PepsiCo decided they would turn the water challenge they faced into a leadership position. They were explicit about how the issue mattered in the world and to the company:

More than 785 million people globally lack access to safe water . . . At the current rate of progress, it is projected that there will be a 40% gap between global water supply and demand by 2030 . . . PepsiCo's business depends on water, and as such, we have a vested interest in conserving and protecting it.[2]

Similarly, when concerns came to light about conflict minerals in tech hardware, many in the industry set out to block moves to introduce transparency on sourcing of raw materials. Intel went in the other direction: instead of avoiding the issue, they aimed to lead on it – precisely *because* it was difficult. As then CEO Brian Krzanich said at the time, 'The solution isn't easy, but nothing worthwhile ever is.'[3]

If you're a pulp and paper company, it is lovely to donate to tiger sanctuaries in Borneo – but the world is challenging you to play an active part in halting deforestation. If you're a grocer who depends on a large population of hourly wage workers, it's an important contribution to speak up on issues of racial justice and inequality in the world – but it may ring hollow unless you're also looking at questions of living wage and in-work poverty in your own value chain. Unless you're addressing the contentious issues that are inherently associated with your business – looking at your own blind spots – anything else you do risks looking like a distraction and opens up the challenge of greenwashing or woke-washing.

At a time when mass shootings were gripping attention in America, one US-based company we were working with surveyed employees to ask what issue in society they would like the company to take a lead on – and the answer came back: *gun crime*. It is an important issue, of course, and clearly one that employees of the company cared deeply about as citizens – but this was a major pharma company and it was difficult to see how this business could meaningfully tackle gun crime other than by adding their voice to the public debate.

To avoid this kind of misalignment, you can use a simple *double materiality grid* to map the issues. The point is to identify the issues that appear in the top right quadrant: not only is the impact of the business a part of the problem, but the issue could have a material impact on the business. To illustrate this, we've played out two issue grids below for two hypothetical US companies – a pharma company and a grocer (see Figure 4).

For the pharma company, we can see that the issue of gun violence is in the lower left quadrant: it's not material for the business, and the business is not material on the issue. While gun violence may be a pressing concern in public commentary and in society at large, a pharma business plays a low intrinsic role in the issue. Conversely, access to healthcare and drug pricing appear in the top of the upper right quadrant: these are critical issues both for pharma businesses and for society. Indeed, these are fraught endemic challenges for the sector, and many pharma companies feel they are doing all they can on these questions: they've got themselves jammed into a defensive position and can't see how there's a win in there. So, it's not news that these issues matter; what often comes as a revelation is that sticking with these thorny issues may be where the opportunity for leadership lies.

It's a different story for the hypothetical retailer, where gun violence may well be a highly relevant issue because the company might face intense social pressure – from employees, from customers, from the media – to make a business decision about whether or not to sell guns. We've worked with retailers who have philanthropic programmes on issues like literacy in schools – which are worthwhile in those communities, but not issues that are materially relevant for the business.

Of course, a company may choose to use its leadership capital

Pharma

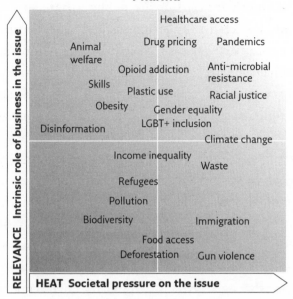

Retail

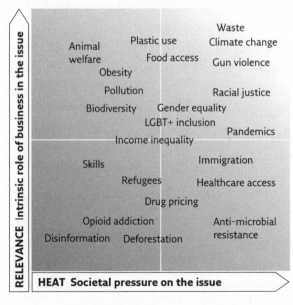

Figure 4: Hypothetical 'double materiality grids'
for a pharma and a retail company

to speak up on an issue that's hot in the public arena but not material to the business itself. Or, to support a cause that offers benefits that matter to the recipients but is not material to the business – because those topics have social traction and feel like a less troubled area to get involved with.

On occasion, a company decides to get behind a topical issue for the simple reason that they see a compelling opportunity to contribute. The refugee crisis, for example, is unlikely to appear in the upper right-hand quadrant of the double materiality grid for any business: it's a crisis that hasn't been created by businesses, and that probably won't have much direct impact on businesses. Still, that issue provides some win-win examples of positive action. Accenture and Microsoft teamed up to create a digital ID for millions of refugees, working in collaboration with the public sector through the ID2020 initiative.[4] In Germany, national hero businesses Volkswagen, Daimler and Porsche ramped up training and jobs for recently arrived migrants, and helped to fill the skills gap in the industry in the process.[5] IKEA designed a flatpack shelter for families in refugee camps, and partnered with the UN refugee agency UNHCR, to deliver them to scale where they're needed around the world.[6] It was an award-winning design and an imaginative response to the crisis, emblematic of the brand that stands for helping everyone to make a home.

However, if you're looking at the dynamics of how big businesses play a role in today's global issues, that is not where you'd go. Usually, the greatest opportunity to make the greatest impact comes from those issues where the business plays a systemic role and is intrinsically part of the problem – and yet, for that same reason, has the potential to become part of the solution.

The climate crisis is, of course, a material issue for all businesses – and especially for a company like Rolls-Royce. It is deeply involved with the issue, as a major producer of aerospace engines and power systems designed to run on fossil fuels. As their former

CEO Warren East says, 'That was a good idea in the twentieth century. It's not a good idea in the twenty-first century and we have to make sure we change and move to a situation where we're not adding carbon dioxide to the environment.'[7] Yet this is one of the very hardest industries in which to make that change. By homing in on where their core capabilities intersect with the search for new low-carbon solutions, Rolls-Royce focused on a few priority areas, including helping sustainable aviation fuels get to scale, the electrification of flight and the development of smart microgrids that can use renewable energy sources for standalone sites. Their stance is: '*Yes . . .* it's *because* this is difficult and we're a part of it that we have to help find solutions.'

Their ambition was not simply that the company should somehow manage to adapt itself to the energy transition but, rather, that Rolls-Royce should become 'essential to it'. As East said, it's all about turning an existential risk into a leadership opportunity:

> This energy transition is a once in two hundred-and-fifty years' event. Over the next couple of decades, we're going to change how the world works; it hasn't happened since the beginning of the industrial revolution. That's a fantastic opportunity and it's great to work for a company that can do something about it.[8]

As Tufan Erginbilgic took up the reins as CEO at Rolls-Royce, he reconfirmed the 'opportunity to take the whole business to low carbon'.[9] For the entire industry, it's the most challenging issue and the one to grip.

There's courage involved in deciding to take on the tough issues to say *yes-because* and not *yes-but*. But if you do take on the contentious and challenging issues – aiming to make a real impact through your business – it can be the path to genuine leadership.

How to bridge paradigms

As a spirit of activism stirs in business leaders, so does a range of anxieties and objections. If you're thinking like an activist, your eyes are on what needs to happen to create change. But this isn't easy – and one of the reasons is that you're in an organisation where doing this hasn't been the operational paradigm.

The idea of taking on a big societal issue can bring up real and legitimate worries. It's a different mindset. As you get started you will inevitably encounter concerns about the fact that you're trying to do something different. It's important to give them space: it helps individuals bridge into the new way of working.

So don't be surprised – the concerns are familiar, and you can even look at them as a signal you're on the right track. They're always there at the beginning – but as the work gets underway, so they recede. Here are some of the common concerns that spring up.

'But we can't deal with *all* of these issues'

That's right; you can't and don't have to – but you do need to tackle those that are most relevant for your business. Yet people can feel overwhelmed by the volume of societal issues crying out for attention – and there always seem to be new ones appearing over the horizon. If you resolve to take on one, doesn't it set you up to have to take on the next – and the one after that – in an unending tsunami of alarm? Sometimes, and unsurprisingly perhaps, there's a desire to retreat back to the more familiar, day-to-day priorities of business. But these issues are now firmly on the corporate radarscreen: the new expectation of business is to act on them, and the risk of not doing so is getting greater. However, no one expects every company to take on every issue in the world. So the question is not whether to respond but how to prioritise and where to focus.

'But nothing we can do will ever be enough'

That's true. But nobody expects any one company to solve for the whole problem – however, they do expect you to *do what you can do*. Still, given the scale of these issues, it can be daunting when you start out. It can feel like stepping into an enormous open-ended commitment and, realistically, as you start making progress, new dimensions of the challenge continually come into focus – that's the nature of progress. There's sometimes an underlying view that maybe it would be better not to get involved at all in trying to tackle problems where so much lies beyond the company's control. But, in practice, companies on this journey gain capacity and confidence in their role over time. The opportunity is to start by focusing in on where to show up in a way that's true to your position and capabilities as a company.

'But we can't fix it alone'
Again, that's true. The scale and complexity of the issues means that no single actor, no matter how brilliant, how resourceful, or how powerful, can 'fix it'. As we'll see, working on the issue opens the way to working across the industry and in collaboration with civil society organisations. This is an attitude shift for many companies: we commonly encounter an entrenched antipathy towards regulators, NGOs or subject-matter experts that makes it feel unfamiliar, and even unnerving at first, to stand shoulder to shoulder in problem-solving on these issues. But doing so makes it possible to reset how you engage with a wide range of stakeholders positively, even critics.

'But we're already doing so much good stuff we don't get credit for'
Most companies have substantial sustainability departments, with people working hard towards goals on environmental and social impacts – everything from reducing carbon emissions, to managing waste, to worker welfare, to human rights in the supply chains and diversity and inclusion in the business – and reporting on these activities in various ESG frameworks. These are the baseline requirements of responsible business today, in the same way that operational or product safety is a given. Most also have laudable social investment programmes – helping on challenges from community resilience to nature conservation. In a big company there may be hundreds of these philanthropic initiatives. You can understand why many business leaders might think, 'Isn't all that enough?' That's why focus is so helpful: decide what

really matters and elevate the most relevant initiatives with a spirit of activist.

'But we're not an NGO, you know'

Sometimes the preconception in business leaders is that we're suggesting these societal issues should take precedence over commercial priorities. 'We're a business, at the end of the day,' they remind us. Absolutely true. But this is a false dichotomy: if you look at the leading companies that approach these issues with an activist mindset, they're well-run global companies with a long track record of delivering shareholder value – and in the coming sections we'll describe how a range of them go about delivering financial value *and* social value, hand-in-hand. Focusing on societal issues is *part of* their business strategy, not separate from it. This is not about becoming a non-profit; it's about how you deliver your profits in today's world.

2.

PERSPECTIVE:
see it as the world sees it

Thinking like an activist . . .	• Step out of the corporate mindset to see the issue as others see it
	• Ask yourself: where's the heat, what's driving concern?
	• Unpack the issue to understand how your business relates to it
	• Find the front edge of the challenge

Step out of the corporate mindset
to see the issue as others see it

The thing that unlocks your ability to be an activist leader is seeing the issues as the world sees them. This sounds like common sense but making this shift in perspective is non-trivial. In fact, for most companies it's counter-cultural because it requires people to look at familiar questions in new ways – and not only through the lens of the interests of the business. Indeed, Mark Carney sees it as essential to leadership: 'A leader in this disruptive age must not only be able to set their eyes on the horizon, they must see from the periphery.' Carney, a former Governor of the Bank of England and Chairman of the Financial Stability Board, has been at the forefront of establishing climate-related financial disclosure and is one of the world's leading advocates on the imperative for business and finance to get engaged with challenges of climate and inequality. Having seen these issues from multiple perspectives over his career, he reminds us of Henry Ford's advice that 'if there is any one secret of success it lies in the ability to get the other person's point of view'.[1]

Most companies will be monitoring the views of key stakeholder groups on key societal issues. They will have teams working on policies and positions. For example, you'd expect a manufacturing company to be alert to the NGOs campaigning on toxins in the water supplies. You'd expect a food company to be fully informed about health concerns and emerging policies on sugar. Or a construction company to be well versed on the debate about the use of sustainable building materials. And you'd probably also expect that the perspective they take is from the point of view of how those issues will impact the company.

So senior management often feel that they're more or less up to speed on the big issues facing the business: they probably receive regular briefings and there may be some level of board oversight on a number of critical issues. But the impetus for the analysis is almost universally risk minimisation, meaning the risk to the *business*: the focus is on how to protect the corporate against likely challenges – unexpected costs, reputational risks, operational setbacks or market disruptions.

This is often spoken about inside the business as 'issue management' – a seductive concept, suggesting that issues can be tamed, somehow brought under control. The term was coined in the 1970s by Howard Chase, author of *Issue Management: Origins of the Future*, who defined an *issue* as 'a gap between your [organisation's] actions and stakeholder expectations'. He goes on to state that *issue management* is 'the process to close that gap'.[2] This is a helpful definition that suggests that the original intention was indeed to more closely match societal and corporate concerns – but the reality is that as issue management has evolved it is most often used as a tool to protect the short-term interests of the business, rather than encouraging a broader perspective that explores common ground and potential solutions.

Cognitive diversity is the theme of Matthew Syed's influential book *Rebel Ideas*. 'We are oblivious to our own blind spots,' he tells us:

> We perceive and interpret the world through frames of reference but we do not see the frames of reference themselves. This, in turn, means we tend to underestimate the extent to which we can learn from people with different points of view.[3]

He likens complex problem-solving to artificial intelligence today which is 'no longer about single algorithms, however sophisticated. Rather, it is about ensembles of algorithms that "think" differently, search differently and encode problems in different ways.' Usefully, for leadership teams wanting to understand the societal challenges they face, he talks about cognitive diversity as a matter of collective intelligence. People can be 'individually perceptive but collectively blind', he explains, citing examples as various as the CIA's response to the threat of Al Qaeda or the experience of the Football Association's Advisory Board. Whenever an institutional response to a complex challenge falls short, it's possible to see how 'a group of wise individuals would almost certainly have become an unwise board'.

To open the aperture on the corporate lens to take in an issue as the *world* sees it can be hard to do – not because of an individual failure of imagination or effort, but because businesses are geared up to consider issues in terms of their impact on the company. That is why shifting your perspective to see the issue from the outside-in is so powerful. Not instead of the conventional analysis, but as well. Even if you're already familiar with the issues, it can give you a dramatically new perspective.

When we speak with business leaders about this, we often liken the traditional corporate to a citadel – a well-defended fortress, built to keep the world out. It's as if the leadership stands up on the parapet to survey the landscape outside the walls and the forces are mustered to shoot down any issues before they become a threat. It often raises a laugh and a rueful recognition of this as a deeply entrenched corporate mindset. It can be recognised by these characteristics:

- **Corporate-centric:** the world is only seen through the lens of the business interests, with little consideration or even curiosity about the perspective of other stakeholders and what's driving them.

- **Short-termism:** an intense focus on near-term outcomes – expressed in quarterly results, seasonal sales figures, next week's headlines – to the exclusion of a longer view on the societal issues.

- **Zero-sum outcomes:** priorities are based on a 'winner-takes-all' mentality that places financial value at odds with creating broader value to society.

- **Defensive stance:** social challenges are viewed only as potential threats and dealt with as risks, rather than an opportunity to engage.

This may sound like a harsh critique – not all businesses are like this all the time, nor all business leaders. Even so, many people working inside corporations recognise aspects of this mindset at play. It's what is meant when people say, pejoratively, 'that's so *corporate*'.

Yet this is already becoming an outmoded paradigm. The most forward-looking leaders view it as not fit for purpose for the world they are dealing with today. Executive education courses and business literature warn of the tendencies of big organisations to get locked in their own worldview through 'information bubbles', 'echo chambers' and 'group think'. Warren Buffett cautions about the dangers of 'confirmation bias' because, as he's often quoted as saying, 'What the human being is best at doing is interpreting all new information so that their prior conclusions remain intact.' People leading organisations experience how that type of corporate behaviour makes for bad decision-making, inhibits innovation and ultimately destroys value. Leaders today are striving to build networked organisations, and inclusive and responsive cultures, with the capacity to deal with complexity and fast-changing realities. Thinking like an activist, you'd harness those business capabilities and direct them towards tackling the relevant complex and fast-changing societal issues as well. Not only is that exactly what's needed to make an impact; doing so also contributes towards building a more resilient and future-facing business. Networked, responsive, cognitively diverse, attuned to the outside world.

And that starts by being curious about the issue itself. Explore it without the need to defend a position or persuade anyone of anything. Create the space to listen to different perspectives, including – and indeed especially – the critics. Ask yourself: do they have a point? What is it about this problem in the world that calls for new solutions? What are we to that? Seeing the issues as the world sees them is what makes it possible to think like an activist leader and to explore how the business might become part of the solution to these challenges.

Ask yourself: where's the heat, what's driving concerns?

For companies in the thick of a pressing societal issue, the clamour can be deafening. It is hard to discern what's really driving concerns – to the point that sometimes it can seem overblown, whipped up by ideologically driven NGOs or a combative media in search of an easy bad guy to point the finger at. We've encountered the situation in many sectors and on many issues, and a particularly striking example is palm oil. Palm oil has become ubiquitous as an ingredient in so many products – but how it's produced has become highly contentious.[4]

Most of the major global palm oil players see themselves as respectable companies, valued players in their national economies, providing livelihoods for millions and producing a highly efficient and versatile crop to help feed a growing global population. But the industry has faced increasing pressure – suddenly everyone was talking about it, and the major companies were being vilified. So, what's the problem with palm oil?

Ask many people that question and they'll tell you, 'It's deforestation, obviously.' And, of course, it's not like the palm oil producers don't know that. The companies we worked with were early members of the Roundtable on Responsible Palm Oil, they have teams of people working on sustainability, and they most definitely *don't* do any deforestation in their plantations. So, for these companies, it was frustrating to see calls for a blanket boycott of palm oil gaining pace in Europe. It seemed ill-informed and unfair. It put them on the back foot, creating a stand-off in their relationship with the wider world. To break that impasse means stepping outside the industry's frame of reference and seeing the issue as the world sees it.

On the one hand, it is not easy to tell a palm oil company anything new about the issue of palm oil. They are all experts in the intricacies of supply chains that include hundreds of thousands of smallholder plantations, unenforced certification standards and the competitive dynamics of land use in forest-based industries. All these factors make it one of the most complex agricultural industries to manage. On the other hand, it's possible to take a fresh look at the rising concern among external stakeholders. It shows up in the growth of global media attention on the subject – and not just in the liberal press, but everyone from the *Financial Times* to *Cosmopolitan*, popular journalism in the *Sun* to the specialist coverage in *National Geographic*. It's in the surround-sound conversation about regulation in Brussels and Washington DC. Then, vitally, it's present in the growing pressure in the financial arena – from investors such as Aviva and CalPERS asking questions about deforestation, to lenders such as HSBC and the IFC toughening their lending standards. An increasing number of major manufacturers and retailers are promising to become 'palm oil free' and putting pressure back through their palm oil supply chains to deliver on that commitment.

And, of course, this was being energised by the campaigns of NGOs such as Greenpeace – who led creative and concerted campaigns, played out on social media, aiming to alert consumers that their toothpaste, chocolate bars, pizzas and shampoos were contributing to the clearing of the rainforest and driving orangutans to the brink of extinction. The orangutan became the lead protagonist in the campaign, even featuring in TV ads from Greenpeace. This was a puzzle to some people in the industry: *why are people so concerned about the orangutan?* one executive asked us. From the point of view of the NGOs, shining a

light on the plight of the orangutan is the fastest way to engage
the public with the issue of deforestation. And the reason that
NGOs are so concerned about deforestation is the climate crisis.

So where was the heat in the conversation; what was exercising
all these different stakeholders? In the case of palm oil, a few
data points anchor the debate. For example, every single minute,
the area of about ten football pitches of trees is lost due to
deforestation.[5] Every day, about 81,000 hectares of rainforest
– an area nearly fourteen times the size of Manhattan – is
burned around the world.[6] Satellite data shows that tropical
forests are being destroyed at a rate of about 8 million hectares
a year – an area equivalent to the Czech Republic every year.[7]

The sense of urgency about deforestation has increased as
the climate crisis has continued to intensify – and this is before
the subject of the collapse of biodiversity ecosystems became
such a prominent issue on the public agenda. Three-quarters
of the world's biodiversity is found in forests so that's become
a new front edge of the deforestation issue.[8] And the rate of
deforestation continues to rise: more than 12 million hectares
of tree cover in the tropics was lost in 2020 alone, according
to the World Resources Institute; most alarmingly, that included
4.2 million hectares of previously undisturbed primary tropical forests.[9] And latest trend data show how the spread of
wildfires is starting to turn forests, that have been carbon sinks
for the world, into carbon emitters.[10]

Meanwhile, even a quick look at the rise of deforestation
over the past decades highlights how it tracks closely with the
rise of palm oil production. Jumping from 22 million tonnes
in 2001[11] to 73 million tonnes in 2020, global production more
than trebled.[12] And while there has been some increase in yield
and efficiency along the way, the underlying business model
remains the same: clearing land to drive growth. So, the industry
is bound to be in the frame.

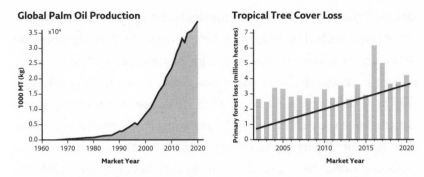

Figure 5: Global trends in palm oil production and tree cover loss[13]

One of the reasons why it's so hard to make the switch in perspective is that, from the vantage point of the businesses, this has been a great success story. It's been an extended period of increasing global demand for the product, driving rapid growth in the industry. These companies are large employers, and have brought prosperity to the communities and nations in which they operate. Lauded in their home markets, they are understandably proud of those achievements. Put simply, looking at Figure 5, the business leaders are seeing the left-hand graph; the world is seeing the right-hand graph.

It's not that people in the industry don't know the facts. They monitor the issue closely but, at first pass at least, the corporate instinct is to deflect the challenge. 'But it's not just our industry causing this,' some point out. 'Talk to the loggers or the soy farmers.' Others object that the regulators have political motivations and are protecting their own interests. Most explain that the NGOs don't get how difficult it is operationally to deal with the problem. Or, even, the response of a weary veteran in the industry: 'This is just a fad – we've been on the receiving end of these criticisms for a long time; people get bored and move on.' All of those points have truth in them. But the problem is that taking that perspective on the issue points the finger of blame at everyone else – and leaves the business itself out of the picture.

When you stop and look at what's uniting all these different stakeholders and the underlying reality of the impact of the issue in the world, it becomes clear that global pressure on the industry is here to stay. Thinking like an activist about it, you'll ask: is this a real and urgent issue that demands action? Do those concerned about deforestation have a point? Where do we fit in that picture? What levers could we pull to change the game?

Deforestation and palm oil producers is not a one-off. The pattern repeats in other sectors. The health impact of sugar, and the role of food and drink producers, is another: we've heard, 'The obesity challenge is not just the fault of this industry . . .' And 'Ultimately, consumers make the choice . . . we put the information on the label so people can make informed decisions . . .' People complain, 'Regulators are focused on the wrong levers for change.' Or, on the transition to low-carbon fuels, and the role of oil and gas producers, we've heard, 'The climate crisis is not just the fault of this industry . . .' And a warning: 'The world will need what we produce for some decades to come . . .' And inevitably, 'It's harder than people think to make the shift to low carbon . . .' All fair points. It's corporate instinct to defend the territory but, as the impacts of these societal challenges intensify, so does the call for a different type of corporate response.

Whatever issues a company is facing, getting a real-world perspective on where the heat is for those stakeholders who are so concerned is a crucial step to bringing a spirit of activism to your business. And the risks of not doing so are clear to see: companies can become dug in, entrenched in positions that seem increasingly indefensible. They start to appear remote and out of touch. This isn't only a licence-to-operate threat, this is about the kind of company they become: increasingly cut off from society, stuck in a corporate mindset, unable to respond to the world around them with agility and creativity.

Unpack the issue to understand
how your business relates to it

Societal issues are wicked problems. One topic leads you to another and the pathways intersect, so it is easy to get lost. Teasing apart how different facets of the same big issue show up in multiple overlapping conversations helps to identify where the business is likely to be able to engage most effectively. That's nowhere more evident than on the subject of inequality. Inequality has become the all-encompassing term for many of today's social issues – indeed, much commentary distils all societal issues into the two uber-themes of climate change and inequality. Almost all major companies today are working out how to respond to this challenge, so it's worth looking at the dynamics of this in a little more depth.

As the covid pandemic swept around the world, it exposed and exacerbated existing inequalities, within and across communities. Front-line workers, not just in the healthcare sector, became heroes in the popular imagination because of their role in keeping necessary services going and supplies flowing. The recognition that these were 'essential workers' jarred with the realisation of the underlying vulnerability of so many of those people, often earning below what's reckoned to be the living wage in their communities, with minimal or nonexistent health benefits and nothing to fall back on. The Federal Reserve reported that over a third of Americans would find it tough to meet a $400 bill for an unexpected financial emergency.[14] Front-line workers were also especially hard hit by the disease,[15] while the rich enjoyed a stock market rally.[16] Many businesses found themselves in the firing line for laying off employees while increasing CEO pay or raising dividends to shareholders.[17]

Yet, while media outlets around the world continue to discuss the fault lines of inequality, for business leaders it can seem like a macro issue that is too large and abstract to act on. With many companies asking us to help make sense of it, we published an *'inequality map'* as a tool to help leadership teams think through where, among the many dimensions of inequality, they have the greatest opportunity to make an impact. We share it here as an example of how any complex issue can be mapped out in a way that unlocks new conversations inside a business about where it fits in the broad landscape of the issue.

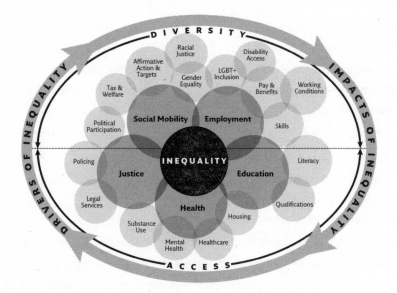

Figure 6: An 'inequality map'

Laying out the many faces of inequality as simply as this helps to illustrate the link between the conceptual debate around systemic inequalities and the real-world manifestations that a company might decide to act on. It provides a context to consider where your business is best placed to respond in practical ways: exploring whether that is likely to be growing skills gaps in an uncertain employment future, for example, or food insecurity, access to the justice system or mental health or any other.

While determining where to focus your efforts is a start, it also requires a vital shift in perspective to see those problems as the people closest to those issues understand and experience them – and how the world at large perceives them. For example, we worked with a retail company that was very proud of its long-standing programmes to help employees move up from shop floor to store manager. These were strong programmes with good results and the company wanted credit for them. But they were missing that a significant underlying source of societal concern was the economic inequalities reinforced by incomes below the living wage. We worked with a gig economy company that wanted to celebrate the progress it was making on diversity and inclusion, but it was tuning out that, in the public perception, the real friction point was that the company was shirking its responsibility in areas such as employment rights and benefits for its workforce.

Inside a business, tackling the inequality issue has re-energised efforts on diversity and inclusion. After all, that is where most companies have most direct influence over facets of the inequality challenge and it is keenly felt in the experience of employees. Building a diverse workforce has become an essential part of any people strategy. The recent history of businesses on this subject illustrates how the front edge of any issue keeps moving. First showing up as just *Diversity*, it began as an exercise in counting heads – an important first step, but meaningless without creating a supportive and inclusive workplace. And so *Diversity and Inclusion* was born – which many companies quickly switched around to calling *Inclusion and Diversity*, to emphasise how an inclusive culture is the prerequisite for fostering all forms of diversity, as well as mental wellbeing and a sense of belonging that are now so often part of corporate efforts on inclusion. Today, reflecting how Black Lives Matter succeeded in highlighting deep structural inequalities, many companies are referring to *Diversity, Equity and Inclusion*

(DE&I) – signalling their intent to ensure not just inclusion but *equity* in the workplace – with a focus on pay and promotions, participation, fairness and transparency. Of course, many might regard this as simply shifting the language while not fixing the problems – but how you frame the problem does have the power to guide the action. For activist leaders, the journey from *Diversity* to *DE&I* shows how having a live understanding of where the heat is on any issue can significantly shift what you actually do: where you put your effort and what actions you decide to take.

Find the front edge of the challenge

At the heart of being an activist leader is a restless impatience to make a difference to the issue. That means looking for the new and even contentious front edge of the problem, where it can get knotty and difficult. Usually, this is where real progress can be made, and where businesses can show meaningful leadership. But how do we find the front edge? How can we understand where to look for the real opportunities to find solutions?

The concept of a 'solution space' – or problem space, or innovation space – may be useful here. A mental model for this space comes from the famous story of the six blind men and the elephant. It's a 2,500-year-old Indian fable in which a king invites six blind men to touch the elephant to determine its nature, but without telling them what it is. One of them touches the tail and thinks it's a snake; another thinks the leg is a pillar, and so on. Similarly, we often only understand an issue from what's immediately in front of us; the full solution space – the whole elephant – often eludes us. This is why it's so important to step outside the usual corporate reference points and see the issue as the world sees it. By doing so, we can form some powerful new perspectives and connections.

Take the relentless rise of diabetes globally, for example. Novo Nordisk, the world's largest producer of insulin, has long seen its purpose as 'defeating diabetes'; in other words, not merely treating the disease but eradicating it. So, with diabetes rising calamitously around the world they decided to take a more activist stance on the issue. They began by reframing the way they looked at the challenge. Historically, their perspective on the role they could play had been centred on how to improve treatment outcomes for patients with the condition. But with more than half a billion people already living with diabetes and the trend set to reach over 700 million over the next twenty years, the question being asked all around the world became how to prevent it. Novo Nordisk called it 'an emergency in slow motion', and turned towards understanding more about the drivers in wider society that put people at risk in the first place.

Diabetes was already a priority in the global health community, but it quickly became clear that diabetes was rising up the agenda of another major global conversation: urbanisation. Driven by city lifestyles, Type 2 diabetes is rising fastest in the most rapidly urbanising parts of the world. This was the front line of the challenge. So Novo Nordisk crystallised the concept of *urban diabetes* – which became the touchstone for a global programme. It began with the publication of a substantial piece of research in partnership with University College London into the 'social determinants' of health in cities.[18] Novo Nordisk became advocates on the issue of diabetes prevention and launched a campaign that's established a network of more than forty cities around the world, from Vancouver to Shanghai, Johannesburg to Copenhagen, sharing knowledge between city leaders, health professionals and communities to bend the curve on the acceleration of diabetes in cities.[19]

Finding the front edge of an issue takes you into the solution space. Listening to what people are worried about – especially those who are experts in that subject matter – allows you to hear what they are hoping for, too. What do they think needs to happen, what are the urgent challenges that need answers? What do they fear and what do they think would change the game? The answers to those questions provide you with clues as to where the solution space is. They equip you to ask of the business: what are we to that problem and how can we help?

Looking back at the problem of palm oil: the front line of the deforestation problem is traceability in the supply chain. Most of the major producers with large global customers may have driven deforestation out of their own plantations, yet the challenge remains out in their supply chains, out in the forest, where it's hard to see. Leading environmentalist Jonathon Porritt, who led an industrywide study in 2015, concluded, 'You cannot carry out proper forest protection . . . without proper mapping; it's just not possible.'[20] According to the World Resources Institute, 'One of the big challenges facing corporations is tracing palm oil through large and complex supply chains to commercial product' – and they pointed to visibility to the mill level as a necessary next step.[21] 'Brands should open themselves up to public scrutiny by publishing complete lists of the mills and producer groups in their supply chain,' declared Greenpeace.[22]

When the Malaysian palm oil producer Sime Darby published Crosscheck they were responding to the universal call for greater transparency. An open-access digital tool that mapped the company's supply down to the mill level, Crosscheck was an industry first. Putting their data, developed in collaboration with NGOs, into the public domain was a recognition that increasing transparency is critical to creating a deforestation-free industry.[23] At around the same time, the arrival of RADD – Radar Alerts for Detecting Deforestation – represented a major step forward for the entire sector. Ten leading palm oil players, producers in Malaysia and Indonesia along with global buyers, came together to invest in satellite monitoring with new geospatial technologies that can penetrate even the dense cloud cover of the rainforests.[24] Now, using European Space Agency satellites and facilitated by the World Resources Institute, near real-time alerts are making a whole new level of visibility possible – way beyond South East Asia and beyond palm oil to other forest-based industries.[25] There's a long way to go to halt deforestation, but it's a vivid example of how mobilising to create solutions to the greatest intractable problems is where the greatest opportunities to create value lie.

Sometimes an opportunity is further out than what is immediately visible on the horizon today. When we worked with one of the world's largest food retailers, for example, a problem in the global food system was emerging that had not yet captured public attention, but all the signs were that it soon would be. And it was one that Tesco was perfectly placed to help tackle: food waste. An initial reaction from operators inside the business was that the company had a good record of managing food waste in their stores and, as they pointed out, stakeholders had never challenged them on the issue. However, when you look at the same question from a different perspective, the opportunity looks different: you see the intersection between the challenge that an extraordinary one-third of food produced globally is wasted and a business which is one of the largest players in the global food system.[26] 'We're talking about food, fresh food, that's being wasted on a colossal scale,' said the campaigner Tristram Stuart in his TED Talk, which has been watched by nearly two million people worldwide, as he set about 'confronting large businesses in the business of wasting food'.[27]

There are many perspectives in the global food waste debate. 'Food loss and waste squanders natural resources,'[28] said UN

Secretary-General António Gutteres, calling on governments and businesses to step up efforts. The global consultancy BCG laid out the many possible routes to tackling the challenge[29] – and once you start exploring you find many different types of organisations pointing at where solutions are needed. When the company made the decision to embrace the issue, they began by analysing where the problem of waste was across their value chain, from the field to the fridge, and used that as the basis for shaping solutions. For Tesco it became an opportunity to demonstrate how they could deploy their huge scale as a positive force in the wider world. A decade on, the issue is centre stage in the global food agenda, and connects to the adjacent challenges of feeding a growing population and combating climate change. And Tesco has become recognised as a corporate leader on the issue and has helped to catalyse change across the industry.

Making sure you understand an issue as the world understands it isn't so different from gathering the data and insight that inform all strategic decision-making in business – whether it's launching a new product, improving a process or committing to an investment. It needs not only to make the upside case for what the business hopes but also to explore the problems and barriers. It should encompass the long-term macrotrends, what others in the space are doing and the perspectives and expectations of stakeholders. Companies have strong strategic planning and market insight capabilities – and those, too, can be applied to provide the data and insights you need to create social value, as well as financial value.

*   *   *

Most of the time, most of us are not even aware of our own frames of reference – any more than the proverbial fish is aware of the water it swims in. In *Rebel Ideas*, Matthew Syed describes this as 'perspective blindness' – and, for an activist, it's a huge barrier. As Syed puts it: 'We become prisoners of our paradigms. Stepping outside the walls, however, permits a new vantage point. We don't have new information, we have a new perspective.'[30]

The corporate mindset is so pervasive, so habitual, we don't even really notice it. Stepping outside the walls, for people in business, can be a radical act. Shifting perspective, seeing the issues as others see them, is what unlocks your ability to think about the problem differently and reframe your view of the solutions you might bring to it.

3.

PIVOT:
adopt the activist mindset

Thinking like an activist . . .	• Turn and face into the challenges • Step up your response – keep asking what needs to happen next • Don't just fix the problem in your business, work to fix it in the world

Turn and face into the challenges

If you've taken a good hard look and seen the issue *as the world sees it* – not only through the lens of the business – then what follows is often a dramatic shift in mindset. We call it the *pivot*: turning to face into that issue, recognising the part your business does – and could – play in it. In our experience, this is the biggest single success factor: once you make that pivot, you find everything else flows from it. Extraordinarily simple at one level, but a 180° difference; it sets you off on a different road.

Three examples will help to illustrate the power of that pivot: for a big food retailer, for an international bank and for one of the major oil and gas producers. They show how the mindset shift from a default, corporate-centric to an issue-led activist position can completely change what a company does. It's not only about the performance of your company on the issue – it goes beyond that to focus on tackling the issue itself. The essence of that shift can be characterised like this:

	From: The Default Position		To: The Activist Position
Tesco: a retailer on food waste	We are committed to eliminating food waste from our stores	⇨	We will help eliminate waste from the global food system
Standard Chartered: a bank on financial crime	We are committed to reducing the risk of financial crime in our operations	⇨	We want to make the financial system a hostile environment for criminals
bp: an oil company on climate change	Climate change is real, but oil is indispensable for the foreseeable future	⇨	We want to be part of the transition to a zero carbon economy

Once you make a shift like this, it radically changes the company's stance on the issue and, indeed, in the world. It has the potential to identify new opportunities and stimulate innovation, as well as resetting relationships with critical stakeholders. Of course, it's not the path of least resistance: it may seem easier to keep your head down, to stay with business as usual. But, as these examples show, today's more foresighted leaders know that there's much to be gained by looking up, getting to grips with the issue and asking: what's our role in this? How can we use our leverage in the system? How can we help?

(i) Tesco: 'We have an almost unique vantage point over the food system – and we must use that scale for good.'

Tesco is one of the largest players in the global food system. Millions of consumers buy from them every week, they have an extensive network of brands supplying them and a substantial manufacturing requirement for their own brand products. We saw in the previous chapter how the scale of the global food waste challenge began to show up in the system – with new data revealing that an astonishing one-third of all food grown globally is wasted, and evidence that between 10 per cent of the world's greenhouse gas emissions are associated with food waste.[1] Against that backdrop, Tesco took the opportunity to step up in a new way.

The company's historic position on food waste was creditable by industry standards; they reported low levels of food waste in their stores; a strong performance in their peer group. However, reducing in-store food waste does not help to solve food waste in the world. Arguably, in isolation, it perpetuates it: the waste piles up along the value chain, in the farms, warehouses and, ultimately, in household trash. So, just doubling down on reducing food waste in their operations would not be enough to make any impact on the issue itself.

Tesco made a pivot. They set out their ambition to lead the fight on global food waste. It was a chance to show how the sheer scale of the company – a source of much distrust – had the potential to be a positive force. 'I've spent the best part of forty years working for Tesco and, whenever I can, I step back to take in the sheer breadth and scale of this business we have built. Not everyone sees that scale as a good thing,' said the CEO when he set out their ambition. 'But it gives us an almost unique vantage point over the food system – and we must use that scale for good, to develop solutions which help tackle this problem.'

Talking publicly about using their 'scale for good' represented a pivot in itself. They moved away from playing down their scale because of its negative connotations in the minds of stakeholders towards a determination to demonstrate how the reach and influence of their business could be directed towards tackling the food waste issue for the world.

The company started by mapping the waste in their food chain end-to-end, from field right through to consumption, for twenty-five of its top-selling products. They kick-started initiatives on demand planning, distribution and storage. They engaged their suppliers across meat, dairy and fresh produce in waste-reduction programmes in their own operations. And, because their 'buy one, get one free' marketing message was driving food into their consumers' bins, they switched their promotions strategy to 'everyday low price'. Store employees organised food donation in their local communities.[2] Led by CEO Dave Lewis, the comprehensive strategy required significant operational change – and we asked him why he decided to take it on.'I think the answer is, why wouldn't you?' he answered:

> Watching that waste happen just feels completely wrong. So, I think the question is why as a retailer would you allow that to happen? Commercially and economically, you'd want to minimise that waste. Then when you accept that in your business model you're always going to have this issue of managing surplus or shortage, you start to think from a broader social value point of view, what can you do about that?

Because of the activist spirit with which Lewis spearheaded the company's food waste ambition, he was invited to chair Champions 12.3, the United Nations Sustainable Development Goal to halve food waste around the world. So, while still CEO of Tesco, Lewis also stepped into leading the international coalition of governments and big businesses focused on fighting global food waste. The company's work on the issue created a leadership platform for him as CEO and for the business globally, and it amplified action on the issue through the commitments made by other businesses that followed suit.

(ii) Standard Chartered: 'Our objective is to become a leader in the fight against financial crime.'

Standard Chartered is an international bank with ventures in about 50 markets and profits coming largely from Asia, Africa and the Middle East.[3] It was taken to task by a number of regulators, including Department of Justice of the United States for processing transactions in violation of the Iranian sanctions, and this was followed by eye-watering fines for poor money-laundering controls.[4] This represented a serious commercial and reputational risk, and a challenge to their very identity, expressed in their brand promise 'Here for Good'.

The bank spent hundreds of millions of dollars overhauling the processes that had made the breach possible. It was a huge programme, increasing compliance teams sixfold and spending tenfold; retraining employees all over the world; strengthening oversight mechanisms. But while it ultimately provided necessary assurance to regulators, for a leadership team with a strong belief in the company's potential to play a positive role in the world that was not enough. The world expected them to fix their compliance processes and doing so wasn't going to win them any special plaudits. They wanted to go further.

Standard Chartered pivoted: they set themselves the ambition to help make the financial system a hostile place for criminals. They began to apply their hard-won expertise to de-risk the global banking system, which the UN estimates moves more than one trillion dollars of illicit financing each year. In some of the most challenging places in the world, they launched

Correspondent Banking Academies to share their expertise, training around 1,200 local banks in due diligence and anti-corruption practices.[5] Taking it on with an activist spirit – working across the financial system with other banks and partnering with law enforcement agencies – they aimed to make a real impact on financial crime.

With an initial focus on modern slavery, and terrorist financing, they expanded the scope to take on the illegal wildlife trade. 'When it comes to the fight over the illegal wildlife trade, the criminals have been winning. This brutal business has become the world's fourth most profitable criminal trafficking enterprise, generating revenues of between seven billion dollars and twenty-three billion dollars a year,' wrote David Fein, their then General Council, in the *Financial Times*. 'We can help prevent wildlife trafficking by targeting the heart of the industry: the money.' Mapping the monetary flows, deploying AI tools, training financial crime investigators, all became part of the effort. And they helped bring together a transnational coalition of partners; banks, law enforcement agencies, regulators and NGOs 'to spot patterns that no one can see alone'.[6] Over time, the bank's dedication to the issue of financial crime helped to earn trust and for employees this work has become a source of pride.

As he launched the campaign, the CEO Bill Winters explained why it mattered to the bank. 'Our objective is to become a leader in the fight against financial crime. We are on the front line in that fight [because of] the privileged position that we occupy as the leading cross-border bank in many of the markets in which we operate.' And this wasn't a side project for the business, he said:

> I would like every one of our clients and employees to know that this is central to our purpose as a bank.[7]

(iii) bp: 'I get it. I get the huge frustration, the anxiety – the anger. I get that people want cleaner energy.'

bp is one of the world's so-called 'supermajors' – alongside the likes of Chevron, ExxonMobil and Royal Dutch Shell. At a time of soaring living costs and fears for energy security, the profits of these big oil companies have incurred public ire and put them back in the limelight once again. Yet the underlying issue facing the entire sector for the future is the climate crisis. For many years these *Big Oil* companies have found themselves in the eye of the storm on climate change – and for many years, many failed even to really acknowledge the issue, while funding industry associations that promoted climate scepticism. bp broke ranks with the industry when in 1997 they left the infamous *Global Climate Coalition* – an industry association opposing action on climate – and soon after they became the first major to acknowledge the reality of climate change and the need for urgent action.[8] This was a big symbolic moment, but fundamentally the position of the industry was unchanged: the world needs fossil fuels and would continue to do so for a very long time.

A big shift happened for bp in 2020 with the appointment of a new CEO. The industry was besieged: targeted by increasingly sophisticated campaigns from NGOs, subject to increasingly negative public opinion, struggling to attract the brightest talent.[9] Commitments by governments looked set to place long-term demand for oil on a downward trajectory. Crucially, investors joined the fray: a divestment movement was growing and the major pensions funds and asset managers were asking difficult questions about regulatory risk and stranded assets. So it was striking that, in his second week in the job, bp's CEO Bernard Looney took to the stage to say, *I get it*:

I get the huge frustration, the anxiety – the anger. I get that
people want cleaner energy. I hear that everywhere I go in
the world. The world's carbon budget is finite, and it is
running out fast. We need a rapid transition to net zero.[10]

It was a real pivot: Looney set out to shift from international
oil company to integrated energy company shaped to meet
future energy demand. He announced a net zero target,
embracing Scope 3 emissions – so including the impact from
cars, homes and factories, as well as from its operations. And
Looney described how bp aims to play a part in getting the
world to reach net zero, with a plan to 'help countries, cities
and corporations around the world decarbonise'.

Within months of setting out this new direction of travel, bp
had announced a raft of significant moves: entering the offshore
wind power market with a $1.1 billion investment in Equinor,[11]
partnering with renewables giant Ørsted on an ambitious initiative to produce green hydrogen[12] and acquiring a majority stake
in Finite Carbon, the largest developer of carbon offsets in the
US.[13] As the war in Ukraine has highlighted, the industry isn't
wrong about how dependent the world is on oil and gas. Yet
even as new contracts are being signed to keep energy supplies
flowing today, the major players are having to work out how to
meet the urgent demand in society to wean itself off fossil fuels.
Nothing about that is easy – but, looking to the future for the
business, Looney is determined to reframe the climate challenge
from *threat* to *opportunity*. He points to the trillions of dollars
that will be needed to invest in 'replumbing and rewiring' the
global energy system, saying:

The opportunity in providing the world with what it wants
and needs is enormous.

In all these examples, the dramatic quality of making a pivot is evident. They represent a 180° shift in mindset − from asserting how good the company's own performance is on this question to seeking new ways to contribute to an issue that is of real and urgent concern in the world, and where it is evident to everyone, internally and externally, that the company has skin in the game. And action is a natural consequence.

Step up your response − keep asking what needs to happen next

Having an activist spirit rebases how a company engages with the major critical societal issues it is intrinsically part of. It's helpful to draw a contrast with the traditional risk-based corporate stance towards dealing with difficult issues − an 'issues management' approach versus an 'issues leadership' approach:

From: Issues Management		To: Issues Leadership	
Corporate-centric	⇨	Issue-centric	Understanding the issue as the world sees it, not only through the lens of the business
Focus on historic performance	⇨	A future-facing commitment	Looking ahead at what needs doing, not only reporting on the past activities of the business
Minimising exposure	⇨	Visibly engaging	Joining the conversations about the issue and taking real action, not just seeking to control risks
Reactive	⇨	Proactive	Getting ahead of the curve and setting the agenda, not waiting to be forced into taking action

From: Issues Management		To: Issues Leadership	
Position statement	⇨	Ambition statement	A rallying cry for the impact you want to make, not a formal statement of policy that feels defensive
About *you*	⇨	About *the issue*	Not promoting how much you have done, but focusing on how to make progress on the issue itself

Taking an issues-leadership approach helps the business and the leadership team to take up a role as protagonists in driving change and enables them to step up their response, looking at what needs to happen next to keep making progress.

Let's look at an example from the apparel sector, which faces multiple social and environmental challenges, from forced labour and worker safety, to waste and water use, and supply chain resilience. This is the globally famous brand Levi Strauss, based in California, in a piece on their website entitled 'We Need to Talk About Conscious Consumption'. They start with a clear *we-get-it* statement of what matters, and why:

> Almost 100 billion pieces of clothing are now made each year, and too many garments get thrown out after being worn just seven times. It's part of a wasteful cycle of overproduction and overconsumption that is clogging landfills, squandering natural resources and hypercharging apparel's impact on our planet.[14]

Their analysis is squarely focused on what needs to be fixed about the issue; not aiming to minimise their exposure to it but proactively locating themselves and their sector in the challenge, and owning their part in it. They go on to make a future-facing commitment to action:

> We don't yet have all the answers, but we know we have to keep pushing in the right direction, in concert with our competitors and customers. We must do away with outdated, damaging industry practices and advocate for new, better approaches . . .

Taking that point of view motivates the step-up in the company's response. So they're directing their innovation at the problem, including developing new materials such as a 'cottonised-hemp' blend that requires much less water and pesticides in the field; they're incorporating recycled fibres into their fabrics; and are facilitating consumers to sell their used jeans into a vintage, second-hand chain via eBay.

Paul Dillinger heads up product innovation at Levi's. He led the design team that came up with the *Wellthread* collection in 2015, a product line that used sustainability criteria at every step of the process. A highly acclaimed designer in the industry, he's gone on to embed that learning across their entire operations and describes the evolution of the idea in the company:

> More important even than the product is that *Wellthread* is the opportunity to learn. We approach the line, every season with a new set of challenges that we work through and try to resolve. There is no single solution but it's more about the diligence of developing that new way of working.[15]

That's a step up from producing a single line of jeans that can tout its sustainability credentials to take into consideration 'the broader system of the business', as Dillinger calls it:

You know you can only do so much by modifying any individual component and recalibrating processing, recalibrating the impact of the form of the materials, you have to take a broader look and see the impact of the full scope of the business and products entire lifecycle.

Levi's was an iconic name but a fading brand when Charles Bergh took over as CEO. He turned it around, taking it through a successful IPO and making it relevant to a new generation of consumers. In 2021, the company launched a new campaign: 'Buy Better, Wear Longer'.[16] The advert starts by proclaiming: 'Global consumption has doubled in the last 15 years – we can change that . . .'[17] The headlines in *Fast Company* voiced the question on everyone's mind: 'Levi's want you to stop buying so many jeans. A new Levi's ad takes aim at overconsumption in the fashion industry. But can the brand sell less and still be profitable?'[18]

Bergh talked about that question in a television interview, calling this their sweet spot: 'Levi's are known for quality, resilience and lasting through time,' he said, explaining how the campaign speaks to the sentiment among many young consumers that they want to shift away from buying, hardly wearing and throwing away their clothes.[19] The campaign is the consumer face of their broader strategy to build business success while taking on the challenge of wasteful overconsumption. Levi's strategy is to tap into the rising level of concern on these issues to future-proof their brand, making it relevant to the next generation of consumers.

Don't just fix the problem in your business, work to fix it in the world

A common thread in the examples above is that they're not just asking, 'How are we performing on this issue, as a company?' they're asking, 'How do we help to tackle the issue in the world?' You can hear it in their language: *to end the cycle of overproduction and overconsumption; to lead the fight in global food waste; to make the financial system a hostile place for criminals; to accelerate the energy transition.* Those are activist positions. For Tesco, success became not just being able to claim that 'We are wasting less food' but 'The world is wasting less food'. For Levi's, the question was no longer just 'Can we make some clothes more sustainably?' but 'Can we get people to buy clothes more sustainably?'

H&M, based in Stockholm, is another global clothing brand intent on challenging the accepted norms of its industry. The company's stated ambition is 'to lead the change' needed in fashion.[20] To do that, they start their story back at the beginning: 'From our very first day in 1947, our business has been about making fashion and the joy it can bring accessible to everyone – democratising what had previously been a privilege of the few.' But, moving on from celebrating the original intent, they quickly turn to face into the challenge that how we live and operate now creates different priorities:

> Today, the world looks different. More people than ever before are enjoying decent incomes and good standards of living. We still want to make fashion accessible and enjoyable for all. But given the environmental and social pressures faced by our planet, we must change how we do that. We have to challenge ourselves, question old assumptions, and reimagine what growth means.[21]

The discontinuity between what was the norm and what is needed now is a hallmark of the activist mindset. And the turnkey moment is evident in those few words: 'Today, the world looks different . . .' H&M are using their well-respected perform-ance in sustainability as a springboard to step up to a different level of commitment.

As with Levi's, H&M is active on climate and environmental issues, delivering a similar set of initiatives on materials inno-vation, increased use of recycled materials and more sustainable sourcing. Alongside all that, a distinctive aspect of H&M's social leadership is their commitment to human rights and working conditions in the supply chain. Following the Rana Plaza tragedy in Bangladesh in 2013 where 1,100 workers were buried under a collapsed factory building,[22] H&M got actively involved in improving the appalling conditions endemic in the garment industry's supply chains. In the midst of the many initiatives kick-started at the time, Karl-Johan Persson, then CEO, was a vocal advocate for a national living wage, meeting with the Bangladesh prime minister to press the argument.[23] And the company initiated several pilots to run factories in a way that gave them full control of working conditions.

'What Fashion Brands Should Do With Wages' was the title of a panel at the Fashion Summit in Copenhagen in 2019.[24] Sitting alongside two front-line NGO activists, just a few months before she became H&M's CEO, Helena Helmersson reflected on that topic. She had been H&M's sustainability director in 2013 when the company published its first living wage strategy, went on to lead production in Asia and was speaking as H&M's COO: 'I think that being part of setting the Fair Living Wage strategy back in 2013 – and then getting a job where you actu-ally get the responsibility to execute and make it happen – has made me learn a great deal about what is working and what is not.' Her biggest lesson from those years was that a siloed

approach, as she calls it, will not have the desired impact –
ultimately, just creating a pocket of excellence in your business
won't work:

> For example, making one factory look perfect, one company
> meeting with the government, designing one product to be
> sustainable. These things have other benefits but if you really
> want to drive systemic change, and raise the bar for the whole
> industry, you need to consistently work on different levels
> and that will require more time.

An area where H&M has a proven track record is working
with their supplier base to implement wage management systems
in factories and make wage levels more transparent. When the
strategy was launched in 2013, it was in just three factories and
by 2019 it was in 800, covering 900,000 workers.[25] But Helmersson
believes 'the true game changer' has been their work with leading
unions, retailers and other brands to push for industrywide
collective bargaining approaches to raise wages: 'This is something I would love more companies and more suppliers to work
on because this is a proof,' she says. She's adamant, though,
that this isn't a way of letting the company off the hook on
driving progress in its own operations: 'It means we have to
look at ourselves in the mirror,' she says.

For H&M, that internal reflection has meant rethinking practices that are accepted industry norms but serve to perpetuate
the challenges in the supply chain – extended payment terms,
for instance, or orders placed at short notice, making capacity
forecasting in the factories hard, leading to knock-on implications for how their suppliers treat their workforces.[26]

H&M's work on a fair living wage shows what it takes to
step up on an issue and keep asking what needs to happen next
to make progress. As well as looking out into the world, you

take that look in the mirror. H&M's goal is for workers to receive a 'fair living wage' not just in their own supply chain, but across the industry. It's an example of the activist mindset in action: don't just fix the problem in your business, work to fix it in the world.

*   *   *

This is a new paradigm and responding in this way can seem counter-intuitive. Often, when we first talk about the power of making a 'pivot' to face into the challenging issues, companies want to explain that they've always been a good company, based on good values. They have a track record of sustainability improvements and philanthropic donations over the years that serve to show that. Typically, all that is accurate but it remains rooted in a corporate-centric perspective where continued incremental improvement in performance on these issues is taken as a marker of a company's good character. It doesn't take account of the changed context within which business is operating today – or of the urgency of the societal issues that are fast becoming business issues.

The opportunity for leadership in these times is to turn the logic around: 'It is because we are a company of good character that has worked on these issues for a long time that we see the need to step up in a different way now.' That shift in mindset sets you off on a different road and with a new energy.

But while it may go against the traditional corporate instinct, it is not against the corporate interest. The companies whose stories we've told here are all global players, leaders in their sectors; they've not made that pivot and stepped up on societal issues in place of driving their commercial success – but, rather, in support of it. They articulate their rationale in terms of underpinning their regulatory licence to operate, connecting with the next generation of consumers, strengthening innovation capacity and building resilience into the operations and supply chain, even creating new product lines and opening up new markets. These are the business benefits of taking an activist approach to the issues; in all of these examples, it's about future-proofing the brand and the business.

4.

AMBITION:
aim to make a real impact

Thinking like an activist . . .	• Take on the issue with a spirit of ambition • Use this ambition to fuel your overall corporate purpose • Make sure the ambition is commensurate with the scale of your business – and the scale of the challenge

Take on the issue with a spirit of ambition

When a business really succeeds in something – pulling ahead of the competition, launching a bold new product, transforming their operations, integrating a major new acquisition – it is because they have applied the core strengths of the business to a new question with a spirit of ambition. This is at the heart of making anything extraordinary happen: you need the desire to go further, to raise the bar, to aim high. Sam Walton is often quoted as saying, 'High expectations are the key to everything.'

Many names in the pantheon of great corporate success stories are built on that. In the early days of Microsoft, Bill Gates articulated the ambition to put a computer on every desk and in every home.[1] Tesla set out to prove that electric vehicles could be quicker, better and more fun to drive than gasoline cars – and disrupted the traditional vehicle industry in the process. They started small and made it big. Adam Morgan, author of *Eating the Big Fish*, captured the essence of a successful challenger brand:

> A challenger brand is defined, primarily, by a mindset – it has business ambitions bigger than its conventional resources, and is prepared to do something bold, usually against the existing conventions or codes of the category, to break through.[2]

Pulling energy into harness behind ambitious goals is how the business world moves itself forward. What we are talking about here is summoning that same spirit and that capability to tackle tough societal challenges. These are inherently complex, difficult issues – unless you are ambitious in the way you approach them, you are unlikely to make any real impact. *The Oxford English Dictionary* defines 'ambitious' as describing a plan or a piece of work 'intended to satisfy high aspirations and therefore difficult to achieve'.

Once you look, you start to notice the many different ways companies take on a societal challenge imaginatively and with ambition. Volvo is a brand built on the promise of safety – yet when the company introduced the modern safety belt in the 1950s many people ridiculed it as a stupid idea. Since then, the safety belt has saved one million lives.[3] In 2020 Volvo introduced a new safety measure in the form of a built-in speed cap, only to get the same response. But they pressed on, setting themselves a new ambition, A Million More, to save another million lives through the set of safety initiatives they have under development in the business.[4]

Coca-Cola has distribution chains that rely on a huge network of female micro-entrepreneurs that extends into villages all over the developing world – and, in 2010, they set in train *5by20*, their campaign to empower five million women by 2020. They activated programmes to provide business skills, financial services, mentors and support networks for women, delivered with civil society partners in local communities worldwide. And by 2020 the company had exceeded their goal.[5]

Intel's chips require minerals sourced from some of the most war-torn places on the planet – and so they made a commitment to drive the conflict minerals out of their supply chain. Described as ambitious by industry commentators, their campaign – called *In Pursuit of Conflict-Free* – captured their spirit of activism: they were on a quest, going after something that is hard to attain but worth it.[6]

The most urgent issue which all corporates today are being called on to step up to with real ambition is the climate crisis. By June 2022, 3,000 companies had signed up to Science Based Targets on climate, leaping a huge increase from just sixteen in 2016.[7] But at a time when business leaders are lining up to make a commitment to becoming net zero by 2050, Microsoft took it to the next level. They announced their intention to be 'carbon negative' by 2030 – meaning that, within the decade, the company aims to remove more carbon from the atmosphere than it emits each year. It is a bold move – and they call it a *Moonshot*:[8] 'It is an ambitious – even audacious – goal, but science tells us that it's a goal of fundamental importance to every person alive today and for every generation to follow.'

In the extensive commentary that surrounded the detail of their announcement, inevitably the fans welcomed the urgency behind the stepped-up ambition and the sceptics focused on the reliance of new technologies that even the company acknowledges are not yet scalable or don't even exist today. Lucas Joppa, the Chief Environmental Officer at Microsoft, readily recognises the uncertainty. 'We have to go out and make some bets on technologies that don't exist, on technologies that are too expensive, and on markets that aren't mature enough,' he told Bloomberg:

> They will never be cheap enough, they will never be scaled high enough, and they will never be mature enough unless a Microsoft comes in right now and starts pushing.[9]

In Joppa's view, the urgency to deliver innovation to scale is an argument for the involvement of the large corporates, not a reason to pull back from the challenge.

Ambition infuses Microsoft actions on other societal issues they take on. Unsurprisingly, as one of the world's tech giants, the company is very active on digital skills. As the socio-economic impacts of covid became evident in 2020, Microsoft launched an initiative to help twenty-five million people worldwide to get access to digital skills by the end of the year. Seeing that the people hit hardest by job losses were those on lower incomes, women and under-represented minorities, they homed in on where they believed they could contribute most effectively: The problem we need to solve, they said, is that:

> The world will need a broad economic recovery that will require in part the development of new skills among a substantial part of the global workforce.[10]

They could move fast in part because they already had a substantial digital skills commitment. One of the long-standing pillars of that strategy is *TEALS* – Technology Education and Literacy in Schools – an initiative focused on students who've become excluded from computer science for reasons of race, gender or geography. It gets tech professionals into US high schools to work alongside teachers. Since it began in 2009, it's built up and trained a network of 1,650 tech professional volunteers coming from 700 companies, reaching 93,000 students, tracking the impact on student performance and sharing what's been learned along the way.[11] As one Harlem teacher who has a TEALS volunteer coming into his classes put it, 'It's seeing that a real professional has taken time out of their day to come into our school that gives my students the confidence to say, "This could be me".'[12] These individual stories are always heart-warming, but what distinguishes leadership initiatives such as this one is the level of ambition – not only to achieve large numbers, of people reached or dollars spent, but to build long-term capacity for computer science education across the entire system.

Both in their digital skills initiative and in their climate commitments, Microsoft is acting with ambition to make an impact, and at a scale you might hope for from one of the world's leading and most systemically important companies. Satya Nadella, Microsoft's CEO, voices the attitude that informs all those ambitions:

> We understand companies like ours that can do more, should do more. Our promise to you is this: we are, and we will.[13]

Use this ambition to fuel your overall corporate purpose

In recent years, many companies have been looking afresh at their *purpose*. It has become a big conversation in the business world; a couple of years ago, *Forbes* described it as 'a purpose stampede'.[14] How does purpose relate to being an activist in business?

When it comes down to it, the live question on purpose is all about whether the company is having a positive impact in the world. The impetus that's driving companies to talk about their purpose is the need to demonstrate that they're not just making profits at the expense of society at large. So it's in the same territory as what we're talking about here: taking on tough societal challenges with a spirit of ambition. And not just any challenges, but those issues where your business is intrinsically involved – through negative externalities or potentially positive contributions. The conversation about purpose lays down the gauntlet to companies to think about their role in the world differently.

And in our experience, becoming an activist on societal issues is a sure step in the right direction. We've seen companies becoming increasingly purpose-driven as they get more and more involved with the critical issues around them. It becomes part of the company culture, part of who they are.

Doing that with sufficient ambition and authentic commitment can help to bring alive the company's own sense of purpose. Financial services businesses, for example, often take on the issue of financial inclusion as a way of making a meaningful contribution in marginalised communities – while, simultaneously, highlighting the essential role that financial services plays in society around the world. Mastercard is acknowledged as a leader globally for their work on access to financial services; it's incorporated into their statement of corporate purpose: 'To connect and power an inclusive digital economy that benefits everyone, everywhere.'[15]

For Mastercard's leadership team, that statement reframed how the company interprets its role in the world. Ajay Banga, Mastercard's CEO for more than ten years, used it to help employees to reimagine the company's purpose: 'It's not to get more cards into the market, but to move to a world beyond

cash, and that's now embedded in everything we do and say.'[16]
From a business perspective, the purpose aligns the organisation
with the digital transformation of the financial services sector
globally. In parts of the world where the cash-based grey
economy is the reality for so many people, working in collaboration alongside policymakers and civil society institutions is
the only way to increase economic inclusion – and at the same
time, build trust and reinforce the company's licence to operate.
Meanwhile, focusing on the direct impact of financial exclusion
on the lives of individuals – who are very far from carrying a
Mastercard in their wallets – they set out their ambitious
strategy to bring one billion people into the digital economy
by 2025.[17] Through delivering on that ambition, they are able
to make a positive impact to scale on a social issue while simultaneously bringing alive for many different stakeholders,
including their employees, the intrinsic value of financial services
in a well-functioning economy and society.

In that crystallisation of purpose the company has succeeded
in synthesising its aspirations for growth with its aspirations
for the role it plays in the wider world. It conveys the value and
values of the business but, more importantly, demonstrates how
purpose is about putting those values into action.

Make sure the ambition is commensurate with the scale of your business – and the scale of the challenge

A question we're sometimes asked is, 'how ambitious should
we be?'. To some it might seem like an odd question: after all,
you probably don't become an Olympic athlete with the hope
of winning a bronze – isn't ambition about going for gold? But
they're asking a real question, a kind of *Goldilocks* question:
on the one hand, they don't want to be *under*-ambitious and

accused of not doing enough; on the other hand, they don't want to be *over*-ambitious and set themselves up for failure.

We often hear leaders saying, 'We don't want to promise something we can't deliver!' Indeed: business is designed to deliver what it promises and business culture is shaped by the ability to do that. One commercial director said to us, 'Our entire performance ethos is based on being clear that you can deliver what you say you can deliver. We don't want to over-claim; we don't want to commit before we're certain we can deliver.' It's a matter of honour. The companies that are most shy of setting a big ambition are sometimes those that are most sincere about their intention to make a positive impact: they see how difficult the issue is, and don't want to make disin-genuous promises. But to flip that around: promising just what you're sure you have the capability to deliver today is not only unambitious, it misses the opportunity. If you are going to achieve anything beyond incremental gains, you've got to have ambition.

The nature of these complex and challenging societal issues is that no one has all the answers. Everyone knows how entrenched these problems are – but what's needed is that people and organ-isations with problem-solving capabilities get involved and work at it.

And, as you start to do that, setting an ambition ups your game. It's a mindset question: it changes your view of what might be possible in your own performance. When you have an ambition, your plans become bolder: you ask for a different level of ingenuity and delivery from the business. Every plan and target then becomes another milestone on the journey towards achieving it. If what you need to do next is beyond the capacity of the organisation today, you've created the motivation to build towards it. We've seen how it can be an 'aha' moment for a leadership team when they see in their minds' eye that setting themselves an ambition is more than a few grand-sounding words, but more a context for the choices they make.

A key test is: when people look at your level of ambition, will it seem commensurate with the scale of your business? Does it stack up against your influence across the systems that you're part of, and against your impacts on the big issues? There can be a dissonance here, which is what fuels the anger of critics such as Anand Giridharadas, whose book *Winners Take All: The Elite Charade of Changing the World*, spotlights the social impact programmes of corporations which he holds to be woefully disproportionate to the scale of the businesses and the impacts they are making in the world. One such example he cites:

> Goldman [Sachs] had launched an initiative called *10,000 Women*, through which it invested in female business owners and mentored them. Doing so, its promotional materials said, was 'one of the most important means to reducing inequality and insuring more shared economic growth' – goals for which Goldman was otherwise not well known.[18]

To many, initiatives like this look like proverbial fig leaves, aimed primarily at projecting an image of a socially engaged company rather than really getting to grips with the issues. Critics conclude that the objective with these sorts of initiatives is little more than having something for the CEO to talk about at Davos. In the case of Goldman Sachs, they subsequently upped their level of ambition and focused it on racial equity in the US: the *One Million Black Women* initiative commits $100 million in investments aimed at 'narrowing opportunity gaps'.[19]

In 2010 when Unilever announced its ambition to double sales and halve environmental impacts, the company knew it was setting out along an untrodden path. The CEO at the time, Paul Polman, admitted: 'We do not yet know how we will do this.'[20] This was the beginning of the now famous *Sustainable Living Plan*, a ten-year companywide initiative.

Ask people to name an activist leader in business and it won't be long before someone mentions Paul Polman. He was early to this journey, and he's often a lightning rod in the discussion of the role of business on these issues. Some people will tell us, 'I'm not a Paul Polman'; one leader even said to us, 'I need to decide where I am on a scale of one-to-Polman.' To others, he's the figure who's set the pace for others for over a decade. Unsurprisingly he's done a lot of thinking about this – so we spoke to him for this book. Reflecting on his experience, he told us, what matters is to be clear that you recognise what the problem is:

> The interesting thing, which I always found, is you don't need to be perfect. It doesn't matter if you don't have all the answers. It doesn't matter if you're not where you should be – no one is. To get credibility what people want to hear is that you understand what is needed. The most important thing is that you acknowledge what is needed. Yes, then the world opens up and people say: he's real, he's a human.

On completion of the plan in 2020, the company estimated it had achieved 80 per cent of its goals and revealed that its most sustainable brands grew 46 per cent faster than the rest of the business and delivered 70 per cent of its turnover growth.[21] As with any stretching ambition, Unilever's *Sustainable Living Plan* had unlocked innovation, new ways of working and new collaborations for the company.

When you look at the ten-year plan Unilever laid out or the approach Mastercard has taken to embrace the issue of financial inclusion into their corporate purpose, they follow what we call *The Leadership Model*, illustrated in Figure 7, as do all the other examples we profile of companies taking on a societal issue with ambition.

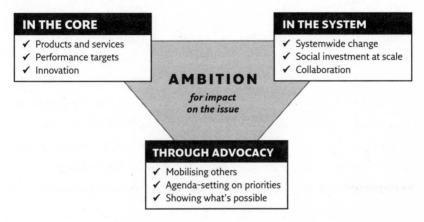

IN THE CORE
- ✓ Products and services
- ✓ Performance targets
- ✓ Innovation

IN THE SYSTEM
- ✓ Systemwide change
- ✓ Social investment at scale
- ✓ Collaboration

AMBITION
*for impact
on the issue*

THROUGH ADVOCACY
- ✓ Mobilising others
- ✓ Agenda-setting on priorities
- ✓ Showing what's possible

Figure 7: The Leadership Model

It's a model we use to help a company build out its strategy on the societal issues they are focused on: you will want to take action **in the core** of the business, through the products and services the company takes to market, your practices and policies, and the targets and plans you set; you will need to work with others **in the system** beyond the business, through collaborations and partnerships that support systemwide change – and to bring your social impact initiatives and strategic philanthropy into harness with these efforts; and you can use your voice **through advocacy** on the issue, speaking up on what needs to change, mobilising others and showing how it's possible to raise the bar. And all of this is in service of a central, driving ambition to make an impact on the issue. These are the dimensions of activity available to an activist leader, and we'll come back to each of them in the chapters that follow.

5.

DISRUPTION:
do something different

Thinking like an activist . . .	• Harness the innovation power of your business to problem-solve on the issue
	• Seek out radical new ways of doing business
	• Ask yourself the 'disruptive question': what if we had to?

Harness the innovation power of your business to problem-solve on the issue

This is what it means to run a business: putting out fires, troubleshooting, overcoming obstacles, managing perpetual turbulence while aiming for continuous improvement, managing for the fact that there's no steady state where everything is fixed, but dealing with radical uncertainty in real time with incomplete information. That's the job. And it's only possible because businesses are by nature problem-solving machines, backed by a significant capacity for innovation. Harnessing all this and applying it to the major issues in the world that your business can help to solve for, is what we mean by *thinking like an activist*.

Once you're facing into the issues, with a sense of ambition to make a meaningful impact, then the work begins. These issues are wicked problems – if there were easy solutions, somebody would have found them by now. It's going to involve some radical thinking and bold new approaches. Every business considers its ability to innovate to be at the heart of its success, and becoming an activist leader means applying that capacity to the societal issues where you have the potential to make the greatest contribution.

Almost certainly that means doing something different from what you have so far done. It takes persistence – when you come up against inevitable obstructions, you find your way around them. It takes insight and fresh perspectives – in the sense famously expressed by Albert Einstein when he said that problems can't be fixed with the same thinking that created them. And it takes a willingness to embrace disruption, to question the status quo and be open to new ways of doing things. These behaviours come naturally to highly innovative businesses – and tackling the world's big issues will take exactly this kind of thinking.

Take Apple's view of problem-solving. In 2017, the company announced a bold ambition: 'to make products without taking from the Earth'.[1] It sounds impossible, but the company enjoys that. 'If you act like you can do something, then it will work,'[2] said Steve Jobs in the early days, as he willed Apple into being. That spirit is present still in the sense of conviction with which the company is applying itself to its ambition to close the loop on its supply chain and to one day no longer mine materials from the earth. 'To do that,' says Lisa Jackson, who has led their work on environmental and social initiatives for a decade, 'we're dedicating Apple's unmatched innovative capacity to get there.'[3]

The allure of Apple products is not only the functionality that they put in people's hands – it is their tactile elegance. And an essential ingredient in the desirability of their products is *aluminium*. 'We use aluminium because it has incredible strength, durability and for its sheer beauty,' said Laura Legros, vice-president of hardware engineering at Apple.[4] Aluminium is one of Apple's most important manufacturing materials and one of the most widely used metals in the world, found in products from planes to drinks cans to electronic devices. But it's a metal with a big environmental footprint: 1.1 billion tons of CO_2 emissions are generated each year by aluminium production, amounting to around 2 per cent of global emissions. And demand is set to increase by more than 50 per cent by 2050.[5] So, to achieve their goal of 'making without taking' requires Apple to radically change how they use aluminium.

In 2018 the company announced the launch of the new MacBook Air made with a 100 per cent recycled aluminium shell. It was a goal they had been aiming for for some time and Apple declared: 'To use 100 per cent recycled aluminium, we had to invent a whole new kind.'[6]

The problem they been grappling with was that standard recycled aluminium accumulates impurities every time it is recycled. They concluded that the material they needed did not exist, so they decided to invent it. Using computational models, they identified the potential of a new customised alloy chemistry that could withstand countless recycling loops. Designed to accommodate sources of scrap aluminium, it can deliver the necessary strength and, at the same time, the flawless finish that is so essential to the Apple brand. Making the casings for the MacBook Air and Mini Mac from recycled material avoided the mining of 900,000 metric tons of aluminium-bearing bauxite in 2019 alone and simultaneously halved the computer's carbon footprint.[7] As Laura Metz, Apple's senior product manager, explained: 'It's designed to use fine shavings of recaptured aluminium that are re-engineered down to the atomic level. This new alloy is as beautiful and robust as any we've used before, and it makes MacBook Air the greenest Mac ever.'[8]

But Apple called the new aluminium alloy 'just the beginning'.[9] The company's next move was carbon-free smelting. 'Aluminium has been made the same way for a hundred and thirty years – until now,' said Legros. Three Apple engineers had set off on a quest to find a better, cleaner way of mass-producing aluminium. Meeting up with large aluminium companies, start-ups and independent labs around the world, they came across Alcoa's breakthrough smelting technology. In 1886, Alcoa was the company that pioneered the aluminium smelting process that's been used in the industry right up to the present day, but its disadvantage is that it's very carbon-intensive. They had recently invented a new carbon-free process and they needed a partner to take their innovation to scale.[10] Apple brought Alcoa together with the mining giant Rio Tinto and the three companies, along with the governments of Canada and Quebec, formed a joint venture to invest in scaling up and commercialising the opportunity.[11] Rio Tinto sees it as a 'revolutionary process'[12] that, when fully developed, has the potential to remove direct greenhouse gases from aluminium smelting globally. In 2019 Apple was able to announce it had bought the first ever commercial batch of aluminium produced with carbon-free smelting.[13]

Those aluminium breakthroughs are only milestones along the way, part of the comprehensive environmental strategy that aims to become carbon neutral across their entire footprint, and to transform their use of resources to make their products and packaging with only recycled or renewable materials. 'At Apple, it's simple. We apply the same level of innovation that goes into everything we create, design, power and manufacture to making things better for people and the planet,' explains

Lisa Jackson: 'In the years ahead, we will all need to think differently and act urgently.'[14]

Seek out radical new ways of doing business

Business model disruptions are the stuff of business legend: think Netflix and how it disrupted the bricks-and-mortar rental model with a monthly DVD subscription model, then disrupted that with a streaming model. Twice Netflix displaced an incumbent business model with a new one and led the industry towards their model. The notion of disruptive innovation was developed by Clayton Christensen and his collaborators,[15] and it's been described by *The Economist* as one of history's most influential business ideas.[16] But corporations find disruptive thinking hard – perhaps because, according to Christensen, 'good managers' like to make evidence-based, data-driven decisions, but 'Markets that do not exist cannot be analysed'. Producers and consumers must figure it out together, he says.[17]

We're interested in how disruptive innovation can work to find solutions to societal challenges, where there aren't existing models to be analysed and so much needs to be figured out. A great example is Philips, which rethought its business model in lighting: Light as a Service – or LaaS – for its business customers. The premise is that rather than selling lighting equipment to their business and municipal customers who then service it as a depreciating asset, Philips retains ownership of the equipment and fixtures and manages them for performance as a service fee. The idea sounds so simple that, once it exists, it seems strange it was not done before. As Philips' CEO Frans Van Houten explained:

We decided to embed circular-economy thinking in our strategic vision and mission, both as a competitive necessity and with the conviction that companies solving the problem of resource constraints will have an advantage. We believe that customers will increasingly consider natural resources in their buying decisions.[18]

The market realities for Philips in the early 2000s were challenging: business and municipal customers were reluctant to make big investments in new lighting systems following the economic crash. Many were playing wait-and-see as the technologies rapidly evolved. Added to this, the company noticed the rising concern in the world about the sustainability of energy use. It became clear to Philips that radical new solutions were needed:

This led us to consider lighting as a service. After all, why do these customers buy light fixtures and luminaires? It's not for the fixture but for the light itself. For business customers, we therefore now sell lighting as a service: customers only pay us for the light, and we take care of the technology risk and the investment.[19]

The company made a bold commitment to deliver 15 per cent of its sales from circular economy products by 2020[20] – and they achieved it. For customers, the new model offered cost reductions of up to 50 per cent over time,[21] with continual access to the latest technologies and a lot less hassle. And in tackling the issue of society's energy use, the model offered a groundbreaking concept in energy efficiency.

The innovation was not the creation of a new business model so much as the application of a proven model in a new context, as the journalist Lauren Phipps observed in GreenBiz. From cars to music, people are now becoming used to buying a service rather than a product. Phipps goes on to comment that in covering circular economy solutions, 'I have learned always to ask, "What happens next?"' Simply selling a managed solution does not in itself require an end-to-end approach and does not necessarily prevent the products finishing up in landfill.[22]

So, next, to make the shift to a circular model for lighting a reality, Philips had to play it out through every part of the business. The company set new criteria for every product, covering design for recyclability, upgradability and service-ability. Even the tendering process had to shift, from a focus on initial price to total cost of ownership and ecological impact. Meeting targets for recycled materials in their consumer products involved workshops with their suppliers where 'we tear down the entire value proposition to see what we might change and how', said Van Houten.

According to Van Houten, including metrics in the Philips KPI dashboard at leadership level was critical to it being taken seriously across the business. 'Above all, operating with circular-economy principles requires Philips people to challenge ourselves and to change,' he said:

> We can't think in terms of designing products that we throw over the wall to customers, but instead we need to design products that are upgradable and maintainable and that can be mined for materials and components that can be reused. Our mind-set needs to be 15 years out – not just 'now' – and it requires us to think in an end-to-end way, involving our suppliers and sales force. I'll admit this was challenging at first. Even though we have a long-standing focus on sustainability – a natural stepping stone toward a circular economy – it still tested us when we initially stepped up our circular-economy work.[23]

Philips had decided to push past its historic understanding of sustainability commitments to shape a new beyond business-as-usual approach. That has, in turn, been a catalyst to a business transformation that aims to bring together economic and social value through circularity.

As 2020 came around, the initial target was achieved. Now known as Signify, after its spinoff from Philips in 2016, the business set new targets, to increase sales from circular economy products to 32 per cent by 2025 and ensuring all new products meet the company's Ecodesign requirements.[24] Meanwhile, Philips is applying the same business model principles in its global healthcare business, aiming to break the traditional mould of hospitals and healthcare providers purchasing and owning equipment which requires big upfront expenditure, such as an MRI scanner, and replace it with offering the use of this sophisticated machinery as a managed service.[25] So, while the process may have involved tearing down the entire value proposition, it created new ones, new revenue sources and even new businesses.

Ask yourself the 'disruptive question': what if we had to?

In times of crisis we can find ourselves doing things we wouldn't have imagined possible. Necessity, the saying goes, is the mother of invention – an insight first articulated by Plato. Researchers at the Open University found a historical connection between rates of innovation and war, famine, pandemic and death: the Four Horsemen of the Apocalypse, if you'll allow 'pandemic' instead of 'pestilence'.[26] Indeed, this has proved to be the case during the years of covid: many of us – in our own lives, in our businesses, in our societies – have seen things happen that we wouldn't have thought possible.

From the perspective of business leaders, this experience has at times been astonishing. Almost overnight, the situation demanded operational change at a speed and scale unprecedented in their working life times – not least the shift to remote working. As CEO of HSBC, Noel Quinn was responsible for making sure that one of the world's largest banks continued operating smoothly. 'Of course, we had contingency plans for the closure of a major office,' he told a meeting of Brunswick partners, 'but nobody imagined that we would have to close down *all* our offices, globally, within just a few days. But we did it – we successfully migrated more than two hundred thousand employees to remote working within a few days!'

The magnitude of this won't be lost on anyone with operational responsibilities. It's the kind of major business transformation that you'd expect to take months – if not years – to achieve. And yet the business world is full of examples like this: companies that took extraordinary measures to keep the show on the road in extraordinary times. It involved supply chain innovation, acceleration of new technologies such as 3D printing, new decision-making processes and, of course, large-scale remote working.

The rapid development of the covid vaccines is another example of achieving something few would have thought possible. It required a radical new approach to research, parallel tracking of many of the steps in developing and approving a vaccine. It forced a new level of collaboration between the pharmaceutical companies, research labs and governments. As with so many tremendous achievements, the next hurdles presented themselves immediately: production to scale, equitable distribution, long-term efficacy and public trust. Still, the announcement of the first vaccines was a historic moment, a turning point in the pandemic. One of the researchers quoted Nelson Mandela: 'It always seems impossible until it's done.'

In the response to covid, business leaders surprised themselves: they learnt that businesses can disrupt themselves and adapt to what has to happen faster than they thought possible. And the experience created a visceral understanding of the colossal strains that come with vulnerability to systemic risk. For many that served as a call out to business to be bolder. At the height of the first waves of the pandemic, Bernard Looney, bp's CEO, commented: 'People talk about "the art of the possible", the current crisis is redefining "possible" day by day. We should reflect on that next time someone says that tackling climate change is too difficult, or too costly.'[27]

Asking the question about what might be possible unlocked innovation they had not dreamed of at the global shipping company, Maersk. Moving twelve million containers a year, with around a fifth of the world's trade on their ships on any given day, Maersk is a national hero company in Denmark. And in the run-up to COP15, due to be held in Copenhagen in 2009, the company reflected on the fact that the carbon footprint of their business was larger than the entire country's carbon emissions – and decided that had to change. The then CEO Nils Andersen set a challenge to Maersk's innovation teams. He asked what we call the 'disruptive question': what if we had to make it possible? How would it be possible to design a ship that was the same size as their largest vessels at the time but used 20 per cent less fuel? He admits that initially they all felt unsure it was even achievable but, as he tells the story, Andersen knew that he had tapped into the passion for problem-solving in their engineering teams:

They went away for some months and came back with this vessel that was actually 20 per cent larger, but also consumed almost 50 per cent less fuel than the average ship on the Asia Europe trade routes. It was a real rethinking of our ship.[28]

The Triple E became the largest but most energy efficient class of container vessels in the world.[29] The three 'E's stand for Economy of scale, Energy efficiency and Environmental impact improvement. Maersk offers up some buzz facts that give a sense of the scale: one of the Triple E vessels is quarter of a mile long, the height of a twenty-storey building and uses as much steel as eight Eiffel Towers. Only three metres longer and four metres wider than what came before, the ship expanded capacity by 16 per cent compared to the previous largest container vessel while reducing carbon emissions by a remarkable 50 per cent per container moved.[30] It was a ground-breaking ship; Maersk ordered twenty of them and the first was at sea by 2013.[31]

But it wasn't only the redesign of the ship itself that made it possible; a whole range of other innovations flowed from that initial disruptive question. As you might expect, there was a long list of engineering triumphs, from waste-heat recovery to more efficient propulsion systems. One of the most significant breakthroughs came from the decision to reduce the speed on all trade lanes: a jump down from the industry average of 22–23 knots to 20 knots brings a saving of up to 37 per cent in fuel,[32] a proposition that customers found compelling compensation for the slightly longer time at sea. And today Maersk's captains map out their passage to make the most of the oceans' currents in order to improve fuel efficiency. 'First and foremost, what we did was we got everybody engaged in it,' Andersen recalled:

> The big difference is that people, once they get to be inspired by this, they get out of bed in the morning and say this is really, really exciting. They've been bitten by the bug for making a better world. So, they also created a recyclability passport. That means that every part of this huge vessel –

every single item – is numbered and entered into a passport. So when the ship comes to end of life, it can be recycled.[33]

In parallel with developing the Triple E, Maersk's engineering teams had created a *Cradle to Cradle Passport* that records every component of the vessels, down to each nut and bolt.[34] Through chasing down an answer to the question about how to reduce carbon emissions, they had hit upon another of the major issues that challenge the shipping sector: the use of steel. Besides fuel, steel is the other major commodity that the industry depends on, with 60,000 tons required for each large ocean-going vessel.[35] Both the enormous quantities required for construction and then, at the end of life, the hazardous consequences of disposal have always presented very significant business and environmental challenges.

Their vision is to be able to make a new hull from the old. The *Passport* will make it possible to separate high-grade and low-grade steel, copper wiring, hazardous materials and waste at end of life in a way that's never been feasible before, meaning that from the design phase ships are intended for full disassembly of the materials and total vessel recyclability. With a lifecycle of around thirty years, the benefits are a while off yet.[36] But the concept holds out the opportunity of circularity in the resource-intensive, carbon-intensive shipping industry. As Maersk said at the time, 'Ultimately, this is not just about shipping; it is about how we manage steel as a resource globally.' In the ten years since then, the question of ship recycling has begun to gain traction and the company was just one of the founding signatories of the Ship Recycling Transparency Initiative (SRTI) that aims to raise the bar across the industry.[37]

But even radical disruption is not a one-and-done exercise. In 2021, Maersk did it again: they commissioned eight ships capable of running on carbon neutral methanol and invested in the scaling up of the fuel production needed to go with them. It was another industry first. Shipping has long been caught in a cycle of inaction: too few ships able to run on green fuels, so not enough supply of green fuels, so fleets don't commit to switching . . . and the company set out to break that stasis. Pointing out that vessels designed and built today will still be sailing in 2050 – when the world aspires to have achieved net zero – Morten Bo Christiansen, head of decarbonisation at Maersk, summed it up succinctly:

> Any talk about so-called transition fossil fuels is simply not relevant from our perspective, it's simply not solving the problem. The last thing we need is another cycle of fossil fuel assets.[38]

The company has made its own net zero commitment, and so have more than half of its top 200 customers – so, for them, this order is a proof that carbon neutral solutions are available and viable today. The activist spirit behind the move was voiced by their CEO, Søren Skou, when he said, 'The time to act is now if we are to solve shipping's climate challenge.'[39]

*   *   *

Whether it's Apple inventing a new kind of aluminium, or Philips reinventing the business model, or Maersk redesigning ships for the future, these are examples of how companies can redefine what's possible. They are responding to the intensity of the global crises. And it's often in response to crisis – the imperative it creates, the courage and ingenuity it can summon up – that people overturn ideas about what is and isn't possible; they throw out unexamined assumptions that something *can't* be done. People in such situations ask a disruptive question:

'What if we had to make it possible? How could we do it?' If told something isn't possible, they're likely to reply: 'Then we have to find another way.' We behave like this in a crisis because, frankly, we don't have a choice. This so often goes with thinking like an activist: an insistence that change is possible – because it has to be.

6.

CORE:
take action in the business

Thinking like an activist . . .	• Act on the issue as you would on any other strategic priority
	• Work through how your products and processes will need to change
	• Operationalise the ambition – with goals and a roadmap, led from the top
	• Climate crisis – moving from commitment to action

Act on the issue as you would on any other strategic priority

Companies are engines of execution – when they decide to make something happen, it's impressive to watch the business mobilise for the task at hand. And that engine can also push forward real change on societal issues. Taking activism into the core of the business means treating it like any other strategic priority. It is intrinsic to the business and its future, rather than a peripheral concern. The leadership rolls their sleeves up to operationalise the ambition.

It is a far cry from the old paradigm of 'giving back', when the great industrialists were free to pursue their profits as long as they wrote some big cheques for good causes and built some libraries and museums for public benefit. The advent of corporate responsibility and sustainability put the focus on how the profits were made in the first place and so social and environmental issues gradually became business considerations. Until the mid-1990s, CSR or sustainability departments hardly existed: now pretty much every business has one. But the historic model was to minimise harm where possible with as little interference as possible to business-as-usual. These departments sat like good angels on the shoulder of corporations, usually without any real strategic traction. Activist leadership today means recognising these issues as significant enough to the business that they must be built into the core and led from the top.

James Quincey is CEO of Coca-Cola, as we'll see shortly a company that has really stepped up in the fight against plastic waste. Interviewing Quincey at a summit on the circular economy, we asked him what it took to get started on a problem of such scale. 'For me, the principal way of galvanising the company is to make it an inherent part of the strategy – which is actually how it becomes a force in driving the economics of the business,' he answered, firmly underlining his point:

> You can look over all business history and anything people have done as some ancillary or parallel objective on the side – it ultimately fails to attract enough attention and sustainability if it's not integrated into the business.[1]

This is central to the proposition of delivering financial and social value hand-in-hand; if you really want to shift the needle, you have to treat the societal issues you work on like any other strategic priority. 'First, comes the objective,' continued Quincey. 'Agree where you're trying to go. That's seemingly obvious but, in the maelstrom of trying to make things happen, the objective sometimes gets moved and diluted. In a company like Coke, it very simply needs to become part of our core business.' In Quincey's view, this is what makes it 'doable'.

Racial justice is another hot issue where people expect to see action in the core of the business, and not just rhetoric. As the wave of Black Lives Matter protests gathered momentum in 2020, many companies contacted us wanting to know: should they speak out – or not? What should they say – or not say? They had seen the 'silence is violence' memes – but they'd also seen companies accused of 'performative activism'.[2] Indeed, many corporations were criticised for being quick to make statements and place black squares on Instagram without seeming to have any real substance behind it. Those intense weeks illuminated the contrast between the companies that spoke, most probably with positive intent but no action to follow, and those that made a commitment to make change in their business.

An organisation called Management Leadership for Tomorrow (MLT) runs a certification scheme that enables companies to report on the actions they are taking to back up their statements on racial diversity. John Rice, the CEO of MLT, told the *Brunswick Social Value Review* why he thinks certification will accelerate action on the issue: 'It falls into the same kind of analytical construct for strategy and execution that leaders have been using and winning with throughout their careers,' he said:

> For any important opportunity, [business leaders] define what success looks like in three to five years quantitatively and qualitatively. They manage to that strategy; they hold their teams accountable; they have interim metrics; they have internal and external accountability mechanisms. The Certification brings the same rigor and accountability to racial

equity that organizations and leaders bring to every other part of their business.[3]

Meaningful corporate action on any societal issue – plastic waste, racial justice or any other – must be rooted in the core business. This means it needs to be part of the business strategy, with a clear objective to deliver change through the business.

Work through how your products and processes will need to change

At the core of a business are the products and services it takes to market, so this is often where companies can most obviously be part of the solution – or the problem – in societal challenges. Can the product be re-engineered to be more energy efficient when it's being used? Can it be reformulated to include less sugar or salt? Can social media services be redesigned to safeguard against online harms? Can paper be produced with more sustainable forestry practices? Can laundry liquid wash at lower temperatures? Can insurance incentivise healthier or more sustainable behaviours? These are all real, live questions aimed at businesses today; answering them requires adaptations at the core of the business.

Many businesses deliver products and services that are inherently a public good – financial services, healthcare, digital connectivity, energy, transport, for example – and a common friction point for these companies is access to these goods. What about the people who can't afford your services? Is it right that pharma companies are making enormous profits while so many people can't access essential treatments? Shouldn't energy companies be doing more to tackle fuel poverty? These questions, and others like them, are a fault line for business in society.

And that's also why this is where you find some imaginative solutions.

Pre-paid *pay-as-you-go* mobile is a great example of product innovation aimed at increasing access to a service that has become, in effect, a social utility. It was first pioneered in South Africa by MTN, as they began rolling out the network in the 1990s. It became clear that the contract-based model that had been dominant in the developed world wouldn't work for many people in Africa. In a largely informal market, there was usually no way to verify credit histories or identities, and most people weren't able to afford big monthly bills. MTN had been founded in post-apartheid South Africa on a promise of being an inclusive business. They were convinced that access to mobile services would deliver a valuable social benefit, and were intent on addressing 'the whole market'. Their pre-paid model was the answer – and has now become a globally recognised approach for lower-income customers, and has extended beyond telecoms into other industries, such as electricity. It was an important part of the formula that has made MTN the largest mobile network operator in Africa.[4]

Attempts to disrupt the car insurance industry by companies like Metromile in the US[5] and By Miles in the UK[6] led to *pay-per-mile* car insurance, where monthly premiums are based in part on the number of miles you drive. Based on the consumer proposition that traditional car insurance is 'unfair', these are companies creating a business model from expanding access to a service that's become a part of the fabric of everyday life. Paying by the mile can dramatically reduce the cost of car ownership for those who only do short local journeys or drive infrequently. And it incentivises lower car use – by 6 per cent, according to a study by Yale – which is good news for carbon emissions and urban congestion.[7] The major insurance companies are slow to embrace this innovation, although the market for pay-per-mile surged during the lockdowns, when people realised they were paying insurance for cars that were not going anywhere.

The auto sector is being transformed by innovation of every kind. The scale and speed of product re-engineering underway is striking evidence of what's possible once the imperative for change is recognised. Until recently, the idea that EVs would become a mainstream product was hard to imagine for many – even those within the sector itself. Tesla's early aspirations were considered as simply a fanciful notion for rich Californians: as the chair of one major car company said, it was 'a joke that can't be taken seriously'.[8] Now Daimler, Ford, GM and Volkswagen are investing between 30 and 60 per cent of their R&D and capital expenditure into electronic vehicles.[9] The intensity of investment in innovation is bringing price parity within reach, with the total cost of ownership for EVs on a level with internal combustion engines almost achieved already.[10] Meanwhile, Chinese car manufacturer BYD – whose initials stand for Build Your Dreams – is focused on the affordability of EVs and expanding rapidly in the US. Their President, Stella Li, confidently declares: 'BYD's mission is to change the world through technological innovation that reduces greenhouse gases and our dependency on fossil fuels.'[11] EVs are only one part of the story of carbon neutral transport of course; fuels are another – and there's huge activity and investment in those as well, as we can see from Maersk's commitments in carbon neutral methanol for shipping (see p. 135) or the coalitions behind Sustainable Aviation Fuels (see p. 172).

Often, the innovative work to reconfigure products goes on more behind the scenes, less visible to the consumer. Consider the toilet: a less glamorous household purchase than an EV, it accounts for about a third of water use in the home in developed countries. Older models typically use 14 litres of water, while newer dual-flush models use only about 20 per cent of that.[12]

That minimises water use and reduces costs for households and major water customers, such as hotels. So far so good, but as the likelihood of water shortages rises, 'water guzzling toilets'[13] become increasingly less logical. So, the search for new techniques continues, from different types of surface coating to using air pressure in place of water, all so that the next generation of toilet design can reduce water use further.

Similarly, think about domestic heating and hot water, which represent around half of a household's energy bills and a large proportion of its carbon footprint. By capturing what used to be wasted heat, escaping through the flue, condenser boilers have brought real energy efficiencies – along with significant cost savings. As a result, the extensive use of condenser boilers has been factored into the regulatory and policy agendas of governments committed to delivering CO_2 reductions. And, as the drive towards zero carbon accelerates, new waves of innovation are focused on developing heat pumps that will be designed to use renewable fuels. These are just a few examples of how companies are anticipating what will be needed for their products to become part of the solution, even when customers are not yet calling for it and, indeed, hardly aware of the need for it.

Yet, often, when a company finds itself in the glare of negative publicity on an issue, it is not because of the product itself but, rather, because of *how* that product is produced. The core processes and practices built into the way the business is run: the chocolate company with child labour in its cocoa supply chain, or the apparel company with suppliers who force people to work in hazardous conditions, or the mining company dumping pollutants into rivers, or the pharmaceutical company with aggressive sales practices that encourage the misuse of painkillers. Sometimes such instances are straightforward corporate crimes and misdemeanours that grab headlines and, subsequently, prompt an overhaul to rectify historic practices.

However, more usually these problems arise from practices long embedded in the ongoing operations that have become normalised but, in reality, throw off significant externalities. As big businesses have grown bigger and the challenges the world is facing become more evident and more pressing, society can no longer bear the scale of these externalities – and increasingly they represent a licence-to-operate risk, through the rise in assertive regulatory action, customer pressure and public censure.

That is why so much of the activist spirit in business leadership shows up in remodelling the practices that generate the greatest externalities. All the companies we feature in this book offer examples of that imperative: whether that's Apple shifting to renewable energy to power its data centres, or PepsiCo reducing the use of water in its operations. Typically, it involves not only the core business but the entire value chain, such as Tesco driving food waste out of its supply chain, Intel driving conflict minerals out of its smelters or H&M working to improve pay and conditions for women across its production footprint.

Yet the point isn't that these are 'good companies' standing apart from 'bad companies' that participate in harmful practices. Rather, these companies have earned a reputation as leaders in social value because of how they've chosen to tangle with those problems and their resolve in trying to reshape those practices.

Operationalise the ambition – with goals and a roadmap, led from the top

When a global survey of plastic pollution identified Coca-Cola as the world's number one source of plastic in the oceans and on beaches,[14] it put them at the centre of a massive global challenge: four hundred million tons of plastic are produced every year and less than 10 per cent of all the plastic produced has been recycled.[15] The problem has captured the public imagination. Take the Great Pacific Garbage Patch: with an estimated surface area of 1.6 million square kilometres, brought together by the currents in the Pacific Ocean, it's a concentration of plastic trash that stretches across an area that's twice the size of Texas – or three times the size of France. It's the largest, but only one of five such garbage patches in the world's oceans, and they only represent a fraction of what there is to clean up, but they certainly serve to dramatise the scale of what there is to deal with.[16]

Coca-Cola made the decision to get a grip on their role in the problem. Turning to face the challenge, they launched an ambitious initiative, 'striving for nothing less than a *World Without Waste*', as they put it.[17] And the company is now seen as one of the leading corporates driving new solutions on the issue of plastic waste.

'You have to start with a vision that's simple and compelling,' says Quincey:

> It doesn't matter that the path from here to there cannot yet be fully seen or understood. People don't have a problem with that. But it does take an act of will on behalf of the leadership to set out the vision.

Inevitably, then, the devil is in the detail – and it's the detail that brings alive what it means to operationalise an ambition of this kind so it's worth taking a look at their plastics roadmap:

– Their target is for 100 per cent of their packaging globally to be recyclable by 2025 and to incorporate at least 50 per cent of recycled material by 2030.[18]

Increasing the use of renewable and recycled
materials, less material per package and introducing
more refillable options or 'bring your own package'
solutions are all part of the plan to reduce virgin
plastic from non-renewable sources by 3 million
metric tons over five years by 2025.[19]

– One of the greatest obstacles they face is the sheer
variety of bottles they produce, with different
shapes, colours and materials across the brands:
recycling systems simply cannot cope. So the
'universal bottle' has been a critical initiative;
multiple brands agreeing to go with the same
reusable bottle, made from a single material, with a
single shape, size, colour. Introduced in Brazil in
2018, the 2-litre universal bottle can be returned,
cleaned and refilled up to twenty-five times and now
replaces 200 million non-refillable bottles a year. It
became the fastest growing packaging format in
Latin America and the concept is being rolled out in
Africa and Europe.[20]

– The company has technology partnerships dedicated
to innovation in the nature of plastic itself. A
collaboration with Ioniqa Technologies, Indorama
Ventures and the NGO Mares Circulares (Circular
Seas) has produced the first ever bottle made from
recovered and recycled marine plastics. It's tiny in the
scheme of things just a few hundred bottles in a
system that produces bottles by the hundreds of
millions – but, as the company says, its significance is
as a demonstrator project with the hope that 'one day,
even ocean debris could be used in recycled packaging
for food or drinks'.[21] Other partnerships like it are

using technologies that be commercially scaled,
pioneering plant-based plastics produced from sugar
cane and other materials, such as forestry waste.[22]

Bea Perez, recognised as one of America's most powerful Latina business leaders, heads up the plastic waste initiative for Coca-Cola and she's very clear that this is about how they 'leverage the scale and scope of the business' to make change. But it will take time: 'Meeting our goals will not be easy but we will push ourselves to reach them.' As she explains, operationalising their ambition has led them into 'radically rethinking how we produce, recycle, and reuse our packaging – and even how we get our products to consumers in the first place'.[23]

An example of their 'radical rethinking' has been bringing together their innovation and sustainability functions to unlock ways of doing things differently in the core business. Their plant-based plastics successes have been the result of that synthesis. And more and more companies are following that path.

In a very different industry, Anglo American, one of the world's leading mining companies, has also brought together the two agendas under the banner of FutureSmart Mining: 'technology, digitalization and sustainability working hand-in-hand'. In that concept, they link the immediate-term benefits of innovative technologies, such as cost reduction and efficient resource use, with their roadmap for long-term sustainability into a single view of the future:

We are applying technologies that more precisely target the desired metals or minerals, delivering greater than 30% reductions in the use of water, energy and capital intensity, and producing less waste in the process, in line with our overall trajectory towards carbon neutral mining.[24]

Nike led the way in 2009 when they created their Sustainable Business and Innovation function (SB&I, as they call it).[25] It was a breakthrough: 'Looking through the creative lens of innovation, we aim to create breakthroughs that improve our world and are also better for our athletes and our investors,' Mark Parker, CEO at the time, said when SB&I was announced:

> This is a fundamental rewriting of the old belief system in which sustainability was so often cast as a cost to business, or a drag on performance.[26]

Innovation for high-performance has always been essential to the Nike brand and there was an activist impetus behind the creation of the SB&I unit: rather than continue to design new product lines the consumer loves and then, after the fact, measure how environmentally damaging that was, they flipped over the construct. They embedded the knowledge, expertise – and motivation – of the sustainability team directly into the design and innovation team. That unlocked an entirely new perspective on innovation and generated a series of hugely successful new 'on-brand' product lines. The *Flyknit* trainer was a first; instead of being made traditionally from cut-and-glued-together materials, the entire trainer is knitted from a single thread, reducing waste by 80 per cent[27] and producing a light, high-performance sports shoe that became a winning billion-dollar design.[28]

In 2020 they launched the *Space Hippie*, designed entirely from cast-off waste. Inspired by the challenge that exercises minds of experts in the field of space exploration that if humankind were to settle on the moon or on Mars we would need to make use of what we had with us to survive because there would be no resupply mission, they concluded: 'There's no resupply mission coming to Earth either.' So at Nike they say that Space Hippie is the result of asking themselves a disruptive question:

What if . . . waste becomes our future feedstock?[29]

But embedding environmental parameters into product design doesn't override commercial viability or consumer appeal at Nike; the ground rules are that there's no compromise on performance or price for sustainability, 'or you will do a disservice to sustainability and you will continue the mythology of *sustainability equals less*,' says Hannah Jones. Vice-president of SB&I when it was established and one of the most highly respected advocates of sustainability-led innovation in the corporate world, Jones talked to GreenBiz about the lessons that she and other enthusiastic sustainability practitioners have had to learn at Nike in order to get this new mindset embedded into the commercial core of the business:

> We've had to let go of things, knowing when to say that this was a great experiment but we need to iterate it and change it, or stop it, because it's not going to work.

Each innovation initiative needs to meet a clear and narrow set of criteria for success, within a balanced portfolio of short-term, mid-term and long-term wins. Aligning sustainability criteria, commercial success and consumer appeal embodies what Jones calls 'the Nike lesson'. But the Nike team doesn't count on existing consumer-pull – they believe it's for them to create the pull:

> Give the consumer something they didn't even expect. It comes down to how you create demand for a new way of doing things.[30]

These examples of taking action in the core of the business have another dimension in common: data and transparency. You need the data to get the whole effort moving, and transparency ensures the effort is sustained. Coca-Cola reports their progress on plastics annually – including collection rates, the use of recycled PET and refillable options, down to market level. This means collecting and verifying data that did not even exist in the business a few years ago. That's not unusual: most companies don't start out by thinking this kind of data is relevant management information. Initially, Intel didn't know what was happening in their smelters on conflict minerals; Nike had little operational data on factories in its supply chain until it got to grips with working conditions; bp hadn't considered reporting on methane emissions until deciding to take a lead on the issue. It's hard to over-emphasise the degree to which seeking out the data and reporting transparently, in itself, is a driver of change. It shines a light on problems that have been in the shadows and makes it possible to pull accountability for them into the core of the business for the first time.

Any business is made up of its own internal system of operations and functions and capabilities that keep it running, its planning cycles and lines of accountability, its processes and protocols that capture 'the way things are done'. The ability to shift these internal systems is the stuff of business leadership. Reflecting on Coca-Cola's transformational journey on plastics, James Quincey recognises the creative challenge:

> Unless you provoke some tension in the system, you won't disrupt the status quo. And in a system this big if you don't disrupt the status quo, it won't change. So there has to be some degree of stretching tension – and the role of leadership is to pitch that at the place that generates a positive constructive action.[31]

The climate crisis – moving from commitment to action

A journalist said to us recently, 'I'm sick of companies expecting a pat on the back for setting a target!' And as more and more companies make commitments on a wide range of societal issues, the question coming from the media – and all stakeholders – has become: 'How are you following through?' Nowhere has the push to turn ambitions into actions been more concerted than on climate change.

Every company in every sector is in the frame, and it's on the agenda of every business. Over the past few years, companies have made promises to achieve net zero greenhouse gas emissions by 2050 at the latest, in alignment with the Paris goals of limiting global warming to a rise of 1.5°C above pre-industrial levels.

But the leaders standing up with these bold goals will be long retired by the time the account is tallied. And the reality is that nobody knows with certainty how it can be achieved; it's never been done. So, even as the numbers of companies that joined the *Race to Zero* in the run-up to COP26 in Glasgow at the end of 2021 reached over 5,000,[32] the commentary took on an increasingly sceptical tone. Greta Thunberg voiced what people fear: '. . . as it is now, I dare to claim that these distant net zero targets aren't about that, rather they're about communication tactics and making it seem like we're acting without having to change.'[33]

We've heard leadership teams hesitate about making a net zero commitment lest it open them up to accusations of greenwashing. However, the commentary – especially from investors – is not questioning the ambition to achieve net zero but, rather, challenging businesses to prove their seriousness by moving quickly to set out their roadmap, including near and mid-term targets. What used to be the preserve of NGOs pushing for more urgent and more credible corporate action on climate is now being led by the investment community. Climate Action 100+ is a global investor-led initiative that represents 700 investors and $68 trillion of assets, with a laser-like focus on 166 companies that are systemically significant emitters.[34] Their latest analysis finds that even with more than two-thirds of those focus companies now promising net zero emissions by 2050:

> . . . it is alarming that the vast majority of companies [even those with net zero goals] have not set medium-term emissions reduction targets aligned with 1.5°C or fully aligned their future capital expenditures with the goals of the Paris Agreement.[35]

Summed up by the *Financial Times*, the challenge being put to companies is that 'Without measurable commitments about what changes must be made in the near term, companies' thirty-year plans will ring hollow'.[36]

That explains the rapid rise in businesses underpinning their bold goals with science-based targets. In practice, that means that the targets the company has set itself have been independently assessed as being in line with what the latest climate science shows is necessary to meet the 1.5°C-aligned Paris goals. With approval of science-based targets goes a commitment by the company to work across all GHG emissions and throughout the value chain in all scopes. And now a company signing up to science-based targets is also required to produce a plan for rapid emission reductions that represents its 'fair share' of the global goal to halve emissions by 2030 – and to report annually on progress. It's intended as a mechanism to make the big long-term ambition more real, actionable and immediate.

More than that, science-based targets start to get at the all-important questions: is it enough, and is it fast enough? Previously, there was no consistent comparison for corporate commitments which made them inadequate for giving confidence to investors, or any other stakeholders, and there was no context for understanding whether or not what a business was promising to do would amount to a meaningful contribution in terms of rising to the real-world scale of the challenge.

Scrutiny is growing ever more intense around what's hidden inside the calculation of a company's net zero commitment. Think about carbon offsets, for example: they had become a recognised and easy route to telling a positive decarbonisation story but, in the face of the action that's needed to decarbonise the real economy, they look increasingly questionable. To critics, offsets are a 'hypocrisy', taking the place of the transformation that's needed in the core of how businesses operate by 'paying for someone else to reduce or remove carbon, while you continue to pump it into the atmosphere'.[37] Even leaving aside the criticisms of the credibility and mismanagement of offsets, as more big businesses make larger offsetting plans the more it looks like there is simply not enough land on the planet to absorb those commitments.[38] Whether the problem is the integrity and impact of carbon credits or, more broadly, the level at which a carbon price should be set, or the systemic barriers to scaling up new solutions, the leadership opportunity for businesses is to focus on the troublesome areas and start to solve for those.

Investors want to understand how decisions are being made about the transition, from allocation of capital expenditure to supply chain resilience to executive incentives. For them, on one hand, it's a matter of fiduciary duty to ensure their portfolio companies are preparing themselves to mitigate the climate change risks that are brewing – and on the other hand, increasingly, to push them to take the opportunity that's available in this time of disruptive transformation. BlackRock's Larry Fink calls it 'a historic investment opportunity' and lays down a challenge to leadership teams: 'As your industry gets transformed by the energy transition, will you go the way of the dodo, or will you be a phoenix?'[39]

Earlier, we discussed the power of shifting from *playing the game* to *winning the game* (see Focus p. 63). McKinsey applies a similar principle to the climate issue, when they talk about companies moving from *defense* to *offense* to create value in the transition:

> Until recently, many companies have responded to the transition only by issuing net zero plans that show they are keeping pace with rising stakeholder expectations and regulatory requirements. This is playing defense – trying to prove that a company will survive, perhaps generating less free cash flow but avoiding the mortal risks of stranded assets and a nil terminal value . . . Playing offense means showing that your business model is built to outperform during the net zero transition.[40]

This represents a strategic pivot in how leading companies think about the climate question, from navigating societal risk to prospering by being part of the solution. Wherever you look now examples are starting to come through of the actions that companies are taking to reduce emissions. The team at Kellogg's, for example, talk about how the goals have created a 'start-up mentality' in the company, leading to innovations such as introducing fuel-cell technology into their waffle-making facilities.[41] At the international train operator Thalys, the target has been integrated into KPIs across the business: they have halved emissions from onboard catering, through sourcing more local, seasonal produce and less meat.[42] Sony has integrated the targets into product design, developing new TV displays which adjust LED brightness frame by frame, using 20 per cent less energy.[43] These are just a handful of encouraging signs, but only the green shoots of transition.

No matter what the sector, there's a set of questions coming from investors and other stakeholders that can be anticipated (see table below). Testing your action plans against those questions is a practical approach to building a climate strategy that's both bold and credible, aspirational and deliverable.

It's a dynamic situation and the bar keeps rising. When science-based targets first appeared, they were set with the goal of holding global warming to 2° but as the science has moved on, companies are finding themselves needing to rebase their plans to meet a 1.5° rise – and it will keep moving.

And while the focus on net zero has been instrumental in galvanising action, responding to the climate crisis is broader than eliminating carbon or GHG emissions. The biodiversity crisis and the very real prospect of the Sixth Extinction is inextricably intertwined with the climate change challenge, and the role of business in protecting and regenerating natural ecosystems is coming to the fore. Pairing these issues on the international agenda, the G7 has called for 'the world to become net zero and nature positive'.[44] The impacts of climate change and of the transition to a net zero economy is also exacerbating inequalities – communities left behind, low-income countries struggling to adapt – and business is expected to play its part in enabling a 'just transition'. The businesses setting the pace are already expanding their focus to include these challenges; the future mantra for action in this area has become *climate, people, nature*.

*   *   *

When Bill Gates entitled his book *How to Avoid a Climate Disaster*, he intended to instil a sense of urgency. Having taken himself on a journey to learn about the nature of the challenge we're up against, he concluded, 'We need to accomplish something gigantic we have never done before, much faster than we have ever done anything similar.'[45] He dedicates the book 'to the scientists, innovators, and activists who are leading the way' – and includes business in that. And his theme is the need to focus on the interventions with the greatest potential to make a meaningful difference and the imperative to act on those to scale.

More regulations, more shareholder resolutions, more mandated reporting and transparency, more employee protests and more scrutiny will come. But the leaders approaching this with an activist mindset are not waiting for those; they're motivated to action by their own assessment of the imperative. And they search out for themselves the areas that require scrutiny and surface those. As we saw in Perspective (p. 77), in a traditional corporate mindset, the fact this these issues are intractable and the path is not already carved out often becomes the rationale for inaction. Phil Drew, a Brunswick partner and pioneer of business action on climate, regularly encounters the challenge of inertia: 'Naming the challenge is the first step towards addressing it,' he explains:

> It's precisely because this problem is so critical and so hard that the leaders are pushing themselves to grasp it. It's not about just pointing at the problem. You need to take a point of view on what it would take to do something about it – and then bring the system around it.

We are now well into the 'decisive decade' on climate action. The transition to a zero carbon economy depends on activist leaders capable of upping the scale and speed of the business response, moving from making commitments to delivering results. In the core of the operations, it will take a step change in effort and innovation – finding new ways of working, doing things that haven't been attempted before. And beyond the business, too, companies will need to work across the systems they are part of, and advocate for the changes that need to happen. Thinking like an activist, you can do more than simply respond; you can help shape the reality in which your business will operate.

Questions on the road to net zero

Goals and targets

- Have you set long-term, mid-term and short-term targets consistent with achieving net zero emissions by 2050, at the latest?
- Do they cover all greenhouse gas emissions and the full value chain, across scopes 1, 2 and 3?
- How are you committed to your 'fair share' contribution of halving global emissions by 2030?

Strategic roadmap

- Have you published a decarbonisation strategy that articulates how the company intends to achieve its goals, including adjusting its business model where necessary?
- Does your strategy anticipate both the risks and distinctive opportunities to create value by accelerating the transition?
- Is your capital allocation, both R&D and capex, consistent with that strategic roadmap?

Governance and disclosure

- Do you have robust oversight of climate-related risks and opportunities at board level and clear responsibilities in the management team?
- Do you have independent auditing of emissions and climate scenarios in place?
- Is your performance reporting in line with TCFD?

Remuneration and incentives

- Are your executive rewards and incentive structures aligned with the transition plan and measurable progress against it?

Breakthrough innovation

- Are you harnessing your core capabilities to meet changing demands for goods and services due to climate change?
- Can you help the industry, sector or wider society to get to net zero faster, in a more affordable way?

Value chain initiatives

- Are you collaborating with suppliers/customers to deliver rapid emissions reductions?
- Is attention to a 'just transition' incorporated into your climate strategy, taking account of impacts on workers, communities and other stakeholders?

Nature-based solutions

- Is the protection and restoration of nature and resilient natural eco-systems incorporated into your climate strategy?
- Are you helping to protect and restore natural carbon sinks in and beyond your value chain?
- Does your path to net zero rely on carbon credits only where it is not feasible to eliminate emissions; and how certain are you that those are high quality and will achieve robust outcomes?

Policy advocacy

- Is your direct and indirect climate advocacy consistent with the company's stated position and supportive of achieving net zero emissions by 2050 at the latest?
- Have you identified the policies required for you to deliver on your roadmap and are you advocating for those policies?

7.

SYSTEM:
drive for systemwide change

Thinking like an activist . . .	• Understand the systemic nature of the challenge – and the role of your business in the ecosystem
	• Help to drive system innovation
	• Use philanthropy strategically to deliver social impact across the ecosystem

Understand the systemic nature of the challenge – and the role of your business in the system

Business is an inextricable part of today's major global systems: food or health, energy or transport – it's hard to imagine these systems without companies of all shapes and sizes playing an intrinsic role. And when it comes to playing a positive role in society, this is the front edge of delivering social value: being part of the drive for systemwide change.

Of course, the priority for any company is to improve its business performance: to do what it does ever better – whether that's in financial metrics, operational KPIs or brand preference – and every part of the operation is already busy delivering on that. So why would you choose to step beyond the business to look at systems transformation? There are two compelling reasons.

The first reason is straightforward: this has become a natural extension of achieving your own operational goals relating to social performance. Most companies now have targets, for example, on sustainable wood supplies, or water efficiency, or driving forced labour out of the supply chain. It is hard – impossible, even – to make progress on these targets unless you engage beyond the business. No one company can solve these goals in isolation: making operational changes in your business often requires a corresponding adaptation in the system.

The second reason is about impact on the issue itself. Even though progress towards the sustainability of the business is important – and hard to deliver – hitting your own targets on these challenges, improving your own performance, is unlikely to fix the issue in the world. No one business, even the biggest, can make a material difference on its own.

For people running a business, we've found, looking at it this way can be something of a shock. To keep pushing their businesses to perform, they are heads down, eyes locked on the track in front of them. And realising the need – and scope – they have to act across the system suddenly brings a new dimension to their leadership. They start to consider the potential they have to shift the ecosystem, establish new norms, generate new solutions. Sensing that opportunity for the first time opens up their horizon. One commercial director said to us:

> It is very refreshing; it's needed and it's demanded of us, but it's also very inspiring and very motivating. And I think we get better at the other part of the job as well by sometimes putting on the activist t-shirt and just going for the cause.

In this context, shifting the system doesn't mean the economic system, at large – which is important to note because the very idea of engaging to change the system sometimes elicits an initial response that the business cannot hope to change how the capital markets operate. It means working across the ecosystem of organisations that enables your business to operate successfully, in order to tackle a big complex issue of shared concern. The most immediate connection with the ecosystem is through the value chain – and this is where companies first started on this journey. The following three examples show what a radical shift in perspective this entails: Nike's work on 'sweatshop' conditions in its suppliers, Walmart's ambitious biodiversity commitment and the work of global logistics company Brambles with customers on regenerative supply chains.

(i) Nike: taking responsibility for the system

Nike's engagement with societal issues stretches back to the sweatshop scandal of the 1990s. Their rapid growth had been driven by a vigorous global outsourcing strategy to access cheaper labour and they became the poster child of globalisation. Their supply base expanded fast into more and more countries, employing hundreds of thousands of workers to fuel that growth. Then, in the early 1990s, when the realities of sweatshop conditions and child labour in the supply chain were first exposed in the US, Nike's initial response was, in effect, *these are not our factories, this is not our problem.*[1] But the disconnect shocked consumers: it was a rude awakening and challenged the glamorous, feel-good spirit that was driving the success of the brand. In the face of mounting public outcry, the company pivoted.

Nike's founder and then CEO Phil Knight had a famous nostra culpa moment at the National Press Club in Washington DC in 1998, when he declared: 'The Nike product has become synonymous with slave labour, forced overtime and arbitrary abuse.'[2]

He announced a suite of new measures that included that their suppliers would be required to abide by safety and environmental standards that matched those in America and would be subject to independent monitoring of their factory conditions.

But that wasn't – and still isn't – easy. Nike found that simply setting standards and auditing suppliers wasn't enough. Most struggled to meet the new level of expectation and the company soon realised they risked cutting off their entire supply base. So they started instead working to help suppliers raise their performance. They began by training managers, increasing awareness of human rights in the workplace and partnering with civil society organisations – also becoming co-founder of the Fair Labor Association, to this day an influential activist non-profit group dedicated to worker rights. Internally, Nike built up their capacity to enable suppliers to move up through the levels of their newly set out expectations. They penalised persistent non-compliance and rewarded improved performance. As a result, they systematically and measurably improved standards over time – and helped to raise the bar for the entire industry. It was a radical shift in perspective – from denying responsibility for conditions in the supply chain to proactively engaging across the entire system to drive out poor practice and up the game.

In the midst of this, Nike established its Corporate Responsibility department and produced the first ever Corporate Responsibility Report – and at that time, for them, the word 'responsibility' carried a new vibrancy and sense of commitment. They were paving the way for what has become a different model of the social contract between companies and the ecosystem that surrounds them.

How the company transformed from villain to hero is an oft-told tale. And today Nike is among the world's leading activists in the corporate arena. At the National Press Club all that time ago, Phil Knight voiced the essence of the problem:

It has been said that Nike has single-handedly lowered the human rights standards for the sole purpose of maximising profits.

Arguably, the underlying challenge to all big companies on how they step up on a societal issue can be expressed in that thought still: is the business focused exclusively on maximising profit, whatever the cost to wider society, on the assumption that others will deal with those consequences?

(ii) Walmart: mobilising the supply chain on biodiversity

Leading businesses are increasingly using their leverage across the value chain to drive change on the societal issues that intersect with their operations. Walmart, the second largest retailer on the planet with a market cap of $400 billion,[3] for instance, has established a track record in this arena over the past fifteen years: insisting on supplier certification for more sustainable fishing practices,[4] driving plastic waste out of the system[5] and backing female entrepreneurship[6] are all issues on which they are delivering measurable impact at scale. As the urgency of the global environmental crises becomes more evident, Walmart has become more assertive. With Project Gigaton, announced in 2017, their stated goal is to avoid one gigaton – 1 billion metric tons – of greenhouse gas emissions from the global value chain by 2030 and they are working through their supplier network to make that happen.[7]

Most recently, they turned the spotlight on biodiversity. Scientists are warning that the world is at a 'tipping point',[8] facing a sudden and irreversible collapse of natural ecosystems. In 2021 the UN reported that around one million animal and plant species are now threatened with extinction, many within decades. The insatiable demand for food from the growing global population is a key driver of biodiversity loss, and the practices of large-scale agriculture are central to the food system, driving 70 per cent of terrestrial biodiversity loss and 80 per cent of deforestation.[9] One of the principal areas for generating solutions is being termed *regenerative agriculture* – in other words, there's a growing understanding, even in the food industry, that we need to turn this situation around.

In a webcast for more than a thousand suppliers, Walmart explained its commitment to regenerative agriculture. It's an illustration of the activist mindset in action: they started their story in the outside world with the imperative for change. They fielded an extensive cast list of leaders from across the business – including the CEO Doug McMillon, who set the context with his point of view on the realities of the growing global crisis:

> We're losing critical landscapes and biodiversity at an alarming rate. Studies show animal populations have declined by around 68% over the past 40 years, and one-fifth of the Amazon's rainforest has disappeared in just 50 years. As a society, we are at an inflection point. If we don't act now, we may not have an opportunity to do something later.[10]

The company invited their NGO and academic partners to talk to this gathering of suppliers about pollination and species diversity, and what businesses like theirs could do to make a difference. It was anchored in the vital fact that 75 per cent of the world's food crops depend on pollinators.[11] And the leadership team talked personally about what they had learned from biodiversity experts. 'For the last few months, a group of us at Walmart has had a crash course in pollination,' said Diana Marshall, the executive vice-president in operations:

> We've learned the types and sizes of habitats, and the best support for different pollinators. We talked about substances

that were harmful to pollinators and also the latest information from science, and the newest legislative efforts. And we've studied what alternatives are available for growers and how they cope with the changes.[12]

Reflecting on the steps we've talked about so far in thinking like an activist, Walmart had, in fact, started at the beginning: they determined why they needed to focus on the issue, then made a concerted effort to understand it from an outside-in perspective, from those for whom this is a core expertise; pivoted to face into the challenge and set themselves a big ambition with the intention of driving action to scale. During the webcast, they showed suppliers case studies of turnaround stories in farming businesses, big and small. Then, they laid out what they expect of their suppliers – with targets and near-term timelines for change. McMillon has made a commitment for Walmart to become a 'regenerative company' – and while this engagement with their suppliers is just the start of a long journey, as he put it, 'We must go beyond sustainability as it is understood in practice today.' That means looking beyond the performance of the business, working to create change at a system level. McMillon is clear that this will require a new attitude:

The work ahead requires learning and commitment from each of us. It doesn't mean being right in a way that makes others wrong. It means listening intently and respectfully, stitching together differences that separate us from each other. It doesn't mean either hope or despair; it is action that is courageous and fearless.[13]

By mobilising their supply chain on this issue, the impact of Walmart's actions will create a domino effect outwards to thousands, even hundreds of thousands, of companies. It will not only reshape the way these companies supply to Walmart, it will embed new capabilities and practices across the entire food system. Few businesses on the planet have the scope of influence that Walmart has, of course, but all businesses, whatever their size or sector, can use the levers they have for driving change through their value chain.

(iii) Brambles: collaborating with customers to drive out waste

In contrast to Walmart, Brambles is all but invisible to the wider world – but they play an essential role in the movement of goods around the world. A business-to-business logistics company, they operate the world's largest pool of reusable pallets and containers for many of the largest consumer good brands, retailers and manufacturers. Operating out of Australia, the company began in the nineteenth century with a horse and cart[14] and has grown to become the backbone of global supply chains.[15] This gives them a unique vantage point from which to look across the world's logistics system. By asking their customers about their most pressing supply chain issues, the company identified three 'breakthrough challenges': eliminate waste, eradicate empty transport miles and stamp out inefficiency.

They decided to make their customers their partners in finding practical solutions to those challenges, setting up a series of 'working collaborations' right across the logistics ecosystem – backed by the company's data analytics and expertise.[16] In the first five years, they established a network of 250 partnerships, and then set a new goal to double that to 500 by 2025.[17] And, because these problem-solving collaborations provide tangible evidence of how the company can add value to their customers, the initiative became part of their dialogue with investors. Identifying where business issues intersect with societal issues has helped Brambles to define how it sees its role in the world:

By getting to net zero impact and beyond, we will be the company delivering the supply chains the world needs for the future.[18]

While Brambles can't boast the scale or purchasing power of the consumer facing giants like Walmart, they've identified where they fit in the system and what's distinctive about the impact they can have. In 2020, they topped the Dow Jones Barron's ranking as the most sustainable company globally.[19] Sharing and reusing the pallets they own is the basis of their business model, so they see themselves as pioneers of the circular economy – a concept that captures the zeitgeist today on the potential for sustainable systemwide solutions.

Help drive system innovation

Achieving meaningful systemwide change will inevitably step you beyond the immediate relationships in your value chain and out into the broader ecosystem around that issue. It's about collaborating on shared challenges, making links, filling gaps and seeking dependencies to unlock progress on some of the thorniest challenges. Taking on the mounting waste crisis and the search for sustainable fuels offer two examples that bring this to life.

(i) Tetra Pak: ecosystem solutions on recycling

In many businesses, in many sectors, gripping the problem of ever-growing mountains of waste has become a priority. All over the world, governments are trying to get at the problem through regulation, and the policy trend towards Extended Producer Responsibility (EPR) is growing – in other words, the producers of the materials are given a significant responsibility, physical or financial, for what happens to them at end of life.[20] The notion of Extended Producer Responsibility can be seen as a reverberation of Nike's realisation in the 1990s of the need for an expanded understanding of a company's responsibility; one that reaches beyond the boundaries of the business and extends into its ecosystem.

An essential part of the waste challenge in any sector is that none of these producing companies are themselves in the recycling business; recycling businesses are not even in their supply chain. So, finding solutions requires joined-up action across the entire ecosystem. Tetra Pak, the leading manufacturer of carton packaging globally, has begun on that task. They've mapped out the steps of the recycling value chain and have a strategy to take action at each step, at local and global levels, always working with partners.[21] Their efforts show up at the start of the chain by engaging consumers in the need to recycle their waste in the first place – for example, through collaborations with retailers in India;[22] then establishing collection infrastructure and systems – as they're doing with local governments and recycling partners across Thailand;[23] increasing accuracy of the sorting process – by introducing robotics in the US;[24] investing tens of millions of dollars to expand the capacity of carton recycling facilities in Europe – for example, tripling capacity in Poland;[25] and a step at a time increasing the value and use of recycled materials – supporting businesses in Ecuador, for instance, to sell products made from recycled cartons for the construction industry.[26] Each intervention alone doesn't change the game, but together, strategically, across each step in the recycling value chain, these specific examples and many other initiatives like them in markets all over the world have the potential to drive systemic change.

Of course, the essential functionality of a carton is to keep the food and drink it contains safe and fresh, and this is achieved through polyAl, the fine layers of polymer and aluminium that keep the oxygen out and the nutrition in. Back in the 1960s, it was Tetra Pak's invention of the aseptic technologies and processes that made the mass production of carton packaging possible and, with it, the massive expansion of access to safe food without refrigeration for consumers globally.[27] But today this is also at the core of the waste challenge for carton producers because polyAl remains so problematic for recycling systems as they are.[28] Tetra Pak is directing its innovation capability towards this challenge from different angles: developing new forms of plant-based polymers,[29] finding new recycling technologies that separate the layers more effectively and, crucially, exploring new ways to drive up the quality and economic value of the materials generated by recycling the aluminium and polymer layers so that they can go on to be used in more new products. To make a transformative difference means being intentional about designing in recyclability from the start – as we saw with Nike's Sustainable Business & Innovation unit.

So Tetra Pak has built up what they call an *innovation ecosystem*. 'The old notion of a linear supply chain is gone,' says Laurence Mott, Tetra Pak's head of R&D. 'We need to work in an ecosystem of close partnerships with our development partners.'[30] The company's collaborations encompass small tech start-ups, digital developers, academic researchers and existing suppliers. They're working with recycling companies and raw material producers, with global customers and local governments, as well as taking a leading role in industry-wide coalitions.[31] As a business producing almost two hundred billion cartons a year, stepping up to take greater responsibility across the ecosystem for the effectiveness of the recycling process has become essential to Tetra Pak's licence to operate. And it's intrinsic to achieving their overarching innovation ambition: to

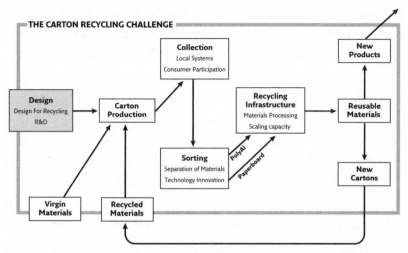

Figure 8: A systemic view of the carton recycling challenge

create a package that's made entirely from renewable or recycled materials, fully recyclable and carbon neutral. Designing for recycling and planning for reuse to eradicate waste and keep materials in the system for longer is what's driving circular economy initiatives in Tetra Pak and an increasing number of other companies.

At a time when the words *partnership* and *collaboration* have become so ubiquitous in business lingo that they seem bland, it's easy to miss what's different in this form of partnership: it requires a new mindset towards innovation, not just partnerships that aim to deliver on the company's business strategy or even to solve industry problems in the pre-competitive space, but collaborations that aim to do both those things in tandem with finding new solutions to the challenge for wider society.

Many of the leaders we work with recognise this picture: they know the scale of the problems that have been accumulating, in part as a consequence of their success, and that this now means they're on the hook to become part of the solution. Critics will call out that the historic practice of business has profited by creating these problems in the first place. That's incontestable. All the more reason, then, to harness that massive implementation capability to help the shift towards more sustainable systems.

(ii) Clean Skies for Tomorrow: decarbonising aviation

Aviation offers a further illustration of how systems thinking is opening up possibilities for activist leadership – in particular, the complex question of how to decarbonise flying. In this instance, we can see not just how an individual company reaches out across the system but how many companies can coalesce around a shared challenge. Aviation is designated one of the 'hard to abate sectors', which tells you that it's really challenging to achieve the necessary system shift. Currently, it represents 3 per cent of greenhouse gas emissions and, even in the context of the industry battered by covid, it is expected to increase by 300 per cent over 2005 levels by the middle of this century.[32] Hitherto the industry has been based entirely on fossil fuels. It's classic territory for pre-competitive innovation; the problem is a risk to the entire industry, solutions would benefit all the players and the interdependencies are complex.

Sustainable Aviation Fuel – SAF, as it is known – is widely recognised as by far the fastest and most viable route to reducing the industry's GHG emissions in the near and mid-term. Most people have not even heard of Sustainable Aviation Fuel and, to many, talking about sustainable aviation is an oxymoron; the only sustainable aviation is *no* aviation. But in the face of continued and growing demand for aviation, there's a need to radically change how the system works.

Multiple routes for decarbonisation are being pursued, including hydrogen-based fuels and battery-powered electric flight, but the technologies needed to make those a practical proposition are a way off yet. The technologies for producing SAF, however, already exist. Multiple pathways to scaling up supply are mapped out and some are even certified. Produced from many different materials, such as municipal waste or even cooking oil, and from sustainably grown non-food crops, such as woody biomass, it has the potential to reduce lifecycle emissions in aviation by up to 80 per cent. Yet two dauntingly high hurdles stand in the way: price and scalability of supply. While, by definition, success is not guaranteed, SAF represents a leverage point in the system.

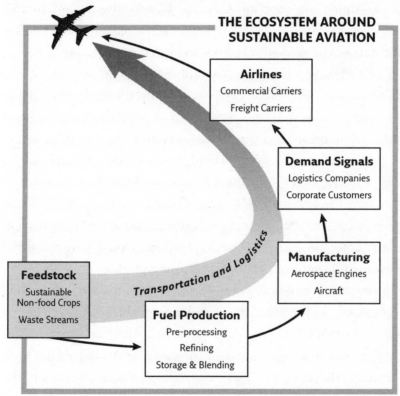

Figure 9: The ecosystem behind Sustainable Aviation Fuel

Systemwide action is the only way forward, but how to get started on such a complex problem has in itself been an inhibitor. For years, the producers were waiting on progressive policy, while policymakers were waiting on certainty that producers could deliver, creating a stand-off of inaction. Meanwhile, time is running out. In 2019, the World Economic Forum put together leaders from across the aviation ecosystem in the Clean Skies for Tomorrow (CST) initiative to 'break the impasse'.[33]

Around eighty organisations are now gathered around the initiative, with different players focused on the interventions where they can make the greatest impact, while joining up with others. These are just some examples of the companies in the ecosystem coming at this problem from different angles:

- **Fuel producers:** Major global fossil fuel producers are starting to incorporate SAF in their strategies. Shell, for example, now plans to produce 2 million tons of SAF a year by 2025. While that's still a small number, it is ten times as much as the volume produced by the entire industry in 2019. Their new biofuels plant in the Netherlands will become one of the largest SAF-producing facilities in Europe, helping the company to deliver on its target of SAF representing 10 per cent of sales by 2030. Others are scaling up production as well; oil and gas majors, such as bp and Total, and dedicated innovators in low-carbon fuels, such as Neste and Fulcrum, among them.

- **Airlines:** Airlines are gearing up to deliver on their decarbonisation targets and incorporating SAF is a vital part of that – EasyJet, Lufthansa and Qantas, for example. United Airlines committed to buying three million gallons of SAF and became the first airline to offer customers an option to buy into securing SAF supply, as an alternative to simply relying on carbon offsets to reduce environmental impact.

- **Logistics businesses:** On the demand side, global logistics companies, including DHL and Amazon, are significant commercial customers of the airlines and are signing deals to purchase SAF, which underpins demand in the system and, in turn, supports their own climate action commitments and the footprint of the logistics industry at large.

- **Corporate customers:** As an organiser of business travel globally, American Express is coming at it from a different angle. With the top 200 corporate customers accounting for around 80 per cent of business travel, they're working to aggregate the demand for SAF among their big corporate accounts in order to provide further confidence to the producers that the market will be there and, crucially, to reinforce the signal to the financial system about the opportunity for accelerated investment.

- **Manufacturers:** The contribution of the manufacturers in this effort is to enable the engines to run on SAF. Engine manufacturers GE and Rolls-Royce are both running trials to show that it's possible. While in practice the industry expects SAF to be introduced slowly, blended with traditional fuels, Rolls-Royce has stepped forward with a commitment to prove that all their long-haul jet engines are compatible with the use of 100 per cent SAF by 2023. In 2021, they carried out a successful test flight using 100 per cent sustainable aviation fuels on a Boeing 747 – as did Airbus on an A350.

It is a composite picture made up of traditional fuel producers, alternative fuel producers, airlines, logistics and transport operators, large-scale commercial customers, and engine manufacturers, along with civil society organisations, including governments. No one can abdicate responsibility to the collective; each needs to do their bit effectively according to the role they play in the system. But everyone sees how their individual efforts are given a greater chance of success by being actively part of this drive for systemwide change.

All this business action needs policy support and, in the context of the evident commitment of the ecosystem, it's beginning to come. Proposals introduced into EU regulation include a 'blending mandate', obliging all aircraft operators to use fuel that contains a minimum share of SAF – starting very small with 2 per cent in 2025, increasing in steps to a minimum of 63 per cent by 2050; the US now provides a credit for blended fuels and has established a $1 billion fund over five years to expand production facilities in America.

Everyone knows they only have part of the solution, but the shared imperative exists. This is no small task: at 200,000 metric tons, SAF production in 2019 amounted to less than 1 per cent of today's demand. So the goal now is to establish commercially viable production for industry wide adoption by 2030, aimed at surmounting today's biggest hurdles of cost and scalable, resilient supply. That shared ambition is what brings everyone onto the same team, as it were, to find practical ways of achieving that.

Clean Skies for Tomorrow is an example of the activist coalitions that are springing up around the big systemic challenges (see Activist coalitions, p. 265). Working collaboratively, and in public–private partnerships, these actors in the aviation ecosystem are applying their combined innovation capabilities, engineering and manufacturing strengths, purchasing power, data and analysis to restructure how the system operates. They're not aiming to get their arms around the entire system in one go. Systems theory holds that there are places where making a focused intervention has the potential to deliver a disproportionately broad impact systemwide. For the aviation industry, SAF represents such an opportunity.

Use philanthropy strategically to deliver social impact across the ecosystem

For the most part, corporate giving has followed a philosophy largely unchanged since the days of the great nineteenth-century industrialists. It's summed up famously in *Carnegie's Dictum*, named for the steel tycoon who spent much of his fortune on good works. Carnegie recommended we think of our careers in thirds: the first third should be spent learning as much as we can; the second third earning as much as we can; and the final third giving it all away to good causes. The Dictum is alive and well in our times. In the US, business billionaires egg each other on to give away ever greater sums. And corporate philanthropy overall is significant, over $21 billion in 2021.[34] In India, big businesses are required by law to give 2 per cent of net profits to charity – amounting to an estimated Rs 1 trillion since the law came into effect in 2015.[35] Typically, it's seen by those companies as giving to good causes and is indicative of an organisation with good values, but the work it funds lies outside the boundaries of the company's sphere of operation.

Among the leaders in social value, there's a more strategic model in play: it's issue-focused and impact-led – meaning that the philanthropic funding is directed intentionally towards the societal issues that the business has prioritised and the activities are designed from the outset to deliver measurable social impact. It's concerned not just with the input but the output:

how is the money being spent and what does it achieve? It aims for scale, in collaboration with partners working towards a common goal. It's aligned with how the core business is tackling the issue and the goal is to help move the whole system forward. In that new paradigm, philanthropy is used strategically as an integral part of the company's efforts overall to deliver social value.

To show how this works, we'll look at two stand-out examples: Mastercard's work on financial inclusion, and JPMorgan Chase's *Advancing Cities* programme.

(i) *Mastercard: a systemic approach to financial inclusion*

Currently, almost two billion people lack access to financial services and that fact alone perpetuates many other forms of exclusion in their daily lives and work. Susan Kelsey, an Executive Vice-President at Mastercard who heads up Global Prepaid and Financial Inclusion, articulates the challenge for those individuals:

> 'People who transact exclusively with cash are effectively invisible in the financial system. They lack access to credit beyond personal networks and informal lenders, who can charge exorbitant rates that trap people in cycles of poverty. Invisibility contributes to inequality. That is not a developed- or developing-world problem alone. And it is not for either the public or the private sector to solve single-handedly.[36]

The World Bank views financial inclusion as a critical enabler 'to reduce extreme poverty and boost prosperity'. Digital and mobile technology as a route to financial inclusion has been around for decades. Against that backdrop, as we saw (Ambition, p. 113), in 2015 Mastercard set a bold ambition to help bring

500 million excluded people into the digital economy and achieved that through 350 programmes on the ground in eighty countries.[37] As ever, the hallmark of this work is collaboration across the ecosystem – with governments, with NGOs, and with other businesses. And as the social and economic cost of covid became clear, the company pledged to expand access to a further 500 million people, including fifty million micro and small businesses by 2025. Ajay Banga, then CEO, put the commitment in the context of building back from the pandemic:

> If we're going to recover in any sort of long-term, sustainable way, we have to make sure that everyone is included. Getting people access to the digital economy is a critical part of that. This is an opportunity to develop commercially-sustainable and scalable social impact with government and private sector partners.

Philanthropy from the Mastercard Impact Fund has played a significant part in achieving those goals – making donations of over $260 million in eighty-nine countries since 2018.[38] Under the broad umbrella of inclusive economic growth, their grants are channelled towards strategic areas of need: micro and small businesses, for example, which in developing economies account for 70 per cent of jobs but more than half of which are unbanked or underserved by financial services, according to the International Finance Corporation (IFC).[39] Through their Strive Community awards they back innovative projects from the Philippines to Colombia that can rapidly strengthen the digital capability of small businesses[40] or, in partnership with Grameen America they're expanding access to credit for female microentrepreneurs.[41] Whatever the focus or the geography, the philanthropic programmes operate on a set of common principles: acting to scale, designed for measurable impact, delivered in collaboration with civil society partners.

Data.org is a $50 million partnership between the Mastercard Center for Inclusive Growth and Rockefeller Foundation to create a platform for data science applied to social impact. Announced in 2020, it's just one of the Center's initiatives using data to amplify their reach beyond the impact of each individual programme into systemic and transformational change in the areas it funds.[42]

But even with this profusion and imagination in the philanthropic work, the key is that the issue of financial inclusion is embedded in the core business as well. Mastercard Labs drive the company's innovation agenda, exploring everything from the consumer experience to online security threats – and the Mastercard Lab for Financial Inclusion, based in Kenya, has brought almost half a million East African farmers into the digital economy in recent years through a platform that provides access to producers, buyers and services right across the agricultural value chain, for instance. Meanwhile, in the commercial business, Mastercard continues to expand access: in Egypt, to take one market, in 2016, Mastercard set up a partnership with the major banks and telecoms providers which allowed 'every Egyptian citizen to perform money transactions via mobile'. In a population of ninety million, 85 per cent of people were unbanked but mobile penetration was more than 100 per cent. For the National Bank, the objective was financial inclusion and through this collaboration, as Madgy Hassan, Mastercard's General Manager in Egypt, explained:

For the first time all Egyptians will have the ability to pay electronically, regardless of whether they have a bank account or not, or whatever mobile device they use.[43]

It's hard to decipher where commercial activity ends and philanthropy begins; they're interwoven in service of the ambition to make a meaningful impact on this particular societal issue. For Mastercard, and all other corporates working with this activist model, making this happen involves a dynamic ecosystem of partners across all sectors of society. The critical success factor is a commitment to work towards a shared goal determined at the outset. Shamina Singh, founder and president of the Mastercard Center for Inclusive Growth, knows what that looks like. 'Remember this rule of thumb,' she says:

> If you want to go wide, go with government. If you want to do deep, go with NGOs and academic institutions. If you want to go fast, go with the private sector. And if you want to go far, you must go together.[44]

Mastercard is explicit that their approach to financial inclusion is not philanthropy. The model they're operating is a creative mix: it leverages the digital payments technology that's at the core of their capability as a business, invests in the application of data-led solutions, supports the efforts of many NGOs and non-profits on the ground, and collaborates across a network of public and private partnerships to deliver progress on the issue at scale and systemically.

(ii) JPMorgan Chase: a 'power grid of opportunity' for cities

JPMorgan Chase's *Advancing Cities* initiative aims to make an impact in economically and socially disadvantaged communities in the developed world. In many ways, the secret to the long-term sustainability of their programme is not the large-scale philanthropic funding and even the commitments of the core business; it's the orchestration of the extensive ecosystem of partnerships. They work through what they call *anchor institutions* in the community – such as the community development financial institutions, the CDFIs. They draw a network around the initiative that creates a shared responsibility for lasting impact: made up of the municipal authorities, local minority owned businesses, academic and skills institutions and community-based non-profits, that together have the potential to lift up the community.[45]

Detroit was the proving ground for their model – because, as they explain, 'Detroit exemplifies both the challenges many cities wrestle with as they work to create greater opportunity for their residents and the conditions for solving them.'[46] With decades of intensifying racial tensions and a weakening automotive sector, the city was struggling. After the financial crash, GM and Chrysler declared bankruptcy, the jobless rate was running at 29 per cent, and in 2013 the city itself went bankrupt.[47]

Back in 2012, as the story is told by Harvard's Joseph Bower and Michael Norris, CEO Jamie Dimon had asked Peter Scher, the bank's head of corporate responsibility, to review their philanthropic activities. What he found aligns with the experience we've had so often when taking a scan of the scattered array of philanthropic initiatives that have built up over the years in many a company. Scher recollects:

We were spending $200 million a year in philanthropy, but it wasn't having the scale of impact we could be getting with a more targeted strategy. I asked, "What do we stand for?" We were technically an educational foundation, so anyone who wanted money would pitch it as an education thing. We ended up being a mile wide and an inch deep. So I said, "If we're going to spend $2 billion over the next 10 years, let's spend 85%-90% of that in a really impactful way." We had to figure out where we had unique expertise and leverage that.[48]

The situation in Detroit provided a focus for the more strategic approach. JPMorgan Chase is the largest bank in the region and they came in to support the revitalisation initiatives that were getting underway. Tosha Tabron, working for the bank in Detroit, was drawn into the early stages of determining what should be done by Jamie Dimon directly:

> We got the call from Jamie in 2013. He told us to go out and start to understand what's happening in the city and figure out how JPMC can help.

The simplicity of the question voiced by Dimon, in our experience, is a great starting point for all such ventures: 'How can we help?' As Scher explained, the bank 'can't go into a city and decide what its priorities should be. That would never work.' The decision to go out and listen first was welcomed in the city and meant that the plan was rooted in a local ecosystem of relationships that created trust and shared purpose.

The *Advancing Cities* initiative launched in 2014 with JPMorgan making a commitment to the city of $150 million over five years, dedicated to four focus areas for impact – what they call the 'universal pillars of opportunity'; small business expansion, neighbourhood revitalisation, skills for the job market and the financial health of households.[49] Able to demonstrate measurable results, they exported the model to other cities, including Chicago. The bank put $200 million of strategic philanthropy into Chicago to kick-start the work, underpinned with a commitment of $600 million of home lending for Black and Latinx families through to 2025. And their Community Development Bank business closed $70 million's worth of deals to revitalise some of Chicago's most vulnerable neighbourhoods. To understand what would be the most valuable local projects to develop, the bank conducted

new on-the-ground research to map out the gaps in access to
everyday services for low-income residents. A year into the
initiative, Whitney Smith leading the project for the bank in
Chicago, shared what she had learned:

> Perhaps chief among our reflections is a renewed appreciation
> for the ways that non-profits don't always have access to the
> data, expertise and other tools that will enable them to most
> effectively translate their work into greater opportunity.[50]

An intrinsic part of JPMorgan's social impact model is the
use of data, both to focus local efforts at the start and to
measure impact along the way. And the model, which has been
replicated in other cities, always involves the mix of commitments from the core business: expanding access to affordable
housing, increasing lending to small businesses in those communities, investing in community development – alongside the
strategic deployment of philanthropy. And always working
through the network of local anchor organisations that Dimon
has called the 'distributed power grid of economic opportunity'.

Eye-catching large-scale philanthropic commitments often
make the headlines, but in this new paradigm what delivers the
real-world impact is the ecosystem approach. These companies
are not just signing cheques for good causes, but using their
philanthropy as a part of their strategy to deliver social value.
As we showed in the *Leadership Model* (see Figure 7, p. 123),
they're working through the core business and beyond the core
business through partnerships.

Social impact initiatives like those of Mastercard and
JPMorgan Chase have taken years to build up. We sometimes
find that, for companies just starting on the journey, the evident
strength of these programmes can seem intimidating. Yet all
these programmes start relatively small and focused, and they

mature in stature and confidence over time. But the common success factor is that they all begin with a similar mindset: a sense of activism and an ambition to bring their resources and expertise to bear in a strategic way, mobilising across the entire ecosystem to make an impact on the issue.

Even as the approach to corporate philanthropy becomes more sophisticated, we're seeing a blurring of the edges of philanthropy and investing. Impact investing and venture philanthropy are becoming part of the corporate activist's toolkit. These invest-ments are expected to deliver a financial return and a strategic value to the company, as well as tackling a societal issue. In the corporate world, Patagonia was a pioneer in this space, setting up a venture fund in 2013 to invest in start-ups 'building renew-able energy infrastructure, practicing regenerative organic agriculture, conserving water, diverting waste and creating sustainable materials'.[51] Corporate interest in this has grown steadily since then, according to the Stanford Social Innovation Review (SSRI) in 2020 alone, Amazon, Citi, Microsoft, Salesforce, TELUS and Unilever each announced venture commitments exceeding $100 million.[52] As the Social Innovation Review puts it, these funds are 'aligned with and amplified by their company's strategic priorities, market position, and resources, in order to generate measurable, mutually reinforcing social and financial returns'. The space between for-profit and not-for-profit is an increasingly interesting and innovative arena – a coming together of a company's capabilities in both social and financial value.

*   *   *

It's hard to exaggerate what a radical shift in business thinking this is: not only tackling the issue through the core of the business, but also aiming to be part of system transformation. Because achieving the company's own ambitions and targets requires it.

And because making an impact on the issue itself demands it. This is a defining aspect of social leadership for these times: showing up with a commitment to drive change systemwide, beyond the performance of your own business. Leaders with an activist mindset are looking for new ways of working with and through others to mobilise change.

How to think systems

Actively engaging to help create change in the system, not just in your business, is a radical shift in the nature of leadership. For people on the inside of businesses it demands a different way of thinking. In the examples shared in this chapter, it's possible to see some underlying principles at play. Inspired by the work of the late Donella Meadows, a scholar of systems theory, we've drawn out some key learnings as prompts to help *think systems*.

1. **Map out the ecosystem your business is part of.** On any societal issue, the ecosystem is made up of the many organisations and interdependencies that enable your business to operate successfully. It starts with your value chain but encompasses innovators, academics, industry bodies, governments and policymakers, NGOs and community-based organisations – even customers and competitors. All the actors who have a stake in the system.

2. **Be clear about your role in the ecosystem.** The more well defined your role, the easier it is to form meaningful collaborations and to understand the leverage you have in the system. What is the contribution your business could make? Where is your business an enabler, or a block? How do other stakeholders see your role and your potential to be part of developing solutions?

3. **Think about the edges of your company.** The 'inside' and 'outside' of a business is no longer as defined as it was; companies today are more like clouds of collaborations, networks and relationships. Proactively engaging at

the edges of your business, the places where you inter-
face with others can increase your understanding of the
ecosystem and prompt the possibility of new partnerships.

4. **Upend your model of innovation.** Systemic problems can't
   be solved in an R&D lab alone – solutions will come from
   the system itself. Starting your innovation out with the stakeholders closest to the issue enables you to more effectively
   identify the most acute pain points in the system and shape
   your strategy accordingly.

5. **Find the 'leverage points'.** Systems theory holds that
   there are places where a small shift in one area can
   produce a much bigger change across the system. These
   leverage points may be outcomes your business can influence positively – through procurement or innovation, for
   example. Seek out the interventions that may have a
   disproportionately positive impact on the issue.

6. **Create data flows and feedback loops.** Comprehensive
   ecosystem data are crucial to understanding the issue and
   tracking progress. That is likely to mean developing new data
   sets in areas the business has never considered before. And,
   as an ecosystem player, you probably have significant data
   that would be valuable to share with others, working in collaboration with independent third parties if necessary.

7. **Look for the pre-competitive spaces.** Critical societal
   issues usually present risks to entire industries, and
   companies have a shared interest in tackling them. For
   example, strengthening recycling infrastructure benefits all
   companies struggling with plastics waste; scaling up
   production of sustainable aviation fuel would be a significant step on the path to decarbonising the entire aviation
   industry. Finding these opportunities is a route to accelerating progress in your business and systemwide.

8. **Use your philanthropy strategically.** Companies often
   find they can act across the ecosystem in alignment with
   their foundation or philanthropic efforts – through civil

society partnerships tackling, for instance, environmental
practices of smallholder farmers or economic resilience in
local communities, delivering measurable social impact to
scale, generating new research on the issues and model-
ling new solutions.

9. **Get everyone on the same team.** All players in the
ecosystem are potential partners, so take an open-minded
and creative approach to who is involved. Don't rule
anyone out – even the noisiest and most critical NGOs,
even competitors, when that makes sense. The opportunity
is to bring people to the table and work in common cause,
towards a shared goal.

10. **Don't let systems thinking stop action in your business.**
By definition, systems are complex – and the issues are,
too – so there's a risk that getting absorbed in system
transformation takes away the impetus from action under
your direct control. Pioneering new solutions in the core
business is an essential contribution as well; it sets the bar
higher for expected industry norms, shows what's possible
that wasn't seen as possible before, and helps moves the
whole system forward.

8.

ADVOCACY:
find your voice on the issue

Thinking like an activist . . .	• Advocate for what needs to change on the issue – rather than lobbying for the interests of the business
	• Aim to set the agenda and mobilise others
	• Speak up on the actions you're taking and why – so others can follow

Advocate for what needs to change on the issue – rather than lobbying for the interests of the business

Most people wouldn't see 'corporate advocacy' as a source of great hope for the world. Even as we write this, there are stories appearing about the efforts of business to block change. The *Financial Times* has reported that major chemical and plastics manufacturers are lobbying to weaken a proposed UN treaty on plastics;[1] TechCrunch has reported a concerted push by the major tech firms to 'weaken EU rules' on data and consumer privacy;[2] Vox describes how lobbying from the meat industry caused the removal of plant-based policy recommendations from the latest International Panel on Climate Change (IPCC) report.[3] This is everything people distrust about business: working to serve its own direct interests and delay action, block change, dilute progress on major societal issues. And it lays the ground for populist rallying cries to 'drain the swamp'.

Unsurprisingly, this isn't the kind of corporate advocacy we're recommending. We've been describing how businesses can take action to make a meaningful impact on societal issues – and can draw on that experience to add their voice to the public discourse in order to mobilise further action. When this happens, advocacy becomes an important contribution that a business can make. Three examples show how this can work in practice: corporate advocacy on the climate crisis, business speaking out on LGBTQ+ inclusion and brands engaging their consumers directly on societal issues.

(i) *The climate crisis: corporate advocacy to accelerate progress*

Take the business response to the climate crisis as an example. This has certainly been an area where the dark side of lobbying in the business world has come under the spotlight, with media stories about parts of the fossil fuel industry funding climate deniers and lobbying against policies for climate action. Increasing scrutiny and transparency are making it harder for companies to sustain a Janus-faced dual stance, seemingly aligned with policies to enable faster progress while simulta- neously lobbying for the opposite through industry bodies. Alongside that is the more straightforward challenge of inac- tion: companies signing up to promises but not yet following through with action. And it hasn't been just fossil fuel producers: Influence Map, a data-based NGO that tracks climate-related advocacy across all sectors, including aviation, technology and consumer goods, finds that, even among companies signed up to the Climate Action 100+ initiative, just 10 per cent have 'fully aligned their direct climate lobbying practices with the Paris Agreement'.[4] But there are also some striking examples of what business advocacy on climate can look like.

At first pass, Søren Skou is an unlikely corporate activist. Known for being painfully shy and averse to seeking public profile, Skou, who leads the global shipping business Maersk, has stepped out to advocate for carbon pricing. He's called on the International Maritime Organisation, the UN's global regulator for the industry, to put in place a carbon tax starting in 2025 and $50 a ton, ramping up to $150. As Skou sees it:

> Combined, a global carbon tax and an end date for fossil fuelled ships would be a strong signal to the shipping ecosystem – including yards and fuel producers – about which way the wind is blowing.[5]

Citing the EU's determination to end production of combustion engine cars by 2035, he wants to see the same resolve to decarbonise shipping globally. Because it's not easy, not cheap, and no individual business can achieve it, the company is looking to the regulators to create a level playing field that supports an industrywide shift.

Maersk is not alone. When in 2020 Microsoft announced its plans to become carbon negative by 2030, it wrapped up its statement saying: 'And lastly, all this work will be supported by our voice and advocacy supporting public policy that will accelerate carbon reduction and removal opportunities.'[6] When Bernard Looney became CEO at bp, his first move was to halt all corporate reputation advertising, diverting that spend towards 'advocating much more actively and forcefully' for policies that promote carbon pricing and an accelerated transition to net zero.[7]

As more corporates get to grips with what needs to happen in reality to decarbonise their businesses rapidly, more voices are speaking up on two of the biggest questions of the day for their industries – legislation on emissions targets and carbon pricing:

- Iberdrola, the Spanish utility company, has promoted the need for a green recovery from the covid pandemic, urging EU policymakers to increase the ambition of climate regulation. Ignacio Galán, the chairman and CEO, said, 'Climate change is a global emergency, so we need everyone on board to fight it.'[8]

- Unilever, in the consumer goods sector, has directly advocated for legislated net zero by 2050 targets in the UK, the EU, the US and Australia: 'We call on all governments to set ambitious net zero targets, as well as short-term emissions reduction targets, supported with enabling policy frameworks such as carbon pricing.'[9]

- PepsiCo has advocated for a US federal-level carbon tax and supported raising the ambition of the EU's Climate Target in 2020. 'There is simply no other option but immediate and aggressive action,' says Ramon Laguarta, their chairman and CEO.[10]

- Aviva became the first major insurer worldwide to commit net zero by 2040 with the goal of cutting the carbon intensity of its investments 60 per cent by 2030 – calling on policy-makers to put a robust price on carbon. CEO Amanda Blanc says, 'Facing up to this challenge and getting ahead of it is the best thing we can do, not only for our customers and shareholders, but for all of society.'[11]

(ii) LGBTQ+ rights: businesses speaking out to advance inclusion

Against a backdrop of steady progress towards inclusion globally, millions of LGBTQ+ people are experiencing a new
intensity of discrimination, harassment and violence. In some
regions, LGBTQ+ rights have become a geopolitical wedge issue,
an assertion of national values in opposition to a global culture:
in Eastern Europe, for example, or some African countries.
Against this backdrop, many global businesses struggle to recon-
cile how they operate in these territories with their vocal support
for LGBTQ+ inclusion as a company. As this situation developed, we were hearing business leaders wanting to speak out
but finding it hard to do so – not only because of the potential
impact on their business but also because of the safety of their
employees. To help find a coherent and collective business voice
on this subject, Brunswick established *Open For Business* as a
coalition of global companies working to advance LGBTQ+
rights even in challenging countries.

The Open For Business approach is 'data-driven advocacy':
rather than become embroiled in a clash of moral systems, the
coalition makes the case that open, inclusive societies are better
for business and better for economic growth. Marshalling
evidence that shows how open, inclusive policies are associated
with increased levels of entrepreneurialism, stronger high-value
business sectors, greater foreign direct investment and, ultimately, greater economic competitiveness and resilience resonates
with economic policy makers. The coalition has grown to more
than forty high-profile global companies that include Accenture,
Burberry, Diageo, Facebook, GSK, Google, LEGO, Mastercard,
McKinsey and Unilever.[12]

The data-led approach has delivered a track record of
successful advocacy. Used by tiny local front-line non-profit

groups, highly vocal global LGBTQ+ champions and business leaders alike, Open For Business reports have become part of court proceedings in Uganda, Hong Kong and India, each with positive rulings for LGBTQ+ equality. They've been part of winning campaigns for marriage equality in Costa Rica, the Czech Republic and Taiwan. The reports on the economic case for LGBTQ+ inclusion have made headlines and changed the conversation in countries in East Africa, Eastern Europe and the Caribbean.

But why would the global drinks business Diageo, or the tech giant IBM, or the cosmetics brand L'Oréal speak out on LGBTQ+ rights? At first pass, it might seem somewhat random. However, for these companies and others in the coalition, their advocacy is grounded in strong positions and hard work to establish an inclusive culture for their own workforce, often built up painstakingly over years. It's not a sudden response to media headlines. They know their employees want to know where they stand on this issue, in the light of their stated principles as global companies. They feel conflicted by the rise in anti-LGBTQ+ sentiment and policies in some places that are dissonant with their long-held principles and are seeking mechanisms that enable them to speak up. The power of the collective voice elevates the potential of each individual company to advocate for inclusion to policymakers and other influential corporate stakeholders.

(iii) *Engaging consumers directly on societal issues*

For consumer-facing companies, their brand and marketing capability is at the core of the business. Their success is based on a finely tuned understanding of consumer perceptions and behaviours, giving them the potential to engage their consumers directly on societal issues that are relevant to them. And today that often encompasses questions of inclusion. P&G is the world's largest consumer goods company, with huge marketing muscle and influence. Ten years ago, the company declared itself to be 'the proud sponsor of mums', speaking directly to the female demographic that represents the main consumers base for its array of household, baby care and feminine hygiene products. Unsurprisingly, it's proud, too, of its ratings as a leading diversity and inclusion employer, with a commitment to working towards a gender-equal workplace with a 50:50 representation of men and women at all levels and in all parts of the company. In 2019, the company updated its commitment to gender equality with the launch of a new campaign, 'We see equal'.[13] Marc Pritchard, P&G's chief brand officer, recognises the advocacy power of brands:

> Brands affect nearly every person on the planet, every day, and can be agents of change – individually and collectively. We believe one of the best ways to solve the challenges facing us today is for brands to spark conversations that mobilise people to take action.[14]

We See Equal is a campaign that aimed to do that. Across P&G's portfolio, different brands took on different aspects of the gender equality question. In India, for example, where research showed that 70 per cent of children believe it's women's responsibility to do the laundry, P&G's leading laundry detergent, Ariel, led with advertising, carrying the message #SharetheLoad.

In the Ariel ad, our eyes follow a young woman around her home, with the phone pressed to her ear talking with a colleague at work, while fixing the children's evening meal. Still talking, carrying the laundry basket in one hand, she fills the washing machine. We see her husband, at the end of a day's work, watching TV. We watch her father watching the scene as she goes back and forth around the family home, and we see her read his apology to her: 'I am so proud – and so sorry,' he says. As we see him back in his own home, putting his own clothes in the machine, the little story finishes with the question: Why is laundry only a mother's job? Dads #ShareTheLoad.

Following the campaign, the brand was able to report that the percentage of Indian men who think that 'household chores are a woman's job' had dropped from 79 to 52 per cent. Meanwhile, in the UK the well-known washing-up liquid Fairy removed the *y* from the Fairy logo to drive their campaign: #MakeItFair. The feminine hygiene brand Always responded to the issue of plummeting self-confidence among young girls at puberty, subverting the age-old insult 'you did that like a girl' to create their campaign #LikeAGirl, designed to boost the self-image of teenage girls.[15]

At the same time, P&G partnered with the youth activist online network Global Shapers Community that reaches across 100 city hubs to 'raise awareness and mobilise action in the fight for global equality'. Through a competition to develop grassroots solutions, P&G provided grants to the winning five to bring their ideas alive. And Global Shapers is just one of a broad portfolio of civil society partners, ranging from Save the Children to The Lean In Circle to We Deliver and many others. UN Women is the campaign's global partner and, at the launch event for the #WeSeeEqual Summit in Mumbai – sitting alongside Dr Phumzile Mlambo-Ngcuka, Under-Secretary General of the United Nations and Executive Director of UN Women – P&G's IMEA and APAC president Magesvaran Suranjan explained:

Gender equality is a core belief at P&G. Creating a world free of bias with equal representation and an equal voice for everyone is both the right thing to do and the right business choice.[16]

Act 2 Unstereotype is another brand-led advocacy position on equity, this time from Unilever, promising to 'provoke inclusive thinking across the end-to-end marketing process', from initial consumer insights right through to production, with creative development behind the camera and on-screen portrayals – and every Unilever brand is creating an *Unstereotype charter.*

Conscious of the potential of their cultural influence, they're eradicating any digital alterations to photography, which includes a 100 per cent ban on changing models' body shape, size, proportion or skin colour.[17] Dove, an iconic brand in the Unilever portfolio, is leading with *Reverse Selfie*, a campaign that highlights the damage that social media pressure and retouching apps are causing to girls' self-esteem. As they did when they launched the Dove Self-Esteem initiative for 'real beauty' fifteen years ago, they've based the campaign on consumer research that highlights the problem they're setting out to fix: 80 per cent of girls said that by the age of thirteen they had already applied a filter or used a retouching app to change the way they look in their photo; 77 per cent have tried to change or hide at least one body part or feature before posting a photo of themselves. So the call to action in *Reverse Selfie* is 'to help girls reverse the damage of digital distortion'.[18] For both Unilever and P&G, advocacy in equality and inclusion strengthens their relevance to consumers, especially the next generation of consumers – and their credibility with employees, especially the next generation of employees.

Stepping into the public arena, armed with data and standing in common cause with partners, underpins the credibility of the company's voice – on any subject from net zero to inclusion – and makes issue-led advocacy an impactful element of activist leadership.

Aim to set the agenda and mobilise others

Anyone that's been to the Consumer Electronics Show (CES) in Las Vegas will know that, in normal times, it's a glitzy show-case of wearable-tech, self-driving cars and consumer-AI. So it was a surprise for the audience when the then CEO of Intel, Brian Krzanich, took to the stage and played a sombre film about the devastation in the Congo, where more than five million people had been killed in a long-running war – many killed by armed groups using profits from the mining of four minerals, tantalum, tungsten, tin and gold. That's why these are known as 'conflict minerals', he told the audience, and these minerals end up in the tech devices we're all using.

This is the difference between the corporate mindset and the activist mindset: while Intel and its NGO partners were working to 'defund the warlords', three powerful business bodies – the US Chamber of Commerce, the Business Roundtable and the National Association of Manufacturers – were asking a panel of federal judges to overturn a provision of the 2010 Dodd–Frank law that requires companies to disclose their use of minerals from Africa.[19] This kind of defensive response on a difficult and contentious issue is hard wired into traditional corporate culture. Intel's approach was to work across the system to try and solve it.

When Enough Project, a non-profit dedicated to bringing peace and good governance to conflict zones in Africa, first challenged Intel on their record on conflict minerals the leadership were taken aback. Should they try to pull out of sourcing from these territories? But apart from the practical and commercial difficulty of doing so, that would not make a difference to the issue itself. Instead, they made a decision to face into the challenge. Recognising that they didn't truly know the situation on the ground, they sent a team of employees out to investigate more than eighty smelters in their supply chain across twenty countries. Based on what they learned, Intel set standards for the first time, they worked with the smelters to raise performance and initiated third-party audits. They also partnered with local NGOs to protect artisanal miners, the most vulnerable communities in the war zones.[20] 'The solution isn't easy,' Krzanich said, 'but nothing worthwhile ever is.'

Intel's campaign was called *In Pursuit of Conflict-Free*. It launched with a big ambition: to produce the first conflict-free microprocessor and, one mineral at a time, over four years they worked to achieve that. In 2014, they were able to announce the full traceability of conflict-free minerals for tin, tantalum, tungsten and gold in their products. And they went on to engage vloggers to reach consumers. Lewis Hilsenteger, whose channel Unbox Therapy has had more than 700,000 views, was a powerful voice to educate tech-users, carrying the message to people, the vast majority of whom had no idea about the issue of conflict minerals, about why conflict-free devices matter.[21]

By choosing to put conflict minerals centre stage in their slot on the industry's most high-profile platform, Krzanich was insisting on the significance of the issue for the sector. By making documentary films that explained the real-world problem of conflict minerals, by highlighting case studies of the work in smelters in the Congo to find solutions, by putting the leadership team on panels alongside NGO campaigners to raise awareness of the human cost of the issue, the company was using its voice to advocate on the issue. In the process, it was also shining a light on the progress and contribution the company had been making – and laying down a challenge to the industry at large to step up on this question.

The purpose of this form of advocacy is to mobilise further action. When Intel published the results of their annual audit each year, it not only reinforced their own credibility, it helped to move the industry forward, and Enough Project applauded their contribution: 'Intel has really driven the whole supply chain reform movement, which has revolutionised buying practices for these minerals worldwide.'[22]

The earned endorsement of a challenging NGO, in this way, is more than a pat on the back; it is an expression of the spirit of the company working in common cause with external stakeholders close to the source of the problem in the world.

When we talk to companies about business advocacy, people will sometimes think we mean *thought leadership*. It's the term people use for finding something smart to say on a high-profile platform or a survey to commission that creates talking points and media interest. Issue-led advocacy is about articulating a clear point of view on what matters about that issue, putting forward an agenda for change that is relevant to multiple stakeholders, backed by commitment to action in the business. Thought leadership is a pale substitute for leadership on an issue.

Any business grappling with an issue is almost certainly generating new information, gaining new insights and perspectives, gaining experiences from the programmes that have been set up. Turning these learnings into content that can be usefully shared with others who are working to find solutions is a powerful act of advocacy, and lays the foundations for productive, trusted engagement with stakeholders. Here are some of the ways we've seen that type of content work.

(i) *Transparency as an agent of change.*

We profiled Coca-Cola's work to reduce plastic waste earlier: when the initiative launched, the company disclosed for the first time that it creates 3 million tonnes of plastic packaging a year, equivalent to 200,000 bottles a minute. It's a startling figure that made headlines. Publishing that fact in a report from the Ellen MacArthur Foundation (EMF), that called for 'an end to secrecy over companies' plastics footprint', they put themselves into the leading pack of companies choosing to grapple with the reality of the challenge.[23] Externally, it sent the message that the company was ready to own their part of the waste issue in the world and strengthened the call for all companies to acknowledge the problem and act. Inside the company, it set the baseline and justified the need to act at scale.

Similarly, when Tesco first published data on food waste in its operations, it was a first for the industry.[24] And it served as a signal of serious intent in the company's ambition to lead the fight against global food waste. When Dave Lewis, while still CEO of Tesco, took on a global leadership role as chair of the Champions 1.23 for the UN Sustainable Development Goals, his call to action was for the transparent publication of data. 'Publishing food waste data can sting,' he conceded, but it must be done:

> You have to understand where food is wasted before you can tackle it. You have to know where to find the hotspots from farm to fork. And you have to share what you know. We're clear that individual companies publicly measuring and reporting on food waste and loss is critical.[25]

During his time chairing the international coalition, the pioneering move made by Tesco was adopted by sixty other companies in the food system.[26]

By publishing its food waste data, Tesco helped campaigners to raise the bar for the industry. Being transparent about its own plastic problem, Coca-Cola was able to kick-start its global transformation programme and its own leadership role. Putting this kind of data into the public domain and engaging with multiple stakeholders in this way can be a game-changer, enabling a company to work constructively with even its most vocal critics.

(ii) Open-sourced data to accelerate the work of others.

Don't underestimate the power of the data you may hold on an issue; it may have value for others. When Nike started to come to grips with the question of sustainable production, they produced a Materials Sustainability Index documenting the environmental profile of hundreds of raw materials in their supply chain. With materials representing almost 60 per cent of their environmental impact, their own product teams had been asking for the data and it simply didn't exist. So they developed it for themselves – and then they published it so that anyone working with those materials could benefit from it. At launch, Lorrie Vogel who headed up Nike's work on sustainable product and open innovation tools, explained:

> All footwear and apparel companies face similar issues regarding the lack of materials information. Because we believe that there should be a system-wide approach to problem solving and innovation within our industry, we are making Nike MSI publicly available.[27]

Through Earth Engine, Google has put a 'vast treasure trove of open-source satellite imagery' at the disposal of NGOs, researchers and environmental advocates to enable them to answer questions about the impacts of climate change wherever they are located in the world – from city planners aiming to augment tree planting in urban areas of California to herders looking for water for their cattle in drought-stricken areas of

Senegal. 'It's just a remarkable level of transparency and information that wasn't available before,' says Mikaela Weisse, a project manager for the NGO Global Forest Watch.[28]

'The raw data is not enough,' says Rebecca Moore, the computer scientist who heads up Earth Engine:

> Government officials now tell us, "We're drowning in data, but we're thirsty for insights".

So Google augments the data itself with software analytics and scientists on staff to generate insights that answer the real-world questions for the users. The entire initiative grew out of Moore's enthusiasm as a user of the Earth Engine's precursor, Keyhole. A natural-born activist, she had so many suggestions for how the data could be improved to make it more effective that Google hired her. And making the most of the company's policy that encourages employees to spend their time on innovative side projects, she used satellite data from Google Earth to lead a campaign in her own local Santa Cruz community that prevented the logging of 1,000 acres of redwoods unity. The impetus of that work took Moore on to establish Earth Engine:

> We invented Google Earth Engine to allow scientists to easily analyse data and ask questions about how the climate is changing and answer in seconds or minutes instead of years.[29]

It's the data that's valuable, but it's not just the data. It's emblematic of a mindset. Sometimes that mindset is made visible by the publication of data that only a big organisation could amass, making it available for others to use in their efforts to drive positive change. Sometimes it's sharing data openly with critical partners in a way that builds trust and accelerates action towards shared goals.

(iii) New insights to set the agenda.

Another pathway to advocacy for companies wanting to contribute on a societal challenge is the generation of new information on the issue. JPMorgan Chase has long been active in disadvantaged communities, focused on building economic and social resilience, in part through the Advancing Cities programme discussed earlier in System (p. 160). As racial equity became a burning issue across the US during the Black Lives Matter protests, it brought to the surface hard questions about income gaps and disparities in economic outcomes. The company published analysis of the systemic challenge, 'Racial Gaps in Financial Outcomes – Big Data Evidence', putting new information into the public debate at a time when the issue was commanding enormous attention. Drawing on data sets of millions of households' banking records and voter registrations, the research explored take-home income, liquid assets and families' consumption patterns in response to income volatility – finding, for example, that Black and Hispanic families earn roughly 70 cents in take-home income for every dollar earned by white families and that racial gaps in liquid assets are twice as large as gaps in take-home income. In the conclusions of the report, JPMorgan Chase spelled out where solutions might come from:

> Policies and programs that boost income and address the underlying challenges Black and Hispanic families face within the labor market could help to close racial gaps in income in the short run. These could include increasing the minimum wage, strengthening the Earned Income Tax Credit, investing in job training programs, and reducing the barriers to employment for individuals with criminal backgrounds.[30]

The findings and agenda set out in the report have relevance and currency for multiple stakeholders concerned about the topic; policymakers across many areas from the economy to employment, skills, justice, health and welfare, as well as to civil society organisations and educationalists. It has implications for the role of the business and finance sectors. Producing research of this nature gives a company a credible, informed and constructive voice on a live issue in the public debate. It literally gives the leadership something of substance to say; something that is of interest and of use to other people.

One of the areas in which JPMorgan has been very active and vocal on racial equity is employment opportunities for people with criminal records. As the company's research highlights, 'this disproportionately affects people of color, with Black adults being over five times more likely to be incarcerated than white adults'.[31] It's hard, often nigh on impossible, to get a job after being in prison, even for a relatively minor offence. CEO, Jamie Dimon, states the problem plainly:

They can't get jobs, they can't rent homes. Socially they're on the margins.[32]

With 600,000 people released from prison every year in America, the human and economic burden on individuals, families, communities and society at large is enormous. *Second Chance* is JPMorgan's response to the problem, with a commitment to help ex-offenders re-enter employment.[33] The bank 'banned the box' – removing from its job applications the questions about criminal records that had no bearings on the job requirements, so as to give every applicant the same chance. As a result of a whole package of such measures, in 2020 they were able to recruit 2,100 people with criminal records, making around ten per cent of the bank's new hires in the US *Second*

Chance candidates. As with all their other community-facing programmes, *Second Chance* is surrounded by a web of civil society partnerships on the ground that deliver support from access to housing to job-and-life skills training to wrap-around services that prevent recidivism.

The bank's experience in making that work – even in the context of a financial institution where security is paramount – makes the company a powerful advocate for 'fair chance' policies that can reduce barriers to employment in all sectors and enable people with a prison record to break out of the systemic inequalities they face. It illustrates the symbiotic relationship between advocacy and action: an informed point of view about the problem naturally leads to action; the experience of delivering that action naturally reinforces evidence-based advocacy for new solutions. With the work rooted in on-the-ground civil society partnerships, it is a credible foundation from which to set the future agenda for progress on the issue.

(iv) Stakeholder engagement to mobilise action.

Becoming an advocate on an issue allows for a fresh approach to engaging with external stakeholders. When Novo Nordisk launched their global campaign focused on halting the rapidly rising incidence of diabetes in cities, for example, it allowed them to reset many important relationships. The trigger for the campaign was the publication of a study they produced in collaboration with University College London (UCL).

Called *Urban Diabetes*, the report showed why cities are the front line of the battle to defeat diabetes: sedentary lifestyles, poor diets and the flow of tens of millions of people in the developing world moving from villages into cities.[34] Lars Rebien Sørensen, Novo Nordisk CEO at the time, explained:

Whilst there are many factors fuelling the growth trajectory of diabetes, the most striking contributor is urbanisation and the growth of cities.

This put a new frame around the debate for Novo, making it relevant to a much broader range of stakeholders beyond the medical professionals and health systems dedicated to treating the condition.

With new insights to bring to the table, the company hosted a series of summits convening their expanding network of partners: mayors and city leaders along with health experts, academics and community groups. Representing organisations large and small, global and local, people came to swap learnings and emerging strategies in a shared effort to stem the diabetes challenge in their cities. Charlotte Ersbøll, who led on public policy for Novo in the early days of the initiative, reflected that the degree of natural engagement and positivity surprised even the company:

We just set it free – and people began to have the conversation amongst themselves. One of the reasons that it's easy for so many different stakeholders to join in the programme is that it's not about Novo Nordisk. It's about diabetes and how we can fight diabetes; how we can control it; how we can eradicate it. And for our company to be seen as taking a leadership role in that dialogue is new – new for us, certainly. This is a way of demonstrating that we are a partner with the patient, a partner with the healthcare environment, a partner in the countries in which we do business. We are here to solve a big, big problem.

The company established public–private partnerships with health systems to understand risk and make change in vulnerable communities; created open-access tools and frameworks for action; and set up media partnerships to increase awareness of the diabetes challenge in cities. As Lars Jørgensen, Novo Nordisk's CEO today, explains, 'We're acting as a catalyst: setting the vision, bringing people together around it and creating a platform for mobilising change.'

By reaching beyond their traditional stakeholder base of diabetes specialists and patients, the company has become a global advocate on the issue of diabetes prevention and a hub for on-the-ground activity in cities that are home to 150 million people around the world.

*   *   *

In this section we've looked at different ways companies have made the case for what needs to happen to make progress on an issue. When Tesco published its food waste data for the first time or Coca-Cola its plastics pollution data, they were setting the baseline for their own transformation initiatives and laying down a challenge to others in their industry. In putting its own Materials Sustainability Index into the public domain, Nike equipped other businesses to improve their sourcing. Through making its environmental data publicly accessible, Google was accelerating the work of climate researchers and activists. By producing new research into systemic racial inequity, JPMorgan Chase helped to set the agenda on the priorities for developing solutions. Through convening stakeholders on the challenge of urban diabetes, Novo Nordisk was able to activate the efforts of others in cities around the world.

Leading the debate on an issue places business leaders alongside other sectors of society, shoulder-to-shoulder, wrestling with these complex problems. It helps to establish common cause with external stakeholders and the basis for shared goals, all in service of mobilising action.

5443

4343243

Speak up on the actions you're taking and why – so that others can follow

Becoming an activist leader is about identifying those issues where you can make the greatest material contribution. And one contribution you can make is using your voice. Raising your voice in the public arena about *why* this matters and how you're working on it is often welcomed with open arms by the NGOs and other social stakeholders working on an issue.

Take as an example Apple's *Earth Day* announcement in 2014 of a bold new environmental initiative. The company had been criticised for being secretive about its environmental impacts, and Greenpeace had repeatedly called it the 'dirtiest' of the technology giants for its reliance on coal power.[35] The issue of carbon emissions from the tech sector was on the rise but the major companies were all saying how hard it would be to switch to renewables and setting out long timescales for adaptation. But Apple invested heavily in solar power, announcing that they were generating enough renewable energy to power 100 per cent of their data centres worldwide. It was a remarkable turnaround: Apple topped Greenpeace's list of technology companies, scoring 100 per cent in their Clean Energy Index.

According to Greenpeace, part of the power of Apple's actions came from their communications: 'The company's challenge to itself also throws down the gauntlet to others,' wrote Kumi Naidoo, the then executive director of Greenpeace in a blog post:

> Far from hiding its environmental goals in the back of an investor report, Apple's very public Earth Day announcement has already reached millions of people worldwide. Apple is now selling environmentalism to the mass market, underpinned by strong commitments.[36]

Often we hear companies say, 'We don't want to shout about what we're doing, we just want to get on and do it.' They're worried that people will think they're only doing it for the headlines. As Apple's story illustrates, communications can itself be a part of creating change on an issue. Speaking about what you're doing, why you're doing it, how you're doing it and what you're going to do next can help others follow your lead – in the industry and beyond. It's about showing what's possible and changing industry norms. And, crucially, it can pave the way for policy that helps the entire industry step forward. As Apple's vice-president of Environment, Policy and Social Initiatives, Lisa Jackson, told the media: 'No one can ever claim again you can't have a data center that runs on 100 percent renewable. Once those proof points are out there, it makes it easier for policies to follow.'[37] That's an activist position.

It's the attitude that Sunny Verghese takes as CEO of Olam International and an advocate for transformation of the global agricultural system. The business he co-founded in 1989 has grown to become one of the world's leading agribusinesses; in the top thirty on the Singapore stock exchange and a Fortune 500 company, with 80,000 people working across sixty countries and a supply chain that encompasses millions of smallholder farmers across Asia and Africa. Speaking at the UN in 2016 about the private sector's role in achieving the Sustainable Development Goals (SDGs), Verghese told the story of his own transformation. He began with 'a confession' that, even though he had worked for three decades to build a successful business, 'it is only in the last eleven years that my sensibility on why sustainability is at the core of building an enduring business began to crystalise'. The company's name, Olam, means 'enduring' and he explained:

At the core of my own transformation was firstly the reali-sation that to live up to our name of being an enduring and everlasting business, how we do business is more important, or equally important, as what we do and how we win.

At a personal level, he reflected, 'After all of this hard work and overwhelming effort, if you're not going to be leaving the world a better place for our children, what is the point of it all?' As a businessman, he concluded: 'I saw the direct link between sustainability and creating long-term value for our owners.'[38]

In 2018, Olam launched AtSource, a digital dashboard that provides transparency for their customers to track to the source all the raw materials they produce, with data on ten sustainability topics and 350 metrics.[39] In 2019, the company created the Cocoa Compass, mapping out their ambition to 'make the future of cocoa more sustainable'. In that plan is a commitment to Cote d'Ivoire, the world's largest cocoa producing country – where most farmers live in extreme poverty. Working with NGOs on the ground, the goal is to enable 150,000 smallholder farmers to achieve a living wage by 2030.[40] These initiatives, and others like them, are part of Olam's purpose to 'reimagine global agriculture and food systems'. But the company cannot deliver on that alone.

So advocacy is critical to the strategy. 'Governments and policymakers have to come to the party,' says Verghese. 'When everybody is forced to do it, everybody will average up the game in terms of what is required to be done.' He calls on regulators to require mandatory disclosure and reporting from companies on their environmental footprint and living wage; on NGOs and businesses to collaborate; on academics and scientists to innovate, and coalitions of sector peers to mobilise action – in what he calls a 'public, private, plural society partnership':

We need to come together to bring all our configuration of assets and capabilities to bear, to deal with these intractable problems.[41]

In contrast with the kind of corporate lobbying that sets a business at odds with other sectors of society, this kind of 'issue-led advocacy' places business leaders alongside critical stakeholders, shoulder-to-shoulder, wrestling with these complex problems. It helps to establish common cause with external stakeholders. And, as significant, it can also catalyse a shift *inside* the company, breaking down the walls of the corporate mindset, making it easier for people inside to see these challenges as the world sees them. People start to feel braver – bolder in ambition, more confident to speak out.

9.

MOMENTUM:
get going, keep going

Thinking like an activist . . .	• Create a *discontinuity* to show you're serious and to signal ambition • Learn out loud – with a spirit of openness • Keep up momentum – treat each new challenge as a springboard

Create a *discontinuity* to show you're serious and to signal ambition

Sometimes companies start with a bang – a big, bold first move that gets people's attention and sends a signal about the kind of company they're aiming to be. When CVS rebranded as a health services company in 2014, for example, it announced a new purpose: *Helping people on their path to better health.* Soon after came another announcement – one that would surprise the retail world: CVS would stop selling cigarettes, reported by the media as a $2 billion decision. Many were puzzled: there was no competitive pressure to do this, no media furore or social media campaign. It was a bold decision, taken on the company's own initiative – and received positively by the public. Shareholders, however, were less convinced. Many voiced their displeasure, and the company's stock price fell 1 per cent the day after the announcement.[1]

It recovered the next day, and the company was bullish about its decision. Larry J. Merlo, their CEO, said in a statement: 'Put simply, the sale of tobacco products is inconsistent with our purpose.' As the largest pharmacy chain in the US, according to the *American Journal of Public Health*, CVS's decision to stop selling cigarettes contributed to reducing levels of smoking countrywide.[2] The company was confident this would strengthen relationships with customers and employees, as well as health-industry partners who appreciated their commitment to healthcare. It wasn't painless, but it was critical for their new direction.

For CVS, it was a move that signalled commitment to their new positioning and ambition for creating social value. We think of it as a *discontinuity* – a break from the past, emblematic of making a pivot, a sign that you're serious. It can be a crucial step in prompting reappraisal, getting people to take a fresh look at the company, starting to rebase perceptions. Making a first move like this – something unexpected, ahead of the game – can earn you the benefit of the doubt from even strident critics.

As we've seen, sometimes a company makes a *pivot* – turns to face into the issue and recognise the problem, rather than focusing their efforts on how to minimise exposure. And we described how a week after becoming CEO of bp, Bernard Looney announced that the company would become a net zero emitter by 2050 or sooner, cutting oil and gas production by 40 per cent by 2030, and setting out to help the world make the transition to a low-carbon economy. Looney had to convince sceptical stakeholders that this was a sincere shift in strategy.

A bone of contention for critics had been the company's *Possibilities Everywhere* corporate reputation campaign, which was typical of industry efforts to persuade the world that they were serious about the climate crisis. He took the campaign down, literally. He created a *discontinuity* – a move of both symbolic and real value, He posted pictures on LinkedIn of empty billboards, commenting 'Not the prettiest pictures – but there's an important message behind them'. The company removed ads from sites around the world and announced it would redirect the spend to actively advocate for climate policies that support net zero.[3]

With less fanfare, the company also publicly parted company with a number of industry bodies that had been associated with anti-climate lobbying.[4] For bp – and for the industry at large – this has long been a controversial area, with NGOs pointing to a history of lobbying designed to block the transition from fossil fuels. Taking down the advertising and proactively supporting climate transition policies signalled a change in direction for bp. That first step may only represent a change in stance towards the issue, but it laid the foundation for the strategic commitments to come.

Both CVS and bp made dramatic first moves; they made discontinuity their friend. Sometimes, getting going can be less dramatic – but bold nevertheless. LEGO's journey on plastic use captures that spirit. When the company realised it needed to act on the growing challenge of plastic, it seemed like an impossible task. LEGO's bricks use a type of plastic prized for its strength and rigidity. It takes lifetimes to break down. Solving this will be critical for the company: at the time of writing, LEGO uses around 100,000 tonnes of polymer each year to make twenty different kinds of plastics, to produce 110 billion bricks designed to have just the right durability, colour fastness, strength and 'clutch power' – their word for how securely bricks fix together. It's a big task to replace all that.

They started in 2015 by bringing together the resources to tackle the question into one hub, setting up a *Sustainable*

Materials Centre with $155 million funding and more than 100 employees. The mission is to make LEGO from fully sustainable materials by 2030.[5] By 2018, just under 2 per cent of the products were made from a new sugar-cane-based poly-ethylene rather than oil-based plastic; that sounds like a small beginning, but that's still a lot of plastic, and you've got to start somewhere. In 2020 the company ramped up the efforts further with an additional $400 million of funding and said it will also be removing single-use plastics from its packaging – encouraged along the way in part by the many letters they received from children.[6] In 2021 they made a breakthrough and announced that they will begin retailing recycled plastic bricks within two years: one recycled 1-litre PET bottle can make ten 2x4 LEGO bricks.[7] LEGO's journey on plastic shows it's also possible to start small – but with a bold ambition. The key thing is to get started.

Learn out loud – with a spirit of openness

This goes against most corporate instincts: being transparent about what's working *and* what isn't. We all know that compa-nies tend to keep their cards close to their chest. They like to keep problems contained and to project an air of calm compe-tence. You can understand why: we take it for granted that the food we buy will be fresh and uncontaminated; or that our data will be protected from criminals; or that the planes we fly in aren't about to fall out of the sky. The consequences of getting this stuff wrong can be disastrous – we rely on companies to get it right. So it's understandable that corporates are unnerved by the appearance of fallibility; any failures are kept out of view, or hurriedly tidied up and managed away. Similarly, in the capital markets a lack of certainty or a failure to deliver what was promised is the cardinal sin. Even the development of innovative solutions and product pipelines must yield to the expectation of controlled outcomes.

Societal issues are messy and noisy in comparison. These are hard problems and they are shared problems. Solutions lie beyond the direct control of the business. Grappling with them means admitting you don't have all the answers and success is delivered through collaborations. Thinking like an activist involves being open about what's not yet solved and shaking off that habitual corporate defensiveness that can go with the need for certainty.

This attitude of openness is evident in the companies we've profiled in the preceding chapters – including LEGO, Microsoft, PepsiCo and H&M. Here's how the people leading the work in those businesses talk about it:

'We set goals and then we go and work really hard to achieve them. But you've got to be transparent along the way about what's working, what's not. We don't set goals that we don't think we can achieve. We don't know always how we're going to achieve them because they are big goals, and they're bold, and they're aggressive. But that's what's needed.'
Jim Andrews, Chief Sustainability Officer, PepsiCo[8]

'[We need] the courage to be as transparent as possible in the progress, as well as the challenges ahead. It's not about being perfect and it certainly isn't easy to always feel confident in what you know, but we need to dare to be honest and vulnerable to open up for impactful collaborations change.'
Hanna Hallin, Global Sustainability Manager, Treadler, H&M Group[9]

'When it comes to our plan it's not like we've got it all figured out. We're just trying to do what the science says the whole world needs to do. There's really no other choice.'
Lucas Joppa, Chief Environmental Officer, Microsoft[10]

'Even though it will be a while before they will be able to play with bricks made from recycled plastic, we want to let kids know we're working on it and bring them along on the journey with us. Experimentation and failing is an important part of learning and innovation. Just as kids build, unbuild and rebuild with LEGO bricks at home, we're doing the same in our lab.'
Tim Brooks, VP Environmental Responsibility, LEGO Group[11]

In our experience, the fear of not having all the answers yet plays a big role in the hesitancy that leaders express about getting involved. So it is quite simply helpful, and something of a relief, to see that it's possible to say so. Initially, it takes courage to take this stance – because, in traditional corporate culture, it's counter-intuitive. But in practice, it becomes a great asset to the business. Fuelled by the conviction about what needs to be achieved and the determination to find solutions, it enables you to take people on the journey with you. And it marks out the activist leader.

For any business, an innovation journey is about treating setbacks not as failures but as course corrections, the next problem to get to grips with. When it comes to tackling societal issues, being transparent about this can be a contribution to shared progress. We call this *learning out loud*. As Henry Ford put it: 'The only real mistake is the one from which we learn nothing.'

Learning out loud is an attitude. It's a shift away from thinking, 'We'll get clear on what we can deliver, get it all done and *then* we'll talk about it.' Often, companies will want to wait before making their commitments public: first, they want a fully baked plan. They want to be able to reassure all stakeholders they're on top of it, in control. The trouble is, in dealing with this type of issue if you wait until you're on top of it, you may be waiting a very long time. Meanwhile, you'll probably have lost the trust of your stakeholders, who want tangible evidence that you're taking the issues seriously, now.

There's a potential trap in the metaphor of the journey, of course. There are some who adopt the idea of being on a journey to tamp down ambition and action: no one action will be the full answer, these things are tough and the timeframe will be long, so there's no need to hurry. It can become an excuse for slipping back towards the corporate instinct for incremental change and initiatives that don't disturb the established parameters of business as usual. So the journey needs an activist mindset, with leaders who tap into the urgency and scale of change needed for today's realities.

This attitude is evident in Microsoft's approach to carbon, for example. As the corporate universe began to gear up to net zero emissions targets, Microsoft went for the next frontier with their ambition to become carbon *negative* by 2030, committing to remove more carbon from the atmosphere than the business emits each year. At announcement, they declared, 'While the world will need to reach net zero, those of us who can afford to move faster and go further should do so.' Calling it *Moonshot* – because they know it's yet to be made possible – they see it as requiring 'wholesale business transformation'. As their president Brad Smith acknowledged, 'We recognise that progress requires not just a bold goal but a detailed plan.'[12] So, since no one has it 'all figured out', part of what they can contribute is what they're discovering on that transformation journey.

In the first year of *Moonshot*, Microsoft put out their first request for proposal (RFP) for projects that could deliver 1 million metric tons of carbon removal and the interest they received was much greater than even they had expected: 189 responses from forty countries. In the selection, due diligence and contracting process for the twenty-six projects they went for was a mass of new learning. So the company published a carbon removal white paper, making all the proposals public and sharing the lessons for them about what worked and what didn't, in order that others could use that learning to accelerate their own carbon removal plans.[13] And, because they see stand-ards and measurement as the bedrock of success on this journey, together with their auditors PwC, they distilled what they've been learning about embedding these big environmental commit-ments into the functions and operations of a business, calling it 'a blueprint to help companies move from ambition to action on reducing carbon emissions'.[14]

A year on from launch, Brad Smith published a progress report in the form of a blog. He had lots to say about what they had begun to achieve, including, for instance, applying an internal carbon price to their scope 3 and setting up their $1 billion Carbon Innovation Fund to invest in new technologies that could potentially make carbon removal – not just carbon reduction – a reality. But even more significant is that the recounting of their successes is accompanied by a readiness to point out the problems as well:

> We need to get real on carbon math. The current methods for carbon accounting are ambiguous and too discretionary. We need clear protocols to ensure that progress reported on an accounting statement is truly progress in the real world.[15]

That speaks to a challenge for the entire corporate world. Most striking perhaps are the details where Smith pinpoints areas of weakness in how they have been operating, insights about what they, as a company, need to fix:

> Another point of progress, while not splashy, is also indispensable. As we work to decarbonise our supply chain, the role of contracts is key. Supplier contracts today do not include a price on carbon – and they must. Passive purchasing is not sufficient.[16]

In their pursuit of new carbon solutions, the leadership team at Microsoft have shed the corporate instinct to defend their territory and minimise their exposure to the challenges. They have approached it with the activist spirit that continually seeks to focus attention on the next problem in order to begin fixing it. Having this attitude makes it much easier to get going in the first place.

When companies adopt this principle of 'learn out loud', pretty soon they find it makes life easier for them. Far from adding risk or complexity, it can help on three levels:

- **A spirit of openness allows you to take stakeholders on the journey.** Those who are challenging businesses to act on these issues, including policymakers and investors, understand it's not easy: they know the problems themselves are intractable and they know it's hard to shift a big business. They don't expect you to solve it all at once, but they do want tangible evidence of significant effort and progress. Transparency and talking openly about the journey is how you provide that.

- **Transparency is a pre-condition to meaningful collaboration.** The modus operandi for tackling these challenges, as we have seen, requires the business to work across the issue ecosystem.

Learning out loud involves that entire ecosystem, from innovation partners to NGOs: they are on the journey, too. And their active participation reinforces the credibility of the work and shines a light on the company's ability to act in common cause with broader society to tackle the issues.

– **Learning out loud is a catalyst to action by others.** Sometimes it's as straightforward as sharing knowledge of what has been learned so far, to save others from replicating that effort – and so accelerating progress. Beyond that, being transparent about the next challenges helps to set the agenda for action. It provides the focus for bringing the ecosystem around the problem to determine what's needed to take the next steps in the journey.

Keep up momentum – treat each new challenge as a springboard

Often, the more progress you make on tackling an issue, the more challenges you encounter. This might seem disheartening at first, but activist leaders look at it as a part of the journey: today's solutions move us forward while revealing tomorrow's problems. If you're serious about making progress on these complex issues, you know there are no quick fixes: you're in it for the long haul. So the trick is to treat each hurdle you encounter as a new chapter – and when you meet it, you ratchet up your response, rising to the new challenge each time. Every one of the companies whose stories we've told works in this mindset, and highlighting a handful of successful long-running initiatives brings that to life.

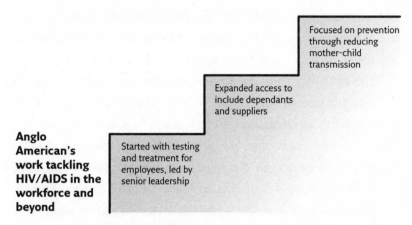

Figure 10: Anglo American and HIV/AIDS

A stand-out example of sustained momentum is the decades-long effort by the mining giant Anglo American on tackling HIV/AIDS. It was a health issue that had become a business-critical issue for the company: as Dr Brian Brink, their former chief medical officer, explained, 'There was a time when investors were getting on the phone and asking whether the disease was going to bring down the organization. We were training two people for the same role, in case one died in the job. It was that bad.'[17] With 120,000 workers in South Africa at the time, the company was faced with a health crisis that threatened their operations, their people and the communities in which they worked. In 2002, Anglo American became the first major employer to provide free antiretroviral treatments for their workforce.[18]

Immediately, they hit the first hurdle: the stigma surrounding HIV/AIDS stalled the initiative – employees were not prepared to come forward to be tested. To make any progress the company had to establish for the first time a clear policy that laid the foundation for trust: no employee would be fired for testing positive and health records would remain confidential – and they mounted a campaign to reassure employees, with senior leaders stepping up to get tested in public. Over a decade, they built up from less than 6 per cent of employees knowing their HIV status to more than 90 per cent testing, and repeating those tests every year.[19]

But as they began to make progress on the testing front, the next hurdle became clear. HIV/AIDS doesn't just affect the workforce, it's a community issue. So Anglo American extended its testing and treatment to wives, partners and dependants, going out to the villages to reach them – and then on to contractors and suppliers.[20] Recognising the power of learning about HIV/AIDS from their peers and informally, rather than from their bosses and through formal channels, the company trained 2,000 peer group educators – volunteers who had tested positive themselves – to work with their colleagues. The very visible presence of this brave and proactive group of people was in itself a mechanism for dispelling stigma. They not only built trust and empathy but also succeeded in getting over 90 per cent of the people they engaged with who had tested positive to get treatment.[21]

There's always a new frontier. As the threat of HIV combined with TB emerged, Anglo incorporated TB into its testing and treatment programmes. And through AngloGold, they established an independent medical research body that, with academic partners such as the London School of Hygiene and Tropical Medicine and the Centers for Disease Control and Prevention in Atlanta, Georgia, has produced a raft of peer-reviewed papers. Then, as the new front line became mother–child transmission, Anglo again built it into their programmatic efforts on the ground and funded medical research.[22]

The company spearheaded the ambition for 'a generation born HIV free', working with UNAIDS and the Business Leadership Council. With 330,000 babies born every year with HIV infection, Anglo's Dr Brink, whose advocacy had done so much to drive the work forward, captured the campaigning spirit:

The transmission of HIV from a pregnant mother to her child is entirely preventable. And that's a burden of disease for life. The cost of that to individuals to families to countries and government is immense. We have the power to stop it.[23]

Anglo American has seen real cost savings in the form of reduced absenteeism, employee retention and improved health in the workforce.[24] Looking to the future, the company lent its weight to the UN 95-95-95 targets – that by 2025, globally, 95 per cent of people with HIV will be diagnosed, 95 per cent of those will be on treatment and 95 per cent of those on treatment will have viral suppression.[25] As Mpumi Zikalala, head of the De Beers operation for Anglo and chairperson of the National Aids Council Private Sector Forum in South Africa, wrote, 'Fighting HIV/AIDS is everyone's business.'[26]

Tracing the story from its beginnings to the present day, what comes across is the company's determination to keep up momentum. They got started when the huge health crisis gripped the world, with particular ferocity in Africa – in their core base and among their employees. When they decided to take it on, providing free antiretroviral treatment was a simple but bold first commitment. There was no certainty about the way forward – indeed, their early efforts showed them just how difficult it would be. But each hurdle they encountered became the focus for the next phase of their programme. From the outset, they've sought out the front line of the problem and they've kept doing that. They built what became the world's largest workforce HIV/AIDS initiative and have become trusted experts and advocates on the issue globally. That activist mindset has been the source of their leadership.

Figure 11: Unilever and the living wage

Step one in Unilever's journey on the issue of a living wage was their commitment to become an Accredited Living Wage Employer in their home market of the UK, which they achieved in 2015. They were by no means the first; they were in fact the 2,000th. As the Living Wage Foundation, the accrediting organisation, explained, these were all businesses moving voluntarily and ahead of the levels expected by new regulation on the minimum wage. 'These employers are not waiting for Government to tell them what to do; their actions are helping to end the injustice that is in-work poverty in the UK now.'[27]

The issue of the gap between minimum wage expectations and the living wage was high on the public agenda at the time in the UK. At the start of 2016, the UK government ran a 'name and shame' campaign against hundreds of employers not paying even the minimum wage.[28] But the reality is that the minimum wage is not a living wage. Hence the emergence of organisations around the world over recent years working on what constitutes a 'real living wage' locally, meaning, as Resolution Foundation describes it 'what families need to get by'.[29]

Unilever linked their decision to take a position on the issue of the living wage to their purpose – *to make sustainable living commonplace* – and when in 2015 they reported that they had earned the accreditation, they also announced the second step: their commitment to achieve at least the living wage for all their employees globally by 2020.

To deliver on that, the HR teams in every one of the 160 markets in which Unilever were operating assessed the wages for their lowest paid employees against the standards of the living wage benchmark for their country, as defined by the Fair Wage Network. Remediation plans were put in place to close the gap where needed, with Unilever reporting progress annually, and in 2021 they won accreditation as a global living wage employer.[30] Immediately, they ratcheted up their level of ambition again.

The company announced a new goal: that everyone who works in their supply chain would earn a living wage or income by 2030.[31] It came at a time when the health and economic impacts of covid were shining a cold light on the vulnerability of low-paid workers around the world; people who on a day-to-day basis face a struggle just to make ends meet and have little resilience and little to fall back on in a crisis. *Inequality* became the shared language for the rising heat in the global debate on systemic disadvantage and injustice.

At launch, CEO Alan Jope was talking, on one hand, about the impetus for Unilever's action in straightforward human terms and the practical impact on individual lives: 'Our ultimate ambition is that everyone in our value chain earns a living wage or living income – just as our own employees do.' It's an ambition that many business leaders might well share. On the other hand, he was joining the live conversation about the nature of the capitalist system:

> As capitalism evolves, more equitable value distribution will become a central feature and living wages as a minimum threshold will become the norm.[32]

Responsible Investor, the news outlet on sustainable investment, called Unilever's global ambition 'a masterclass in ESG'.[33]
And the view that the future will require greater investment in
the workforce had been reflected also in the milestone statement
from the Business Roundtable (BRT) in the US in 2019 on the
purpose of business and Jamie Dimon, chair of the BRT at the
time, summed it up: 'Major employers are investing in their
workers and communities because they know it is the only way
to be successful over the long term.'[34]

There's no quick fix; the plan is based in a realism that getting
to this new 'norm' will require some things to be changed and
a readiness to find new ways of trying to make that happen, in
partnership with others. Unilever thinks that, in practical terms,
an essential foundation will be 'creating reliable, scalable, transparent, and comparable living wage methodologies and better
visibility of living wage data to raise the floor across whole
industries and countries'.[35] They are well aware that this is what
it will take to deliver on their own commitment and also that,
if they achieve it, they will have hammered out an approach
that could contribute to change systemwide.

Unilever has embarked on a ten-year journey and is taking a
phased approach, working closely with their suppliers to deliver
through plans based on agreed local living wage rates and an
external verification process. The business has calculated that, in
the face of regulatory pressure in many markets, increasing investor
focus on the 'S' in ESG, more challenging labour relations, as well
as a competitive employment marketplace, getting this right will
de-risk the business and make it more resilient. The plan is for
this to reach more than 65,000 direct suppliers, so the uplift will
be felt by millions of individuals and, as Unilever and their partners point out, that will have knock-on benefits for millions more
through the families and communities of those workers.[36] David
Ingram, Unilever's Chief Procurement Officer, explained:

The core of what we're trying to do is make a change that is systemic and wide enough that ideally sectors and governments institute living wages as a natural base.[37]

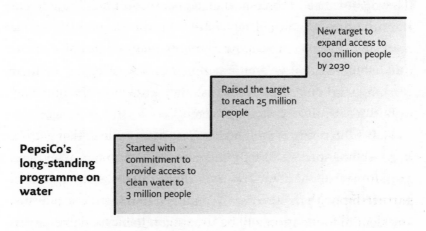

Figure 12: PepsiCo and water

PepsiCo is one of the world's largest producers of soft drinks, so water is their essential raw material. In the early 2000s, the company came under fire for the huge quantities of water used for their manufacturing in some of the most water-stressed places in the world. In India, they faced protests on the street and criticism from lawmakers; the issue of water had become a licence to operate threat and they were getting a very real sense of what it meant to lose it. They pivoted and set out an ambitious approach to tackling the water problem. In their core business, they put in place a tough target to reduce water use in their operations by 20 per cent by 2015 and exceeded it, saving the business $80 million in the process. Alongside that, beyond the business, they began in 2011 with a goal to provide access to safe drinking water to three million people who didn't have it. When they hit that early, they doubled it to six million.[38] Then sixteen million, then twenty-five million.[39] Gaining in confidence and capability, they kept going.

When covid spread across the least-developed economies it became evident how many communities couldn't protect themselves with even the most basic of defences – hand washing. The significance of access to clean water was heightened, and the initiative became all the more relevant and urgent. So the company quickly introduced a raft of new programmes, from building community water systems in rural Colombia[40] to hand washing stations in South Africa's dense urban environments.[41]

But, as PepsiCo says, one in ten people still lack access to safe drinking water and nearly 700 million are likely to be displaced by intense water insecurity by 2030. So, in 2021 – ten years on from their early water commitments – the company reported it had provided safe drinking water to fifty-five million people, and once again upped the target, this time to reach 100 million by 2030. This was part of a newly framed big ambition to become 'net water positive by 2030'.[42]

In practice, it means aiming to replenish watersheds with more than 100 per cent of the water used by their operations in high-water-risk areas. It's the activist mindset in action: being ambitious about the impact you can make – and continuing to rachet up your efforts in pursuit of that ambition.

They continue to push up the operational efficiency of water use in their business and through their supply chain – and to do that there's more than a dozen innovation projects running. In partnership with N-Drip, for example, they've created a new micro-irrigation method powered only by gravity for farmers in India that halves water use compared to the traditional method of flood irrigation. And the R&D team has worked out how, during the frying process for chips, to capture the water that escapes as steam from the potatoes and reuse it to clean the potatoes as they come into the facility.[43]

Bringing together these efforts in the business with the work of the PepsiCo foundation under the umbrella of their shared ambition, they fund work across myriad local water projects around the world – with a portfolio of globally renowned non-profits and research institutions from Water Aid to the World Resources Institute, from the Water Resources Group to Water.org. Each one of that powerful cluster of partners comes at the problem from a different angle that together represents the many aspects of the water issue in the world; watershed management, conservation, distribution, hygiene and sanitation, agricultural practices and more. And the network creates a symbiotic relationship which enables the company to contribute to and learn from leading-edge thinking and practice globally. They use that to inform their public advocacy on 'smart water policy' with governments at all levels all over the world. So, if you come across their work on water now, it's clear that PepsiCo knows their subject. The issue is deeply embedded in the company and has big numbers associated with it; big investment, big targets for reach and even bigger ambitions. But it started small.

The first move was simple: a study of just five watersheds around the world to understand the challenge of watershed management, close up on the ground – in order to see where the greatest challenges lay and the greatest opportunity for impact. Produced in partnership with an expert global NGO, Nature Conservancy, the report was published along with those first commitments from the business for both operational efficiency and social impact.[44] By keeping up momentum over the years, the company has earned a reputation as a global centre of excellence on the issue of water management.

* * *

Momentum is the last of our nine steps. We've seen what it takes to get going – but what marks out the leaders is not just that they get going but that they keep going. They keep up momentum – always focused on the horizon and the next move. In the previous chapters we've seen some examples: Maersk, having delivered the world's largest and most energy efficient ship, made another ground-breaking move in 2021: an order for eight large container ships capable of running on carbon-neutral methanol – the first of which will be on the seas in 2024. JPMorgan Chase, with long-standing initiatives to build resilience in inner cities in the US, upped their commitment to racial inequality following the Black Lives Matter protests, committing billions more in funding to help close the wealth gap among Black, Hispanic and Latino communities. Intel, having led the way for their industry on tackling conflict minerals, has expanded its efforts to the next tier of the supply chain, new geographies and new minerals.

These companies take it in their stride that there will always be a new front line in tackling these issues. They treat it as a journey; when inevitable challenges and setbacks come, they're seen not as a reason to turn back, but as a springboard. This is the spirit of activism, and it gives you stamina and staying power for the road ahead.

III.

The Activist's Guide to the Conversation About the Role of Business in Society

The Activist's Guide to the Conversation About the Role of Business in Society

There's a live and often heated debate about the role of business in society. It forms a noisy 'surround sound' in the business world today. It can be confounding: you might be asked to take a view on whether investors really care about ESG, or whether this whole purpose-thing is just marketing. You might be accused of woke-washing, or expected to explain the circular economy, or pontificate on the future of capitalism.

So this section aims to be a guide, helping to make sense of all this. We outline the dimensions of the debates so you can form your own perspectives and look at what you, thinking like an activist, might need to take out of it all.

First, we look at what's driving the rise and rise of ESG – which has been meteoric, reflecting the new expectation of the financial community. Second, we look at the power of *purpose*, and the problems that can arise from it. Third, the front edge of the conversation we have with companies is about system transformation: societal issues are systemic in nature and businesses are key players in those systems. Fourth, corporations are increasingly finding themselves on the fault lines of contentious political issues and culture-war controversies. Fifth, there is a new and dynamic shared agenda emerging with governments, as well as a formidable 'third wave' of regulation. Finally, all of this forms part of a broader 'big debate' about reinventing capitalism.

Anyone in the business universe today encounters these concepts, so we look at the main drivers of these conversations. There's one important point above all to keep in mind – a point that can be hugely empowering for activists: they may seem like different conversations, but they all spring from the same impetus – the growing demand for businesses to step up on environmental and social issues.

The Activist's Guide to the Role of Business in Society

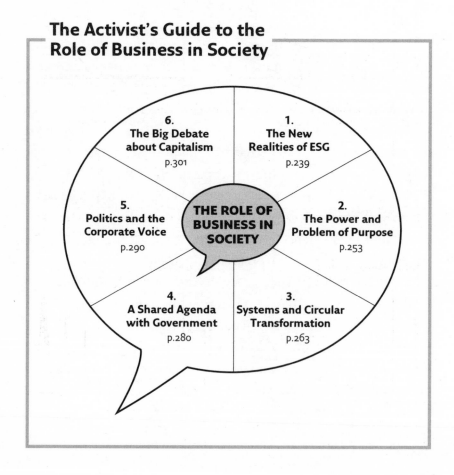

6. The Big Debate about Capitalism p.301

1. The New Realities of ESG p.239

5. Politics and the Corporate Voice p.290

THE ROLE OF BUSINESS IN SOCIETY

2. The Power and Problem of Purpose p.253

4. A Shared Agenda with Government p.280

3. Systems and Circular Transformation p.263

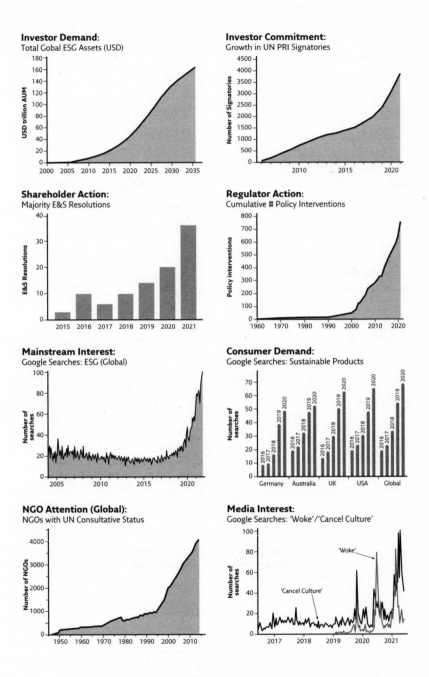

*Figure 13: Rising interest in the conversation
about business and society*[1]

1.

The New Realities of ESG

The growing intensity of societal issues, looked at through the lens of investors, has propelled ESG to the top of the corporate agenda. A decade ago, when we were working with a CEO, or the CFO, the Strategy Director or the Sustainability lead, to identify where their company could make the greatest impact on a societal issue, even the most willing among them would at some point say, somewhat ruefully, 'but the problem is our investors don't care'. It's different now. ESG is making boards and leadership teams look again at how they respond to societal issues.

It's the speed with which ESG has moved into the mainstream that's astonished many people. Rising from $22.8 trillion in 2018 to $35 trillion in 2020, global ESG assets are on track to exceed $53 trillion by 2025, representing more than a third of the $140.5 trillion in projected total assets under management, according to analysis by Bloomberg.[1] When the asset manager power-block of BlackRock, Vanguard, Fidelity Investments, Capital Group and State Street throw their weight behind ESG, that's a force to be reckoned with. The Principles for Responsible Investment (PRI), started in 2005 and supported by the UN, is on a mission to build sustainability into the global financial system.[2] When PRI won its 4,000th signatory – the China-based life insurance firm Taikang Insurance – they said that it had taken them six years to reach the first 1,000 signatories and just one year to get from 3,000 to 4,000. The combined signatories now boast $110 trillion assets under management.[3] And in the spring of 2021, Commissioner Herren Lee of the US Securities and Exchange Commission (SEC) declared:

> There is really no historical precedent for the magnitude of the shift in investor focus that we've witnessed over the last decade toward the analysis and use of climate and other ESG risks and impacts in investment decision-making.[4]

Stepping out of the wings and into the limelight has made ESG a hot topic. Recently, like so much else in the US, the term's become politicised, caught up in the fractious debate around 'wokeism'. If you're following the subject in the business media, every day you'll come across another voice with another opinion on what it's all about. Some commentators celebrate ESG as an idea that's time has come at last, while others claim it's already come and gone. If you're tracking the deliberations of the accounting profession, you might get lost in the important but arcane technicalities. It might all create the impression that there's more heat than light, that there's no substance, no consensus, only discord. You might miss that there's a seismic shift underway.

ESG has brought questions about non-financial reporting into the mainstream and that will transform what businesses are held accountable for. These questions are by no means new, yet in most businesses they have felt peripheral, until now. But the pressing nature of these multiple crises is forcing the pace on data, metrics and transparency on non-financial issues in corporate performance. It's not yet fully formed but it's maturing fast.

Leaders in the asset management industry have been setting

the agenda. Larry Fink, founder and CEO of the world's largest investment institution, BlackRock, writes an annual letter to CEOs and he put a stake in the ground in 2018 when he said:

> Society is demanding that companies, both public and private, serve a social purpose. To prosper over time, every company must not only deliver financial performance, but also show how it will make a positive contribution to society.[5]

He spelled out that this means engaging directly with those issues that are most relevant to the business:

> Your company's strategy must articulate a path to achieve financial performance. To sustain that performance, however, you must also understand the societal impact of your business as well as the ways that broad structural trends – from slow wage growth to rising automation to climate change – affect your potential for growth.

The increased activity around ESG is being driven in part by the changing priorities of the people with the money; individuals choosing not to invest in activities that are harmful to the environment or society at large. And for the wealth and asset management industries, capturing the significant flow of client funds into sustainable investment has become interwoven with the structural generational shift in wealth. An unprecedented wealth transfer is taking place: an anticipated $30 trillion in the US over the next twenty years passing from baby boomers to millennials[6] and trillions more in Asia as family-owned private businesses pass to next generation leaders.[7] The evidence shows that younger generations are more likely to prioritise ESG.[8] One survey found that 90 per cent of millennials want to tailor their investments to their values;[9] Another reports that 87 per cent of high-net-worth millennials see a company's ESG track record as an important investment consideration.[10]

However, not everyone is onboard with ESG, so let's pause to consider where the scepticism comes from. The critics point to the muddle of acronyms: TCFD, GRI, CDP, CDSB, SASB, VRF – unsurprisingly, you often hear people describing ESG as an 'alphabet soup'[11] – and the proliferation of institutions and frameworks creates confusion. A single company can receive wildly different ratings from different agencies and that calls the whole premise of ESG performance into question.

Geopolitical tensions have played into the debate as well. War in the Ukraine has brought defence stocks top of mind – and that's led to a conflation in the conversation with the notion of 'ethical investment' (which is a long-established value-based approach to investment choices and carries an anti-arms stance) and ESG (which is focused on a company's measurable performance on environmental, social and governance factors). Meanwhile, fears about energy security have led to new fossil fuel deals being forged that seem counter to the momentum that's been building behind climate commitments – in spite of the recognition that the road to a zero carbon economy cannot be linear and, indeed, many think that disruption in energy markets may well accelerate the transition to renewable fuels.

On top of that, there's the irony that as ESG's moved centre stage – in an attempt to bring rigour and transparency to the environmental and social performance of corporates – the sudden enthusiasm for ESG funds has led to greenwashing in the financial industry. Many funds appear, to all intents and purposes, to have simply been relabelled as ESG funds. The concern in the industry is that 'advisors can mint money by calling their products and services "green" without doing anything special to justify that label', according to Commissioner Peirce at the SEC.[12] And some high-profile investigations, for example, those into Goldman Sachs and Deutsche Bank, have made it pertinent to define what can justifiably claim to be an ESG fund.

In this fistful of criticisms levelled at ESG, it's clear that there are plenty of angles to fuel contentious debate. Strikingly, however, they're mostly wrestling with the problems of ESG as it shows up in the world today; few are questioning the under-lying drive towards more robust non-financial reporting. Only a few years ago, ESG was a backwater in the financial flows of the capital markets. It didn't warrant the scrutiny it has now. Its rapid rise has surfaced what the *Financial Times* journalist Andrew Edgecliffe-Johnson describes as 'a backlash' but, as he goes on to conclude:

> . . . harnessing it still seems one of the most promising ways to address our greatest collective challenges. But to beat the backlash, ESG must be held to a higher standard, with a more honest focus on its impact.[13]

To make it possible for ESG to work more effectively and to a higher standard, the most significant obstacle that ESG scep-tics point to is the patchiness of data and inconsistency of standards. As it's become more mainstream, so it's become more evident how little data there is on ESG issues – as yet. What exists is not reliable or consistent. And, more than that, many are questioning whether it can ever be meaningful to bundle so many disparate issues into a single ESG score.

In November 2021, the International Financial Reporting Standards (IFRS) Foundation announced the creation of the International Sustainability Standards Board (ISSB). It repre-sented a big step forward, achieved by merging the major competing players on the ESG landscape – going a long way to sorting out the 'alphabet soup' problem – years earlier than anyone in that arena anticipated was possible. 'For anyone familiar with financial standards, you tend to measure progress in decades,' Dr Jeremy Osborn, then at the Value Reporting Foundation, told us. 'The reason this has moved so quickly is because there's huge corporate support behind the regularisation of sustainability standards.' Designed to be compatible with IFRS and established as a global benchmark, its arrival was welcomed by the G20 economies and the Financial Stability Board.[14]

With the arrival of the ISSB comes the development of the first ever comprehensive and consistent global framework for disclosure of sustainability standards. Application of the framework won't be instantaneous, but the implication is profound. None of the trends behind it are going to let up. The multiple crises in the world will continue to drive increased demand for high-quality information. Regulators will continue to press on the areas of the greatest corporate externalities. And in the capital markets, intangible assets constitute around 80 per cent of market value these days, up from just 17 per cent forty years ago[15] – so investors looking to understand that 80 per cent are moving beyond the traditional scope of financial and manufactured capital. Ideas around other 'capitals' are gaining traction – intellectual, human, social and natural capital – and establishing reliable metrics on sustainability is bound into that trend. Bringing non-financial data and disclosure into the mainstream changes the nature of reporting which, in turn, will change what's required of business leaders.

Professor Robert Eccles, recognised as the foremost pioneer of integrated reporting, today calls himself a 'capital markets activist'. Founding chair of the Sustainability Accounting Standards Board (SASB), he went on to become the first chair of Arabesque Partners, the world's first ESG quant fund. Begun as a management buyout from Barclays Bank in 2013, Arabesque set out to combine two of the disruptive forces in the capital markets, ESG and AI. Eccles characterised the concept as bringing together 'the smart guys who do quants and the financial stuff and the nice people who do ESG and responsible investing' with the ambition of making sustainable finance mainstream.[16] Analysing millions of data points across thousands of companies, what Arabesque is doing is a sign of the times. Right now, it's easy to bemoan the lack of reliable data on ESG issues but with every passing reporting season, the amount of data available increases and AI technology is accelerating what it can tell us. Data is pushing the frontline of the ESG.

Businesses are all geared up to report on their financial performance. And Osborn observes that typically in the large accounting firms today for every 100 financial auditors there's only one sustainability assurance professional – until now. The Big 4 auditors are investing billions of dollars in hiring and training the next generation of auditors able to rise to the challenge of an integrated approach to reporting, underpinned by robust data on non-financial issues.[17] Gillian Tett, who co-founded the *Moral Money* newsletter that tracks ESG developments at the *Financial Times*, coined the term 'activist warrior accountant':

> Sparking a revolution is no longer 'just' about placards or street protests; chaining yourself to a bulldozer feels as outdated as 1980s shoulder pads. Instead, the new front for activism revolves around something that anti-establishment hippies used to scorn or ignore – the world of accountancy and finance. Or to put it another way, we are entering an era when balance sheets matter more than protest barricades – and a new breed of activist warrior accountants could be the biggest revolutionaries of all.[18]

First and foremost, investors look at ESG investing as a risk and resilience strategy. The hypothesis is that companies with poor ESG performance are less viable long term: more prone to supply chain disruption, more exposed to regulatory pressures, more likely to encounter the opprobrium of consumers and employees. Ron O'Hanley, who heads up State Street, is one of the leading asset management voices advocating for the inclusion of societal issues in corporate strategies. Talking to McKinsey about resilience, he reflected on the huge government funding poured into holding together the fabric of communities and economies in the face of societal crises, from the fallout from the global financial crash to the covid pandemic, and posed a question:

> You have to ask: Are we going to run the world anticipating that there will be the kind of government interventions we have seen to make up for the lack of investments in resilience? Boards have to look at it too. How do you think about a stock buyback, for example, versus investing it in shoring up the company's resilience?[19]

O'Hanley's provocation that companies should invest in resilience to societal shocks ahead of investing in a share buyback takes aim at a practice that has come to represent, literally and symbolically, the prioritisation of shareholder interests ahead of all other considerations – in the case of share buybacks, including management as shareholders.

In truth, among the detractors of ESG, the greatest criticism is not that it's not yet fully formed, but rather that it draws focus away from the legitimate business of business to deliver financial returns to shareholders (see The Big Debate about Capitalism, p. 301). But the investor voices setting the agenda on ESG are doing it precisely because they believe it will produce better long-term returns. This isn't *instead* of value creation, but rather it opens up the understanding of value creation in the capital markets, to bring societal value alongside financial value. As Fink declares:

> We focus on sustainability not because we're environmentalists, but because we're capitalist and fiduciaries to our clients.[20]

In his 2022 letter Fink turned the focus to opportunity. While acknowledging that the transition to a net zero carbon economy represents a significant cost in the near term, he predicted that the next raft of Unicorns won't be search engines or social media companies, but 'sustainable, scalable innovators' for a zero carbon world, whether they are start-ups or 'bold incumbents'. BlackRock is mobilising the corporates to tackle the climate crisis and encouraging them to see in it an enormous innovation opportunity:

> I believe the decarbonizing of the global economy is going to create the greatest investment opportunity of our lifetime. It will also leave behind the companies that don't adapt, regardless of what industry they are in.[21]

A lot of people have invested a lot of hope in ESG. Many in the financial community are hopeful that ESG promises the ultimate win-win of value to society *and* value to shareholders. Businesses hope that ESG can repair frayed stakeholder relationships and reverse the long trend of declining trust. Civil society hopes that ESG can rein in the negative externalities of corporate operations. However, there are also those among the sceptics who fear that ESG may be a 'dangerous placebo',[22] giving the appearance of substantial action while nothing much changes in terms of impact in the real world. In our view, there's some truth in those fears.

The conversation around ESG has pushed societal issues up the agendas of investors and boards. At the same time, if taken on with a compliance mindset, it can become narrow, focused on checking the boxes rather than fixing the problems. When we look at how ESG is commonly interpreted in most businesses today, we see a number of ways in which it can actually undermine the activist impulse in business:

- **Focus on incremental improvement:** Management attention can get overtaken by a focus on delivering incremental improvement based on historic performance and existing business models, and benchmarked against peer group accepted practice – which takes the place of ambition to set new standards, to reinvent business models or invest in innovation.

- **Focus on risk to the business:** As long as the business risk is mitigated and the operations become more resilient, that's enough: the investor demand can be satisfied. The attention goes to preparedness to meet anticipated regulatory trends or potential reputational damage – rather than making an impact on the issue itself.

- **Focus on individual business performance:** ESG metrics are about the performance of an individual company, in isolation – rather than taking a systemwide view of issues and encouraging companies to use their potential to drive change as system players. ESG is a single business concept in a world looking for systems solutions.

Yet ESG is evolving. It may well turn out that the bundling of so many important issues into one set of unifying metrics is untenable and un-useful; maybe, for that reason, even the term as we use it today outlives its usefulness. However, the forces that have fuelled the rise of ESG are growing ever more intense and are reshaping the way businesses operate. The power of big data has just begun to make it possible to track each facet of ESG to a level of granularity never achievable before; gender pay, methane emissions, rates of deforestation, and on and on to other material issues. Major financial institutions have been investing heavily to build or acquire data and analytics capability for ESG – among them, BlackRock, HSBC Asset Management, JPMorgan Chase, State Street.[23] What's possible today is only a fragment of what will come. In the coming years, transparency for investors – and all other corporate stakeholders – on how businesses are performing on these issues will move to a whole new level. So, thinking like an activist, the question becomes what needs to happen next to establish a robust view of value creation – one that integrates financial performance and social performance.

As companies move to adopt ESG, you can see their approach mature in three stages (see Figure 14). First, there's what we think of as *Baseline ESG*, which is where companies first begin to grapple with this new demand from investors. It's the start of the journey: it involves an assessment of the material *risks* associated with societal issues, and a commitment to metrics, targets and transparency on key societal issues. Second, companies move to *Strategic ESG*, becoming more proactive: they set a roadmap including the capital expenditure and investment involved in stepping up to ESG issues and the returns for doing so. They focus on the evolution of their products and practices to respond to new trends, and the long-term resilience of their supply chains. They have a more forward-facing interpretation of how they relate to these issues and build that into their corporate strategies. These are the dominant approaches to ESG today, focused first on risk and, second, on return. But a third dimension has emerged, which you can think of as *Impact ESG*. In an article entitled 'How impact seeks to enhance the risk-return equation', BlackRock suggests:

> A major shift is underway as companies are increasingly measured not only on how much money they make, but also on the impact they are having. Rather than judging by risk and return alone, investors are looking at risk, return and impact.[24]

Impact ESG is concerned with delivering impact on the issue, as well as measuring the performance of the business on the issue: *double materiality*, as it's now termed. In practice, for companies, that means understanding the social and environmental issues they have an impact on and how they engage with the wider system to improve it. As ESG continues to evolve, so new concepts come to the fore – and double materiality is the new front line.

The roots of ESG track back to a corporate-centric focus on risk: it's a one-way perspective. Double materiality is a two-way street: as well as requiring companies to disclose the likely impacts of environmental and social on their business, it holds that companies should disclose their impact on environment and social issues.

On climate, for example, double materiality is about enabling fund managers to understand how their investments might pose a risk to the environment, as well as how climate change might pose a risk to their investments. In the US, Moody's have defined themselves as 'champions' of ESG through a double-materiality lens, calling it the cornerstone of their approach.[25] Already,

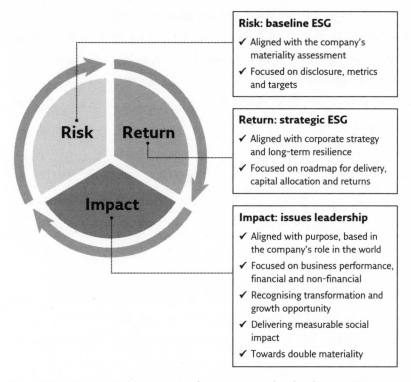

Risk: baseline ESG

✓ Aligned with the company's materiality assessment

✓ Focused on disclosure, metrics and targets

Return: strategic ESG

✓ Aligned with corporate strategy and long-term resilience

✓ Focused on roadmap for delivery, capital allocation and returns

Impact: issues leadership

✓ Aligned with purpose, based in the company's role in the world

✓ Focused on business performance, financial and non-financial

✓ Recognising transformation and growth opportunity

✓ Delivering measurable social impact

✓ Towards double materiality

Figure 14: A new equation for corporate leadership on ESG

it's embedded in the new sustainable finance disclosure regime in the EU.[26] And, as investors seek greater clarity about the consequences of societal issues on their investments, double materiality is likely to gain traction.

Meanwhile, activist leaders in business – including in the companies discussed in this book – are there already. For sure, they've incorporated investor expectations on ESG into how they operate: they're doing the hard graft to seek out the data, they're looking to mitigate risks to and create opportunities for growth but, alongside that, their ambition is to make a real-world impact on the issue itself. In short, the activist frame of mind has double materiality built in, focused not only on assessing the material impact of the world on the company but the company's impact on the societal issues in the world. That captures the spirit of activist leadership in the business world; the ambition for the double win of building a stronger, future-proofed business while harnessing its mobilising power to become part of the solution to today's major societal challenges.

2.

The Power and Problem of Purpose

If you're working in a big business today you will have heard a lot of talk about *purpose*. It's become a preoccupation over the past few years and there's a new consensus emerging about the purpose of business. In essence, it represents a movement away from the historic paradigm of recent decades that delivering shareholder value is the sole purpose of business, and an attempt to express that companies need to be creating value in a way that looks to the longer term and encompasses multiple different stakeholders.

Purpose is *outwards* and *forwards*. That's why, for anyone with an activist mindset, a sense of purpose comes naturally. Employees want to work with a *purposeful* company: according to a survey of its members by LinkedIn, 74 per cent want work that delivers a 'sense of purpose',[1] and we hear that confirmed in all the companies we work with. Two-thirds of consumers prefer to buy from 'purpose-driven brands', according to Accenture.[2] Even the financial community these days is using the language of purpose to express what's expected of business. Purpose as a company's 'north star in this tumultuous environment' was a strong theme in Larry Fink's 2019 annual letter to CEOs:

> Purpose is not a mere tagline or marketing campaign; it is a company's fundamental reason for being – what it does every day to create value for stakeholders. Purpose is not the sole pursuit of profits but the animating force for achieving them.[3]

So, there is a real impetus to talk about purpose. And if you're looking to define the purpose of your business, we've found that a constructive way to approach it is to think in terms of your *role in the world*. It becomes less a soul-searching exercise and more about your footprint in society and your intent. It encourages an outward-looking attitude and an alertness to the perspective of others. And it opens up a set of powerful questions: you look at the *why*, the *what* and the *how* of your company.

Many businesses have re-examined and re-articulated their purpose in recent years and, inside a company, that process can be very energising. The most robust approaches don't, as Fink suggests, treat it as a marketing exercise, but, rather, as a chance to think afresh about what the business is there to do and to engage employees in why what they do matters. Everyone relates to the idea of being *purposeful*, after all, because it is inherently about the future and about what you do that's meaningful.

Indra Nooyi, one of the earliest CEOs to make purpose central to her leadership, sees it as all about the future. At PepsiCo, she had been Chief Financial Officer before becoming CEO in 2006 and then executive chairman until 2019. Thinking back to taking on the CEO role, she says, 'As I looked at PepsiCo, clearly the company was built for a different time. And as times were changing, I felt we had to change the company.'[4] Her rationale for change included the demand for healthier products, the problems of plastic waste and water consumption – in other words the societal issues surrounding the business – and her goal was to deliver 'top-tier' financial performance while taking those on, and while making the business a magnet for future talent.[5] The mantra of her leadership became *Performance with Purpose*.[6] 'It's very easy to run a company for the duration of a CEO. Just hit the pedal through cutting costs, cutting investments. And then let somebody else pick up the pieces. I came at it differently,' she explains:

> To me, purpose was not about doing good for the sake of social responsibility. For me, performance and purpose was about future-proofing the company. All that I did was look at the future trends and say, 'How do we change the company so it remains successful for ever?'[7]

But the purpose movement has its critics. Many argue that the purpose of the corporation is first and foremost to deliver profit to shareholders and their perception of this new-found interest in purpose is that it dilutes that primary objective. On a closer look, however, the influential voices shaping the new purpose agenda are not challenging the profit motive. Indeed, the opposite is true. 'Profits are in no way inconsistent with purpose – in fact, profits and purpose are inextricably linked,' is how Fink puts it.[8] 'To be clear, in creating value for stakeholders, that strategy must be profitable over time. Profit is vital to companies and to society,' is how Mark Carney views the question. Their focus is on *how* those profits are made.[9]

To those who still hold a loyalty to the Chicago school of economic thought and Milton Friedman's philosophy that has proved so influential since the 1960s, Carney points out that Friedman 'gives himself an out'. In the same breath that Friedman talked about the responsibility of executives to 'make as much money as possible . . .' he provided a caveat '. . . while conforming to the basic rules of the society'. That is really where the rub is now: the rules of society are changing, and need to change, in order to respond to unprecedented environmental and societal crises.

This is why the Business Roundtable (BRT) announcement of 19 August 2019 was such a watershed moment in the context of the US. It reversed the statement set out by BRT in 1997 which, in the spirit of the Chicago school, began, 'The Business Roundtable wishes to emphasise that the principal objective of a business enterprise is to generate economic returns to its owners.'[10] In 2019, with the weight of 181 signatures behind it, the new statement marked an acknowledgement in the mainstream of corporate America that the rules have changed. The chair of their Governance Committee, Alex Gorsky, declared that their statement 'redefines the Purpose of a Corporation' and expanded on the theme: 'This new statement better reflects the way corporations can and should operate today. It affirms the essential role corporations can play in improving our society when CEOs are truly committed to meeting the needs of all stakeholders.'[11]

Professor Colin Mayer of the Saïd Business School at Oxford University led an international project to define 'Policy and Practice for Purposeful Business'. Drawing on the input of hundreds of experts and businesses and producing seventeen academic papers over four years, it was described by the *Financial Times* as 'one of the most ambitious programs to reform capitalism for the 21st century' and he talked to us about why that work mattered:

> The problem we're trying to fix is that business should really be there to solve our problems as a society. There was a view until recently that business – almost on autopilot – would do that for us. That was the underpinning theory of markets: that profit seeking firms will produce social benefits because

that's the outcome of the competitive process. Well, we've increasingly come to realise that this very simple and powerful idea which has prevailed over the last 60 years, unfortunately, is increasingly not working like that.[12]

What's driving this refresh of purpose, according to Mayer, is the intensification in business of the single-minded focus on the short-term generation of profits juxtaposed with the intensification of the environmental and societal challenges we're all facing. His central thesis is that the 'role of business is to produce profitable solutions for people and the planet, while not profiting from creating problems for either'. The idea that companies are there to solve problems resonates strongly with business leaders, we find. They often tell us that this is exactly what has brought the company into being in the first place; filling a need in the world, solving a problem for their customers. What they don't hear so readily is the second half of Mayer's proposition, that bit about 'not profiting from creating problems' – in other words, creating profits without throwing off negative externalities that others have to handle. Mayer talks about this as the most important element to emerge from his work on a framework for purposeful business:

At the very least, you don't profit from harming others. That has to be a fundamental requirement. So long as it remains unclear that companies cannot legitimately profit at the expense of others, you undermine the competitive process.

To many, purpose is all about 'why we exist'. In our view, that's part of what's being asked but, as companies discover, only a part. Whether you're a supermarket, a mining company or a legal firm, *why* you exist is probably in common with the rest of your sector. Even *what* you do is often largely shared with your peers. The *how* is where much more differentiation comes in; the story of how the business delivers on its promise of *why* and *what* brings alive the company's character, its values and its promise to customers. Crucially, focusing on the *what* and the *how* alongside the *why* also allows you to demonstrate what you're doing to grip the problematical issue of externalities that are driving concern about the purpose of business in the first place.

The author Simon Sinek popularised purpose with his million-copy best-selling book *Start With Why* and a TED Talk that became one of the most viewed in the platform's history. But he doesn't say *end* with why: he says, 'Start with why, but know *how*.'[13] Sinek's advice is 'Don't forget that a WHY is just a belief, HOWs are the actions we take to realise that belief and WHATs are a result of those actions.' Companies eager to define their purpose are sometimes quick to talk about their *why*, but it's the *how* and the *what* that makes the expressed purpose tangible and credible.

A consequence of the purpose concept catching on so swiftly is that many companies have fallen into some common pitfalls in how they've approached it in practice. These are the ones to watch out for:

- **Pitfall 1 – Not backing words with action:** Purpose is inherently about what you do, not just about what you say. And yet, in an effort to be inspiring or uplifting, companies often fall into the trap of hyperbole. *Forbes* wrote: 'The purpose stampede is increasing consumer cynicism and mistrust at brands insincerely hopping on the bandwagon of ill-fitting social causes.'[14] *Campaign* magazine wrote: '. . . one company after another are jumping on the bandwagon spouting beautiful rhetoric, but not following through. The result is that sound ideals become diluted into yet another purpose-wash.'[15] Words not backed up by action is always the source of the accusation of 'washing' in whatever form.

- **Pitfall 2 – Looking for a 'higher' purpose:** Sometimes, because this new approach to defining purpose stands outside the traditional assumption of the profit motive, leadership teams feel they are looking for a 'higher' purpose. They end up seeking some form of meaning beyond the selling of their goods and services for profit. This creates a risk: boards and, beyond them shareholders, baulk at the idea – it often elicits the response that 'We're not here to save the world; we're not an NGO'. That's why the notion of a 'higher' purpose misses the point. The question coming from all stakeholders is how you see – and justify – the purpose of your core business and the role it plays in the world. Looking for a purpose above or other than your core business overlooks that question. Instead, the opportunity is to articulate how these product and services, and the way you operate as a business, create value for society. Ten years ago, McKinsey described it thus:

Companies that succeed in building a profitable relationship with the external world tend to think very differently: they define themselves through what they contribute. This approach does not mean changing purpose; it means being explicit about how fulfilling that purpose benefits society. [16]

- **Pitfall 3 – Polarising profit and purpose:** Often companies talk about purpose as the parts of the company's life that aren't focused on profit – sustainability, philanthropy, community partnerships – all the activities that may be deemed 'worthy'. Shareholders get profits, and all the other stakeholders get purpose. It's very common to see this seep into the language, and the mindset: there's a purpose-led aspect to the business made up of all the 'doing good' bits. The trouble is that this inadvertently casts the commercial core of the business as the non-purpose-led, profit-making 'bad' bits. This is the antithesis of the original intention. When that happens the quest for purpose loses its way. A sense of purpose needs to drive the profit engine and animate the business.

- **Pitfall 4 – Explaining everything good about you:** Often, the process of defining purpose morphs into an assertion of everything the company thinks is good about itself. The banking sector provides an object lesson. In the wake of the global financial crisis, many banks examined their souls, but the purpose statements that resulted were often attempts at explaining the important role that banking plays in society: banks are there to protect people's savings and help them thrive, to enable investment and trade, to help businesses and the economy to grow. Those statements didn't cut through: people know how important banking is – that's why they were so upset with the conduct of the banks. They know *why* banking matters, and *what* it does for them; they were questioning *how* it was being done. The disconnect between the impetus behind the question and the tone of the answer jarred and opened the gap of mistrust, rather than bridging it. For companies today aiming to re-express purpose, it offers a lesson: it may be natural to want to accentuate the positive but it's vital as well to recognise the challenge in the question.

The idea of purpose is so simple and intuitively understood. Yet these pitfalls show how easy it is, in the corporate arena, for it to get mangled in practice. They are symptoms of the fact that under the surface the conflict continues to play out: whether the purpose of the corporation should be expressed only in terms of its financial value and anything else is flummery, or whether the very purpose of being clear about your purpose is to reflect the entirety of what matters about the business. The intensity of demand that companies should take a broader and longer view of how they play a positive role in the world is relatively new and – and as we saw in the ESG debate – profoundly different from the received interpretation of previous decades. In great part that's why answering the purpose question often sets up many competing impulses within the business.

One of the most helpful contributions to the conversation is Professor Mayer's concept of 'purposes' – *plural*. After all, companies play different roles in the lives of different stake-holders. As Mayer puts it: 'One of the major drawbacks of the traditional view is that it suggests one purpose: profit.'[17] To embrace the idea that a company has multiple purposes relaxes the tension in defining what the company is there for. And knowing, too, that it's not immutable is empowering: your purpose can evolve as the world evolves. Markets get disrupted, sectors become redefined and the needs of stakeholders change over time – and so the opportunity to create social value inevitably changes, too. Some things about a company's purpose are rooted in its origins and endure. But thinking of purpose as future-facing frees you up: it becomes a chance to redefine what you want to be to the future.

The underlying question is clear: what are you going to do differently to tackle the problems associated with historic models? This isn't about whether there should be profit; it's *how* the profit is made and whether that profit adds value to the world at large. The call for leaders to be clear about the purpose of their organisation is strong because stakeholders, of all kinds, want to know how a company intends to play a positive role in the world.

3.

Systems and Circular Transformation

Whether it's climate change, or inequality, or waste, or any of the other big issues, it's become clear that systems are not just the *context* of the challenge; they *are* the challenge. Systems thinking has moved from the background into the foreground, and many of the players in those systems from all sectors of society have realised that isolated, unilateral action will never be enough.

As we saw in System (p. 160), businesses are critical actors in the systems they are part of and there's a dual rationale for businesses to work on systemwide change: it's both essential to achieving the company's own goals for future sustainability and it's the only way to deliver an impact on the issue – any issue. For an activist leader, this is the way forward.

It's been a long road to get to here. John Elkington has been one of the most influential figures along the way: known by many for the concept of the Triple Bottom Line that he defined in the 1990s and which has been adopted by numerous businesses under the banner of People, Planet, Profit. Described by *Business Week* as 'a dean of the corporate responsibility movement';[1] and still at the forefront of thinking in this field, Elkington talks today about the need to 'rethink how we define and create long-term business value and wealth'. He uses a visualisation from the non-profit Future-Fit Foundation that he works closely with to illustrate how the notion of value has been evolving over the past two decades: from the historic model of shareholder value, where business, environmental and social value exist in separate realms; to the well-known idea of shared value where the areas overlap but remain unintegrated; towards a system value model – where business value is built into a broader understanding of societal and environmental value (see Figure 15).[2]

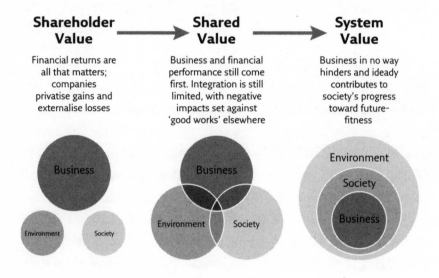

Shareholder Value → **Shared Value** → **System Value**

Financial returns are all that matters; companies privatise gains and externalise losses

Business and financial performance still come first. Integration is still limited, with negative impacts set against 'good works' elsewhere

Business in no way hinders and ideadly contributes to society's progress toward future-fitness

Figure 15: The long road to system value – Future-Fit Foundation

Essential to systems thinking is finding the intervention points which will provide the highest leverage; the places where a 'small shift in one thing can produce big changes in everything', as Donella Meadows said. She warned, however, that while most people have an instinctive understanding of where those leverage points are, when they reach for them, they often push in the wrong direction – because from their unique vantage point, wherever that may be, they cannot see the whole. A professor at Dartmouth College in New Hampshire, Meadows taught systems thinking to many students and her advice was to be prepared to test their own models and assumptions against those of others. 'Getting models out into the light of day, making them as rigorous as possible, testing them against the evidence and being willing to scuttle them if they are no longer supported is nothing more than practicing the scientific method,' she explained. The principles she taught are relevant to systems transformation in the business world today:

> Remember, always, that everything you know, and everything everyone knows, is only a model. Get your model out there where it can be viewed. Invite others to challenge your assumptions and add their own. Instead of becoming a champion for one possible explanation or hypothesis or model, collect as many as possible.

So bringing people together across the ecosystem of an issue is at the forefront of how leading businesses, in all sectors, are approaching the real work of shifting historic paradigms. And though it's undoubtedly daunting to get your head around an awesomely complex system and challenging to secure alignment across multiple stakeholders, Meadows reminds us that, for an individual, in the end this is about a mental model. It's a mindset: a way of looking at things:

> There's nothing physical or expensive or even slow in the process of paradigm change. In a single individual it can happen in a millisecond. All it takes is a click in the mind, a falling of scales from the eyes, a new way of seeing.[3]

Activist coalitions

Coalitions used to be where activism went to die. At best, they were well-intentioned groups, where convening and conversation took the place of meaningful action. These were lowest-common-denominator initiatives, sailing at the speed of the slowest ship rather than accelerating progress. Too often, dialogue was a substitute for – rather than a precursor of – change.

Not so long ago our advice to any business serious about creating social value would be that coalitions aren't the answer; they'll slow you down and dilute ambition. But a different type of model has emerged, infused with a different kind of energy. We call them 'activist coalitions'; they form with the shared intent of bringing the right people around a complex, problematic issue in order to accelerate progress, and we advise businesses to seek them out. These days, no matter what the issue, there's likely to be an active coalition pushing it forward. **EV100**, for example, has the stated aim of 'making electric transport the new normal by 2030' and it brings together the ecosystem needed to accelerate this transition. As well as 'driving the market' for electronic vehicles, EV100 works on policy in energy, infrastructure and built environment – drawing on the combined power of more than 120 corporates, including some of the world's largest vehicle fleet operators, such as BT Group, GSK and Unilever. Such a strong demonstration of cross-sector support can provide confidence to policymakers, as it did in the UK when EV100 worked with the government to introduce a policy that requires 100 per cent zero-emission car and van sales by 2030.[4]

There are plenty of other examples, and they come in all shapes and sizes. **Radar Alerts for Detecting Deforestation** (RADD) was an investment in satellite monitoring by ten of the major players in the palm oil industry working with the global non-profit World Resources Institute. Using data from the European Space Agency's Sentinel-1, it is making open-access, real-time alerts accessible to all stakeholders and provides a step change in transparency and traceability of deforestation on the ground. **The Global Coalition for Animal Welfare**, led by some of the largest players in the food system, is grappling with the nitty-gritty of building global supply of cage-free eggs which requires significant operational transformation. As well as responding to consumer concern, the coalition provides a focal point for the industry as it comes to terms with growing systemic risks to food safety and the looming health issue of antimicrobial resistance that is rising up the agenda in the light of the world's experience of the covid pandemic. **ACT** (Action, Collaboration, Transformation) is a coalition that aims to achieve a living wage for workers in the apparel and textile industry. The big brands and retailers are working with trade unions, governments and industry bodies to create whole sector solutions that can be scaled up in the main garment-producing countries.

There are many more. These are a far cry from the talking shops of which we used to be disdainful. You name the issue and there's likely to be an aggregation of organisations bringing together a mix of different roles in the system, with different vantage points across the value chain, with different skills and capabilities, directed towards problem-solving.

Efforts to tackle climate change have produced numerous coalitions, and coalitions of coalitions, each with a different angle. The UN's **Race to Zero** describes itself as 'a coalition of leading net zero initiatives, representing 1,049 cities, 67 regions, 5,235 businesses, 441 of the biggest investors'.[5] **We Mean Business** is a coalition of businesses partnered with a group of climate non-profit organisations with the shared ambition 'to halve emissions by 2030 and accelerate an inclusive transition to a net zero economy'. The **Carbon Pricing Leadership Coalition** has a specific mission to 'expand the use of carbon pricing policies'. Decarbonisation is an area where investor coalitions have sprung up as well: **Climate Action 100+** is 'an investor-led initiative' to 'ensure the world's largest corporate greenhouse gas emitters take necessary action', and there are several others – the **Global Investor Coalition** (GIC), for instance, set up to encourage capital deployment at scale to finance the transition and progress corporate disclosure on climate risk and opportunity. This may sound like a terrible confusion of organisations, and it can be confusing; but climate is an incredibly complex issue, and these groups are each drawing together a constellation of stakeholders around a specific dimension of the challenge where they see the chance to create change.

Mapping out the contours of a system in order to pinpoint where the opportunities lie for high-leverage interventions is a big part of what these activist coalitions can offer. A multisector, multi-geography coalition that has done that is the **Food and Land Use** coalition (FOLU). FOLU begins its analysis by making the case for change, including the environmental costs, health costs and social-economic costs of the system as it is. It spells out the 'economic prize', the scale of investment required and the business opportunity. That provides the underpinning for what they identify as 'the ten most critical transitions' needed to reshape food and land systems globally over the next decade.[6] In Figure 16 we show FOLU's Transformation Pyramid as an example of what that can look like, ranging across transitions to healthy diets and healthy and productive ocean systems, to stronger local supply loops and stronger rural livelihoods. That shapes the agenda for action and makes it easier for different actors across the ecosystem to see the role they can play.

One of the founding organisations of FOLU is SYSTEMIQ, a self-described 'think and do tank', which counts coalition building as part of its mission. Its managing partner, Guido Schmidt-Traub, explains: 'If you say everything depends on everything, you end up not advancing on anything.'[7] His long experience of systems change has told him that, if you want to move from lofty vision to meaningful action, you need to 'choose

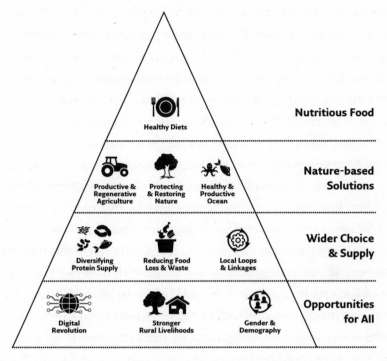

Figure 16: Food and Land Use Coalition –
Ten critical transitions to transform food and land use

a big goal . . . and take it seriously as a quantitative, time-bound proposition'.

SYSTEMIQ was founded by Jeremy Oppenheim after more than twenty years as a McKinsey partner. 'I used to be of the persuasion that a sensible model of well-managed market economic development could get us where we need to go,' he told the *Ethical Corporation* journal:

> Now, I don't think we can get there with an evolutionary model, [with] a bit of good policy here and a bit more markets there . . . Today, there's a need for a really big dose of structural transformation.[8]

Sunny Verghese, Olam's CEO, is a champion for the transformation that needs to happen in the global agricultural system.
For a start, different players in the industry must come together,
but he admits that's not easy: 'That's a tough thing to ask
because we're competitors: we don't like each other! So, coming
together in any kind of pre-competitive alliance is not natural;
it's tough.' More than that, he continues, it means reaching out
to civil society but that too can be counter-intuitive: 'Civil society
and NGOs see companies as evil, and the company sees them
as trouble-makers: we are at loggerheads most of the time.'
And, Verghese says, businesses must advocate for policymakers
to demand mandatory disclosures and reporting on their carbon
footprints, their greenhouse gas footprints, water footprints.
Yet, while all this means overcoming ingrained resistance, he's
learnt that to solve problems and transform systems 'we need
these unusual and unnatural collaborations that we've not been
used to in the past'.[9]

The phenomenon of activist coalitions has grown up out of
the need and appetite for systems transformation. Nevertheless,
the term itself can seem abstract and unwieldy. And, certainly,
working across any system isn't plain sailing: any complex,
collaborative effort is cumbersome and has its frustrations as
well as its wins. Systems thinker Donella Meadows brings the
wisdom of her experience to describing the attitude that makes
it fruitful, when she said:

> Interdisciplinary communication works only if there is a real
> problem to be solved, and if the representatives from the
> various disciplines are more committed to solving the problem
> than to being academically correct. They will have to go into
> learning mode. They will have to admit ignorance and be
> willing to be taught, by each other and by the system. It can
> be done. It's very exciting when it happens.[10]

The circular economy

The most ambitious system transformation concept is the *circular economy*. It has made its way into the business vernacular as a way of talking about the innovation needed to get to grips with the challenge of unsustainable use of resources, the ever-growing mountains of waste – and, ultimately, climate change. The movement towards 'closed-loop' thinking has been intensified by attention from governments and regulators, as well as growing interest from investors. The *circular economy* has become a shared language for a solutions space: radical, systemic and involving all sectors.

The gathering momentum shows up in the ambitious plans governments and regulators have published to create a circular economy. For example, the EU has launched its *Circular Economy Action Plan* – one of the major building blocks of the *European Green Deal* and the *EU Industrial Strategy*.[11] China has announced its *Development Plan for the Circular Economy* – part of the 14th Five Year Plan (2021–5) – which aims to have a circular economy for China 'basically established' by the end of the plan period.[12] Achieving the vision of a circular economy will be a long haul but these are policies that aim to set a direction of travel.

Progress towards the circular economy is also seen by the UN as critical for delivering on the global agenda of the Sustainable Development Goals (SDGs), in particular SDG 12 (responsible consumption and production) as well as SDG 14 (life below water) and SDG 15 (life on land). It's on the agenda of the G7 and the G20.[13]

Financial stakeholders are also on the case. More than thirty chief executives from some of the world's largest banks and asset managers – including Barclays, BlackRock, ING, Lloyds and the European Investment Bank – have backed research on how green finance can spur the circular economy.[14] The Institute of Asset Management sees the circular economy as 'a systems solution framework' that acts as an enabler for organisations 'to move towards more sustainable business practices'. BlackRock launched the first major circular economy public equity fund, which has now passed $2 billion under management and is now one of a dozen or so similar funds. More than thirty-five corporate and sovereign bonds have been issued to help finance circular economy activity. As Paul Bodnar, global head of sustainable investing at BlackRock, put it: 'If you're an investor who's focused on long-term value creation, and you live on a planet with finite resources, you have a vested interest in the circular economy.'

The essential idea of the circular economy is electrifyingly simple. It's best defined in contrast with today's 'linear economy' where we take materials out of the ground, make products that we use for increasingly short amounts of time and then throw away. This 'take, make, waste' model means we are using up the world's resources at a phenomenal rate, because currently most products are designed to be disposable – even our high-value goods. The circular economy concept is radically different: it designs things to be in use for longer and, after use, to be safely biodegradable or to be made in ways that allow the materials to be recovered and reused in new products. The Ellen MacArthur Foundation (EMF), one of the leading institutions advancing the circular economy, has distilled the concept into three principles: eliminating waste and pollution, circulating products and materials and regenerating nature.[15]

The Foundation captures the idea of the circular economy in a diagram, showing that 'technical' or non-biological materials are recovered after use so they can be reused or repurposed, keeping them in the value chain and driving out waste. Biological materials go back into the earth to regenerate our natural systems (see Figure 17). The magic key that opens the door to that circularity is designing it in from the outset – because 80 per cent of a product's environmental impacts are determined at the design phase.[16] All of that needs an economic and policy environment that incentivises it. Andrew Morlet, the EMF's CEO, describes it as a completely different paradigm:

> It's a shift in thinking from an economy that extracts value to one that creates it. It's restorative and regenerative by design. Crucially, the circular economy doesn't aim to reduce the negative effects of the linear economy, it's a fundamental systems-level shift to a new model.[17]

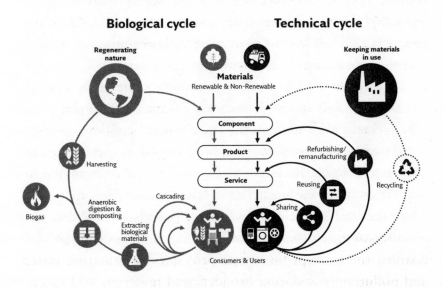

Figure 17: Ellen MacArthur Foundation –
visualising the circular economy

While the public and consumers are scarcely familiar with the term *circular economy*, they are increasingly concerned about the underlying challenges it aims to solve. Perhaps the greatest surge of public concern followed the *Blue Planet II* series narrated by Sir David Attenborough, which brought the problem of ocean plastic pollution to a wide audience. Indeed, few who have seen it will forget the scenes of albatross parents feeding plastic to their chicks. The EMF harnessed the dawning realisation around plastic pollution to drive action on the circular economy more broadly. A landmark report, published in 2016 with the World Economic Forum, showed that on the current trajectory by 2050 there could be more plastic in the ocean than fish. It generated huge media coverage and raised awareness of the scale of the problem – and led to a rapid expansion of corporate interest in the circular economy.[18]

Plastic pollution has become an entry point to the circular economy for many businesses, and a recycling initiative is often their first move. Building recycling systems that work is an essential part of tackling the plastic waste problem of today, and any other waste materials. Yet many companies get stuck there and fail to push on towards the transformative nature of the concept. As the World Economic Forum puts it, 'recycling begins at the end'. There's a lot more to the circular economy than recycling.

Many of the companies we've discussed in this book have significant circular economy initiatives – many of them in partnership with the Ellen Macarthur Foundation. IKEA announced their ambition 'to become a circular business' by 2030 and have released an open-source *circularity blueprint* tool for product designers, based on an assessment of 9,500 products. People can already buy IKEA products made from 100 per cent surplus or recycled materials, and the business is trialling models for repairing, reselling and even leasing furniture. And the company has begun to talk to their consumers about different ways of doing things: 'Do you feel bad about throwing things away? Maybe you want to repair, reuse or recycle, but lack the time, knowledge or energy to do so. We can help.'[19]

Microsoft, which decommissions thousands of servers each year from data centres, is rolling out *Circular Centres* to disassemble, reuse and recycle components. Google also talks about its journey to become *Circular Google*, focusing on data centres. Walmart aims to 'break the link between consumption and waste'. Apple is working towards 'making products using only renewable resources or recycled materials'.

We saw how, in order to build its iconic sleek laptops from materials that can be recycled over and over again, Apple invented a new type of aluminium alloy. And how Maersk, in order to be able to reuse the huge quantities of steel that go into each one of its enormous Triple E ships, created a *Cradle to Cradle Passport* that can keep track of every part of the vessel for disassembly at the end of its life (see Disruption, p. 124). For both Apple and Maersk, such innovations are just one component of an extensive circular strategy and, through them, it's easy to see why so much of the innovation in circularity in industrial and manufacturing businesses is dedicated to reducing the use of virgin resources, to recovery of materials and innovations in materials science. Belgian company Solvay, a global leader in the materials and chemicals industry, is one of those types of businesses that most people are unaware even exists – and yet it holds a key that will be vital to many manufacturing companies achieving their circular transformation ambitions.

Closing the loop in electric vehicle batteries is one of Solvay's most promising opportunities. With the number of electric vehicles set to increase tenfold over the present decade to 120 million, Solvay is in an innovation partnership with car manufacturer Renault and waste management company Veolia to collect end-of-life EV batteries and recover the metals for reuse. Solvay brings their expertise in chemical extraction and purification to the consortium, making it possible to keep essential materials such as lithium, cobalt and nickel in the battery manufacturing value chain. Ilham Kadri, their CEO, is ambitious for Solvay's role in helping to make the circular economy a reality:

> As part of the chemical industry, we are part of the problem but also part of the solution. And we acknowledge that what brought us here will not take us there.

Kadri is under no illusions about the disruptive nature of the undertaking, though. As she sees it, getting to scalable solutions is one of the greatest challenges, 'not to stop at anecdotes, as I call them', and that involves 'embedding the circular mindset in our business and in our strategy'. Solvay's goal is to more than double the revenues it generates from providing circular economy solutions and products based on renewable and recycled resources by 2030. 'We need to keep one eye on the microscope when we are a publicly listed company, and one eye on the telescope to reinvent ourselves,' says Kadri:

> This is a revolution going on, including in the research and innovation arena. Our chemists and our engineers are starting to design new molecules, new polymers and solutions, which can have a second, a third life, from day one. This is new and challenging, but it's exciting.[20]

For businesses that rely on natural systems, the biodiversity crisis has forced regeneration onto the agenda in recent years. More than 90 per cent of biodiversity loss is due to the extraction and processing of natural resources.[21] In the food industry, that's a consequence of ramping up production over decades to feed a growing population with farming practices that have degenerated natural systems, clearing land for agriculture use and overexploiting natural resources. Turning that around means developing circular solutions. Nestlé, the world's largest agricultural business, has decided to take the challenge of regeneration into the core of their business, calling it 'the only path forward'. They put €3.6 billion behind their commitment to climate and regeneration in 2020. That means changing agricultural practices in their supply chain; specifically, reducing dependence on synthetic fertiliser and improving soil quality in 500,000 farms that Nestlé sources from – and, a crucial part of the strategy, paying a premium to the farmers that adopt regenerative practices.[22]

'The actions of big firms carry disproportionate importance,' Chris Barrett, Economics and Management Professor at Cornell University, observed:

> Their multi-billion-dollar-investments are significant in their own right. But those actions especially matter because market leaders compel other firms to follow suit.[23]

Nestlé is only one of a growing number of the industry leaders whose supply chains end up in the fields and forests and oceans who have made regeneration a focus; Cargill, Danone, Mars, Olam, PepsiCo, Unilever and Walmart have all started to rethink the operating models and practices of 'Big Ag'. And though food perhaps comes first to mind, fashion has a part in this, too. H&M have set themselves the ambition of transforming into a circular business, which they say will require redesigning the entire value chain and operations. As Pascal Brun, head of sustainability at H&M, says:

> With our size comes responsibility. The way fashion is consumed and produced today is not sustainable. We have to transform the industry we are in. Our ambition is to transform from a linear model to become circular.[24]

Circularity is a seismic shift from the way our economy is organised today: it requires a whole-system rethink of the way products are designed and manufactured and disposed of, of how they are sourced and sold, and even of how they are owned. We saw how Philips shifted from selling lightbulbs as a product to offering *Lighting as a Service*, enabling them to collect old products and reclaim the materials. New businesses are being built on the opportunity to disrupt the disposability model of established players. RealReal and threadUP, in the fashion industry, have grown to be valued at $1 billion each on a model that offers consumers second-hand or even subscription rental clothing. Kaiyo is pursuing a similar circular model to solve the problem of finding a new home for used furniture for New Yorkers.

The major consultancies all now have client offerings around circular business model and process redesign. McKinsey advises businesses that 'the circular economy is all about retaining value', explaining that:

> Contrary to popular thinking in various companies, the circular economy isn't the latest sustainability fad and shouldn't be thought of as a recycling or green program. It requires top-down management and change across a company, including re-evaluating product design, business models, and the supply chain.[25]

With all the attention and enthusiasm gathered around circularity, it would be easy to think that great progress is being made – but campaigners are keen to point to a sobering reality: the circular economy doesn't actually exist yet. In fact, it's getting further away, not closer. On the basis of the Circularity Gap Report, in 2020 the global economy was only 9.1 per cent circular, and the linear economy continues to grow faster than the circular economy, with some sectors further behind than others: for example, although new business models are coming up to promote the resale and rental of clothing, currently that accounts for only about 0.05 per cent of the global industry.[26] Tech manufacturers are pushing forward circular innovation – but still, the circular e-waste market is only 2 per cent of the linear market.[27] For all the effort that's been dedicated to plastics in recent years, according to the OECD still only 9 per cent of plastic is successfully recycled.[28] And analysis by Just Economics found that currently the corporate sector globally is investing around $800 billion annually into circular business models, which may sound substantial, but they point out that this amounts to less than 3 per cent of the investment in linear models.[29]

The latest estimates of global 'ecological overshoot' tell us that humanity uses the equivalent of 1.75 Earths to provide the resources we use and absorb our waste. Another way of saying this is that it now takes the Earth one year and eight months to regenerate what we use in a year.[30] It's hard to find a clearer picture of *unsustainable*.

The circular economy needs activist leadership. Making the concept a reality needs people who can envisage a new way of doing things, are prepared to mobilise resources to help it happen and are up for transformative change. In the long run, companies have a lot to gain by becoming part of circular solutions, and we all have a lot to lose if they don't.

4.

A Shared Agenda with Government

Companies are dealing with a blizzard of regulation. There's a regulatory change somewhere in the world every twelve minutes directed towards the financial sector.[1] There are almost 750 policies on sustainable finance and investment policies in eighty-six countries around the world, 96 per cent of which have been created since 2000.[2] And there's more of it to come, on more issues and from more places than ever before.

Most would agree that the role and purpose of government includes protecting long-term national security and financial stability, and enabling the smooth functioning of society. But the societal challenges governments need to solve for today – especially the climate crisis and the political consequences of economic inequalities – threaten the ability of governments to deliver on these most basic obligations. This is resulting in a new policy agenda around the world; we call it the 'third wave' of regulation.

The third wave of regulation

When the social and environmental impacts of business intensify, governments respond with regulation. This isn't new: historians talk about two 'waves' of regulation on the activities and impacts of business. The first began in the nineteenth century, in response to the environmental degradation and social problems caused by industrialisation. Anti-pollution laws were passed in the United States and Western Europe, national parks were created and legislation was introduced to improve the lives of impoverished communities living in polluted cities and to protect the welfare of workers. Health and safety regulations were established that changed standards in business. Banning child labour in industrial sites, controlled working hours, sick pay and paid holidays were all hard fought for. All are now seen as basic good practice.

The second wave of regulation began in the 1960s, in response to the negative environmental impacts of accelerating economic growth – most notably acid rain, ozone depletion and the destruction of wildlife caused by pesticides. In industrialised nations, governments acted to get a grip on smog and air pollution in cities. The world's first Department for the Environment was created in 1970. The United Nations published the landmark Brundtland Report, *Our Common Future*, which set the scene for the first Earth Summit in Rio in 1992 and offered a principle to guide regulators: 'meeting the needs of the present generation without comprising the ability for future generations to meet their own needs'. That principle still guides thinking today.

Today's urgent social and environmental challenges have engendered a 'third wave' of regulation. As the systems become overstretched and unstable, so governments are moved to act. The sheer scale of business operations and the consequential negative externalities are also triggering a new level of government response internationally. For example, 175 nations have signed up to a UN resolution that commits them to introducing regulation to limit plastics pollution, the first global treaty on that scale since the Paris Agreement on climate – and many countries are already banning single-use plastics within their jurisdiction.[3] But there are other issues with devastating environmental impact that have yet to be regulated. A super-efficient fishing industry, for instance, deploying sonar and drift nets to catch fish on an unprecedented scale, calls for a new level of policy response; traditional controls are no longer fit for purpose. And, since fish don't recognise territorial waters, these regulations need to be coordinated internationally. As Donella Meadows put it, 'The power of big industry calls for the power of big government to hold it in check; a global economy makes global regulations necessary.'[4]

Most especially, the accelerating impacts of climate change are driving this new third wave of regulation. As these impacts become ever more apparent and the urgency increases, it is inevitable that governments will adopt an increasingly tough approach to tackling it. The question for business is no longer *if* governments will act, but when and how – this is the view of the Inevitable Policy Response (IPR), a UN-backed project aimed at helping investors understand the policy response to climate change. The Inevitable Policy Response argues that neither businesses nor the capital markets have adequately prepared for the wave of regulations that are bound to come, which they expect will be 'increasingly forceful, abrupt and disorderly, leaving financial portfolios exposed to significant transition risk'.[5] Figure 18 sets out the main categories that are anticipated.

The 'Inevitable Policy Response' to the Climate Crisis			
Carbon pricing	Coal phase-out	100 per cent clean power	Zero-emission vehicles
Low-carbon buildings	Clean industry	Low-emissions agriculture	Forestry

Figure 18: UN PRI – anticipated categories of climate-related regulation

National governments around the world are acting on a range of social issues as well – the 'S' in ESG as it's often talked about in the business world – and that, too, is accelerating. The 'sugar tax', for example, is a response to rapidly rising levels of obesity. Triggered by a World Health Organisation report in 2015 on the damaging health consequences of excessive sugar consumption in modern diets, twenty countries brought in some form of sugar tax; six years later the number had climbed to fifty jurisdictions. The effectiveness of that proactive regulation can be measured, showing up both in consumers increasingly taking up lower sugar options and in manufacturers reconfiguring the products they take to market. Interestingly, though, for those corporates, overall sales of soft drinks had not changed and share prices were not affected, suggesting that the drinks industry wasn't unduly hit financially by the tax.[6]

Continuing disparities in pay between men and women is another question drawing a regulatory response. Despite decades of campaigning for gender equality in the workplace, studies show a persistent gap between pay for men and women doing the same work. So a number of governments have passed laws requiring employers to publish data on the gender pay gap in their organisations. In 2017, for example, the UK became one of the first countries to oblige employers with 250 or more employees to publish gender-pay-gap data. Already the signs are that it's having an impact: in companies affected by the legislation, the wage gap has narrowed by almost one-fifth on average in five years – though there's still a way to go.[7] And greater transparency around the issue drives awareness and public debate which, in itself, becomes a lever for further change.

Most people will assume that businesses have a natural antipathy towards regulation – and indeed there is no shortage of examples of companies attempting to water down, slow down, or push back on these kinds of policies. At best, the corporate mindset is to wait. Just sit it out until the regulators get their act together – in the hope that they won't.

On climate, that's started to change: an activist mindset is taking hold. Increasingly, we're seeing proactive corporate advocacy for pro-decarbonisation policies. Take major food companies like Mars and Nestlé, for example: their agricultural supply chains are hugely vulnerable to climate impacts. The farmers in their supply chains, many of them smallholders, lack the resilience to deal with floods or droughts. This is a material business risk, and so these companies – alongside Danone and Unilever – have formed the Sustainable Food Policy Alliance to press for agricultural carbon markets, and other policies that can create a consistent framework for industrywide regenerative practices and transparency for consumers.[8]

The 'third wave of regulation' is gathering momentum. The opportunity for business is to anticipate it and work with it: don't fight it. The scale and intensity of these challenges make government intervention inevitable and puts business firmly in the frame. Rather than pushing back on this, or just sitting on the sidelines, the activist leader will see this as opportunity for businesses to help shape the future. And they don't look at governments only as a source of regulation, but as a potential partner in delivering their own ambitions on societal issues.

Mission-led partnerships

In the same way we're arguing that business leaders need to bring a new spirit of activism to the role their companies play in the world, so the economist Mariana Mazzucato is calling for governments and regulators to infuse policymaking with a sense of 'mission'. In her book *Mission Economy*, she demands a shift in perspective from policymakers:

Missions require a different framing for policy – not about fixing market failures but actively 'co-creating and co-shaping' markets. Shaping markets means moving our language – and our thinking – from a model in which the state's main goal is to fix and 'level' the playing field to one in which it co-creates a direction.

Equally, though, she challenges business to stop seeing governments as only a block to innovation and a drag on growth: 'Conventional wisdom continues to portray governments as a clunky bureaucratic machine that cannot innovate,' she writes. This creates a self-fulfilling prophecy:

[Government] is always reacting and making running repairs to a sputtering system, like someone patching a worn tyre rather than replacing it with a new one, constantly squandering its capacity to be an active value creator.[9]

Businesses are increasingly looking at government not just as an irritant, an obstacle to be navigated, but as a partner in tackling shared challenges. All the examples of activist leadership that we've described in this book have some form of collaboration with government at their core. Standard Chartered's campaign to 'make the financial system a hostile place for criminals' is delivered working closely with financial regulators and national and international enforcement agencies. We saw how Apple's development of a new kind of fully recyclable aluminium was made possible through a joint venture funded by the federal government of Canada and the province of Quebec to scale the new technology, in a collaboration with aluminium producer Alcoa and the mining company Rio Tinto.[10] PepsiCo's work to provide access to safe drinking water is delivered in collaboration with government ministries – a pattern set early on in the programme when they worked with the Chinese Ministry of Agriculture to identify partners who could deliver projects on the ground in their local communities.[11]

Sometimes collaborations at a regional level can direct support to areas of specific need. When covid threatened to disrupt Olam's push towards regenerative agriculture, for instance, the business partnered with the Asia Development Bank to unlock nearly $100 million of working capital for smallholder farmers, in collaboration with the governments of Vietnam, Indonesia and Papua New Guinea. As well as securing supplies of coffee, cocoa and other high-value crops, this allowed Olam to continue rolling out climate-smart agricultural practices in the midst of the pandemic. No one player could have achieved that alone but the readiness to collaborate across public and private sector boundaries answered that need.[12]

Municipalities and local governments are also often highly engaged in corporate social impact programmes. We described how city authorities are anchor partners in JPMorgan's Advancing Cities programme. Citi and the Citi Foundation, too, set up an 'innovation lab' for US cities to create systemic solutions to a range of problems – from economic inclusion to infrastructure finance. In their view, progress is hampered by the cyclical changes in city leadership – new administrations often sweeping away previous initiatives. So the *City Accelerator* was set up to provide a space to test and scale lasting solutions, bringing together public, philanthropic and private investment aimed at 'fostering collaboration across municipal systems'.[13] This kind of cross-sector work is also at the heart of the Novo Nordisk programme *Cities Changing Diabetes*, which has set up city-based networks of policymakers and health systems to identify 'ecosystem pain points' in the prevention, diagnosis and treatment of diabetes.[14]

In India, the city of Delhi struggled to secure a reliable and affordable supply of electricity during the 1990s. The economics were challenging: the public utilities were making enormous losses, largely because of the inability among low-income households to pay their bills and last-mile electricity theft in poor slum areas of the city. Power cuts were the norm. It was a challenging situation and required bold new thinking. That took the form of a joint venture, set up in 2002 between the city government and industrial giant Tata – Tata Power Delhi Distribution, aimed at turning the situation around.

Central to the partnership was improving residents' socio-economic conditions – and therefore their ability to pay. In collaboration with a strong cluster of local NGOs, initiatives included insurance schemes, medical facilities, drug rehab programmes, women's literacy centres and vocational training.[15] The model worked – and the company has helped set up similar ventures across India, as well as Nigeria, Uganda and other countries. It was an ambitious venture, and the CEO, Ganesh Srinivasan, still describes it as an organisation with 'a mission'.[16] That sense of elevated ambition is evident in the most impactful of the business and government collaborations today. There's a new impetus to *Public Private Partnerships*.

Admittedly, Public Private Partnership (PPP) is not a phrase imbued with an activist spirit; it doesn't immediately connote transformative change – rather, it brings to mind wranglings over missed deadlines and budget overruns. Yet over the course of the last decade, these cross-sector partnerships have become a new driving force for business action on societal issues.

Much of the world's infrastructure was built by PPPs – electricity grids, water systems and ports in many countries, for example, or the US railroads. It's been argued that the rise of Silicon Valley, held up as the epitome of the entrepreneurial spirit of business, was, in effect, the result of public–private partnership – principally, investment by the US Defense Advanced Research Projects Agency (DARPA) in developing the Internet.[17] PPPs aren't new; what's new is the complexity and urgency of the societal issues that these partnerships are now being aimed at. And this takes a new mindset – one that Mazzucato would recognise as 'mission-led'.

We've seen in this book the power of ambition to drive business action on society's biggest issues, bringing together different stakeholders to collaborate at scale on shared innovation challenges. When Brad Smith, president of Microsoft, announced the company's plan to be carbon negative by 2030, he said, 'This is a bold bet – a moonshot – for Microsoft. And it will need to become a moonshot for the world.'[18] The US mission to put a man on the moon – the original moonshot – is the defining example of a mission-led partnership. It required unprecedented cross-sector investment and disruptive innovation, involving government agencies, universities and more than 20,000 companies in aerospace and numerous other sectors – all working towards a clear shared goal. The wave of breakthrough innovations that flowed from this are well documented. Mazzucato makes good use of this example and makes the point, too, that the situation we face today is altogether more demanding. Working with European policymakers, she told them: 'Societal challenges are complex. More complex than going to the moon, which was mainly a technical feat.'

In order to handle that complexity, activist leaders are increasingly working across the wider ecosystems within which they operate to create change. And you can't work on system transformation without engaging with the role of governments in it. They are the ultimate 'system shapers' with the ability to change the rules of the system through regulation and to influence behaviour throughout the system. They are also direct actors in the system: they act as supplier by providing goods and services, as well as buyer – public procurement is a substantial slice of GDP in most developed economies. In his book *How to Avoid a Climate Disaster*, Bill Gates underlines governments' role in backing technology innovation that can go to scale. In the transition to net zero, governments 'can be the main investors in scientific research, as they are now,' he says:

> The point is that when we focus on all three things at once – technology, policies and markets – we can encourage innovation, spark new companies, and get new products into the market fast.[19]

There's a new energy in the relationship between the government and business. It means that many in business will have to shake off the view that governments have failed and are good for nothing; and those parts of civil society that are reflexively anti-business will need to deal with the fact that business has a role to play. Already, among the leading businesses committed to delivering social value, you see practical collaborations with governments at all levels, infused with a spirit of activism to create meaningful change. We will need a lot more of that.

5.

Politics and the Corporate Voice

'Each day brings a new and unexpected question', we recently heard from the CEO of a major US company. 'Can we help get an employee's mother out of a Uyghur camp in China? Should we fund employees in Texas to leave the state for an abortion? Where do we stand on the *Don't Say Gay* laws?' Most CEOs didn't expect that responding to questions like this would be part of the job, but this is the new reality of leading a business. And it's not just that you're expected to take a stand – you need to do it fast. From the Black Lives Matter protests to the Russian invasion of Ukraine, companies that hesitated have been portrayed as out of touch, or out of values.

The stakes get higher as societal issues become increasingly politicised, and as the public dialogue around them is more and more polarised. Eurasia, a political science consultancy, ranked 'losing the culture wars' as a top ten business risk for 2022.[1] Researchers at the Carnegie Endowment for International Peace have found that these polarised culture wars are a global phenomenon, including nations as diverse as Bangladesh and Brazil, Poland and India, Turkey and Indonesia.[2] In Europe, a study of thirty countries by researchers at the London School of Economics has shown deepening political divisions, resulting in growing support for 'anti-establishment' politicians.[3] For business leaders being drawn into increasingly politicised debates, the learning curve is proving to be a steep one.

When it comes to taking a public stand, the corporate calculation once focused only on the risks of speaking out. Now it must include the risks of staying silent. Disney's initial decision not to take a position on the controversial anti-LGBTQ+ law in Florida provides a high-profile example. There was widespread media coverage of 'employee outrage' as workers protested against the company's silence on the issue. Employees at the creative heart of the company, such as the Pixar studios, were particularly vocal. As the clamour grew, the company reversed: Bob Chapek, the CEO, apologised and announced that Disney would work to repeal the law. But this time, the company's stance had itself become a political issue, and its position would have material consequences. Florida's governor, Ron DeSantis, denounced Disney as 'woke' and introduced legislation to remove its special tax status in the state. The share price took a hit of nearly 20 per cent.[4]

Fortune magazine published a timeline of the Disney–DeSantis saga, concluding that their response hadn't come quickly enough.[5] By the time the company spoke out, the situation was dangerously inflamed. Disney had in fact previously spoken out several times on contentious issues – often being one of the first companies to do so. In January 2021, it said it would suspend political donations to lawmakers who voted against certifying Joe Biden's electoral victory.[6] In 2016, it took an early stand on an anti-LGBTQ+ law in Georgia – threatening to pull business from the state.[7] The Florida incident illustrates how, once caught up in politicised debate, for every hour you remain silent the stakes steadily ratchet up.

And, increasingly, the issues that companies are expected to speak out on are inherently political. Another US example is business engagement with the voting law in Georgia. In 2021, a number of high-profile companies and business leaders joined criticisms of an election law passed in Georgia that many saw as a concerted attempt to suppress minority voters. Initially, Georgia-based companies were reluctant to be drawn in and issued generic statements of support for voting rights, but they faced a furious backlash and protestors showing up at their headquarters.[8] Ken Chenault, former CEO of American Express, was one of a number of Black executives to call for companies to step up: 'There is no middle ground here,' he said. 'You are either for more people voting, or you want to suppress the vote.'[9]

Delta and Coca-Cola, two iconic Georgia businesses and major employers, were among the first companies to make clear statements against the law, and this was followed by a statement signed by 170 businesses, including BlackRock, Boeing, Cisco, Citibank, Mastercard, Maersk, PepsiCo, ViacomCBS, Verizon and Walmart. With some Republicans accusing these companies of 'woke hypocrisy', many of the companies were keen to stress the link with the interests of business, and of the economy at large: in the words of William George of Harvard Business School, and former CEO of Medtronic, voter suppression 'puts democracy at risk, and that puts capitalism at risk'.[10]

This is how business leaders can rise above the fraught partisan arguments, elevating the dialogue and appealing to the long-term interests of business. There may be no middle ground, but often there is higher ground. Corporate engagement with the issue of marriage equality in the US provides a case in point. In 2013, a group of major corporates submitted a brief to the US Supreme Court against the Defense of Marriage Act (DOMA) which defined marriage as the union of one man and one woman. Nearly 300 businesses signed on, including Amazon, Citigroup, Goldman Sachs, Pfizer and Starbucks. They asserted that the law contradicted their principles and was against their business interests. 'The cost of inequality is a price businesses cannot afford to pay,' commented the late Arne Sorenson, then CEO of Marriott International, which signed the brief. He contended that the core strength of the business was the ability to 'embrace differences'.

LGBTQ+ equality was, of course, already a highly polarised issue, but the language of the brief Marriott submitted to the Supreme Court by the businesses elevates the argument:

> Our principles are not platitudes. Our mission statements are not simply plaques in the lobby. Statements of principle are our agenda for success: born of experience, tested in laboratory, factory and office, attuned to competition. Our principles reflect, in the truest sense, our business judgment.[11]

The Supreme Court struck down DOMA, and the brief stands as an elegant example of how businesses can enter the public dialogue on an issue. In our rapid-response social media age of insta-communications, such fine drafting may not always be possible – but the appeal to broader, enduring values and the interests of business can be hugely helpful. Businesses flourish in open, inclusive societies; they depend on transparency, on trusted information, and on the rule of law. In all of these things they share an interest with their employees and consumers. Alan Murray, CEO of Fortune Media and deeply rooted in the landscape of America's largest businesses, uses the term 'activist CEOs' to refer to the growing number of business leaders who speak out in the polarised public debate of the US. Like us, he observes that those CEOs may at first be surprised to see themselves cast as activists and then surprise themselves by stepping into the role. Marc Benioff, the outspoken founder and CEO of Salesforce, for example, at first resisted the label when it was applied to him, according to Murray. But his view shifted:

'. . . over the next year, it grew on me. Or more accurately I grew into it . . .' Benioff reflected.[12]

Our concept of activist leadership is about businesses taking decisive action on the societal challenges most directly associated with their operations and where they have levers for change. At first pass, that seems different in nature from adding your voice to the noisy and politicised dialogue on the contentious issues of the moment. Yet they intersect. Those who use their voice most effectively on these hot topics root themselves in their commitment to what intrinsically matters to their business and what they are doing about it.

*   *   *

Whereas the modus operandi of populist politicians is to find wedge issues and create division, the role of leaders in business can be to stay focused on enduring values, emphasising the areas of shared concern with society at large. With media attention emphasising the differences that exist on societal issues, it's easy to overlook these areas of shared values. Policy Agenda, a 'nonpartisan' US think-tank, has a programme called *America's Hidden Common Ground*, which uses opinion polling to seek out areas of agreement across the political spectrum – even on contentious issues such as immigration, police reform and economic inequality.[13] The initiative 'challenges the narrative that Americans are hopelessly divided and incapable of working together'. In today's fraught public dialogue, some may find this a little optimistic, but the business leaders are well placed to bring a grounded, common-sense perspective on those enduring areas of shared concern.

This is how many companies explain their commitment to issues of diversity, equity and inclusion – it becomes part of an overarching aspiration: that everybody is able to fully participate in business life, and in society more broadly, regardless of personal attributes such as gender, race, sexual orientation or gender identity. This is not 'woke', and it's certainly not new: many businesses have a long history working towards this. For example, in the early 1950s, as demand for IBM computers exploded, the company opened manufacturing facilities in the heart of the racially segregated American South.[14] By law, services such as housing, medical care, education and transportation were provided separately to white and Black citizens – but IBM made it clear that it would not comply with segregation. As the company's president, Thomas Watson Jr, wrote:

> It is the policy of this organization to hire people who have the personality, talent and background necessary to fill a given job, regardless of race, color or creed.[15]

This bold statement set out the business's position on diversity – more than a decade prior to the passage of the US Civil Rights Act. IBM had taken a similarly progressive stand on women's rights, enacting equal pay for equal work in 1935 – almost three decades before the US Equal Pay Act. Today, IBM's support for issues of equality around the world is a natural continuation of this approach. And sometimes this places them at odds with the political context of the time – just as it did in the American South in the 1950s. Today, IBM is an active member of the Open For Business coalition, working to defend LGBTQ+ rights in countries where they are under threat. If they're attacked for their support for LGBTQ+ equality, they're able to explain how it flows naturally from their enduring values and the actions they've taken to operate based on those values; it is a natural continuation of a decades-old commitment to creating inclusive, meritocratic environments in which to do business.

*   *   *

The biggest corporate sin, particularly for consumers and employees, is *hypocrisy* – any dissonance between word and deed, between policy and practice, between professed values and the actions of the business. As companies have become increasingly vocal about their role in society – talking about their purpose, and making high-profile sustainability commitments – so concern has grown about the dissonance between these public statements and non-public political activities, such as lobbying and political contributions. The term 'corporate political responsibility' has been coined by those who want to shine a light on this misalignment – and it's not hard to find examples of companies saying one thing and doing another. Many people conclude that this is the result of bad intentions and shady corporate practices – and doubtless this is sometimes the case. As often it's just internal disconnects. Elizabeth Doty, the director of the Erb Institute's Corporate Political Responsibility Taskforce, says the problem is usually that the left hand doesn't always know what the right hand is doing:

> I think the biggest issue is that companies naturally tend toward functional siloes. Companies already struggle to act as 'one company' around their brand and normal operations. Alignment is even harder on more complex issues – such as sustainability, inequality, social justice and education; where CSO, brand management, DEI, and government affairs start with very different assumptions, priorities and strategies. Without a proactive, principled way to reconcile these views, companies' words and actions diverge.[16]

Finding a 'proactive, principled way' to engage with these challenging societal issues is a leadership task – and leaders who miss this are running a big risk. The world is looking: NGOs and investigative journalists are actively on the hunt for hypocrisy. For example, A *Popular Information* study titled 'These 25 Rainbow Flag-Waving Corporations Donated More than $10 Million to Anti-Gay Politicians in the Last Two Years' found that numerous companies are vocally supporting LGBTQ+ issues whilst making significant political donations to US lawmakers who support anti-gay legislation.[17] As companies come under increasing scrutiny for their stance on societal issues, we can expect to see more exposés like this.

Increasingly, leaders are asking for help navigating this fraught landscape. They know it's a new source of jeopardy – for the business, but also for their own leadership. It's as if you can get hit at any moment by an unanticipated issue, and you're expected to respond straightaway. Around you on all sides people are poised to denounce you. Preparing for this volatility seems like a challenge – but just because these issues may be hard to anticipate doesn't mean they're impossible to prepare for. After all, most companies undertake comprehensive crisis prepared-ness for key commercial and operational risks. In the same way, it is possible to get yourself ready to respond to unexpected societal challenges when they come.

This doesn't mean exhaustive war-gaming on every possible issue, but it might be useful to have some clear criteria for when you might engage – and when you might not. IBM, for example, has developed five 'guidepost questions' to help with this:

- Is the issue directly linked to the business?
- Does the company have a history of engaging on it?
- What are the stakeholders (employees, clients and shareholders) saying?
- What are competitors doing?
- Could the company make a meaningful difference by engaging?[18]

An example of IBM using this criteria was reported by the *Financial Times*: when asked to engage with 'Bathroom Bills' – legislation that forces transgender people to use the public toilets corresponding to their sex at birth – the company decided to get involved in North Carolina and Texas because they have big employee populations in those states, and so considered the issue directly linked to their business – the first guidepost question. However, they decided not to engage on this in Tennessee: without a presence there, the issue didn't pass the first question. Reflecting on the sheer volume of such decisions that need to be taken, Chris Padilla, head of global government affairs for IBM, told the *Financial Times* that it's 'the biggest single change I've seen in my job in the last 10 years'.[19]

Even with such careful consideration about when to engage, companies like IBM inevitably face criticism for doing so. As a poster-child for sustainable business, Unilever in particular is used to this. 'Go Woke Go Broke' ran gleeful headlines covering criticism that the company's recent sluggish performance was due to being over-engaged with societal issues. The antagonist this time was Terry Smith, one of the company's top ten investors, who said that Unilever's management is 'obsessed with publicly displaying sustainability credentials at the expense of focusing on the fundamentals of the business'.[20]

Smith also ridiculed the Unilever mayonnaise brand Hellmann's, which had declared that its purpose is 'fighting against food waste' – this, he said, showed the company had 'clearly lost the plot'.[21] Indeed, it's not hard to see why it might draw ridicule – this is exactly the kind of misapplication of corporate purpose that we caution against in The Power and Problem of Purpose (p. 253). But overzealous purpose statements aside, Unilever's underlying commitment to sustainability is about future-proofing the business: as the reality of double materiality begins to hit home, and the ESG demands of investors ratchet up, the company will be on firmer ground than those that have been neglecting these issues. And this was the sentiment expressed by several other Unilever investors, who spoke up in response to Smith's criticism.[22]

This kind of criticism will keep coming – the key is not to let it bend you out of shape. After all, success in business is not the avoidance of criticism. A statement from the Adam Smith Institute think-tank lambasted 'woke capitalism', saying: 'Companies should stick to traditional profit-driven shareholder capitalism rather than pursuing "woke capitalist" social objectives that often require political action and leave firms facing accusations of hypocrisy.'[23] It's true, as we've been discussing, that getting involved in 'social objectives' and 'political action' do bring real tensions and contradictions to the surface. And hypocrisy, in these times, is indeed a cardinal sin. But society is looking for businesses to take a position. Because of the scale of today's companies, people want to know how you see things. *What do you stand for? What's your agenda? Who are you, exactly?* And employees are calling for it in their employers. They expect to hear your voice at moments of crisis, like the pandemic or the war in Ukraine. Business leaders are increasingly aware of the risks of not rising to these expectations.

* * *

More than anything, the ultimate way to prepare for the slings and arrows of these turbulent times is to follow the steps outlined in *How to Think Like an Activist*. If you're clear on what issues matter to the business, and why; if you've seen those issues as the world sees them, not only through the corporate lens; if you've set an ambition to be part of creating change, and then set it in motion in the core of the business, and beyond, then people will see that you're serious about grappling with difficult societal challenges. Specific questions will come and go, and you may decide to engage (or not) – and you'll incur inevitable criticisms if you do (or don't). But nobody will be able to say you're unengaged with your role in the world.

This means keeping focused on the big picture. The urgent crises facing the world require new innovations, disruptive business models, systemic transformations. For the activist leader, businesses are at the heart of delivering change that the world needs. Political storms rise and fall, often driven by the underlying imperatives – and staying focused on where the business can make change, demonstrating your commitment to this, is the best way to ride out the latest political storm. This can be obscured by the intensity of the moment, but the world is really asking a much bigger question about the role business plays in the world today.

6.

The Big Debate about Capitalism

For years, people have been talking about the need to reinvent capitalism, giving rise to concepts such as *responsible* capitalism, *inclusive* capitalism, *ethical* capitalism, even *conscious* capitalism, and most recently *stakeholder* capitalism – reflecting concerns that our current market system does not encourage companies to take responsibility for their environmental or social impacts, and that the reality today is that listed companies are run primarily for the interests of shareholders to the exclusion of other stakeholders: employees, customers and society at large.

For anyone interested in the role their business plays in environmental and social issues, this is not a remote, theoretical conversation, you're part of it already.

A new CEO of a FTSE 100 company, having just done his first town hall meeting talking to a large crowd of employees, recently joked to us, 'I just got several questions about fixing the capitalist system. I didn't know that was in my job description!' As Harvard's Professor Rebecca Henderson says in her book *Reimagining Capitalism*:

Welcome to the world's most important conversation.[1]

The debate about reinventing capitalism is reaching a tipping point. Long the preserve of radicals, think-tanks and academics, the question about whether capitalism is fit for purpose has moved from the margins into the mainstream. But shareholder capitalism *versus* stakeholder capitalism is a phony war. Couched in those terms, it's bound to polarise – you get to choose one or the other. Yet in practice, while there will be much debate along the way and much still to be thrashed out, the direction of travel is clear.

When in 2019 the US Business Roundtable published their statement on the *Purpose of the Corporation*, they called for a departure from 'shareholder primacy' to 'stakeholderism' as a core principle of corporate governance, and the signatories committed to 'lead their companies for the benefit of all stakeholders'. The World Economic Forum has been on a similar journey – from being emblematic of the global elites protecting their own interests to convening discussion about 'reforming capitalism'. In 2020, capturing the gathering momentum in the conversation, they put out the Davos Manifesto, a set of principles to guide companies 'in the age of the Fourth Industrial Revolution', declaring that 'the purpose of a company is to engage all its stakeholders in shared and sustained value creation'.[2]

Marty Lipton, a founding partner of the New York law firm of Wachtell, Lipton, Rosen & Katz, has been an advocate against short-termism and for a longer-term, multistakeholder capitalism since the 1970s. And it was to Lipton, with his years steeped in the subject, that the World Economic Forum turned to author the 'New Paradigm', the paper they published in 2016 that was a precursor to the Davos Manifesto. Lipton identifies the financial crash of 2008 as the turning point in the broad acceptance of 'the adverse impact of short-termism' and thinks of 2020 – with the covid pandemic and the Black Lives Matter protests forcing systemic inequalities into the forefront of everyone's consciousness – as 'a greater inflection point than any we've had in the past'.[3] When we met him on zoom in the midst of those huge events, he was clear where the problem lies. 'The problem is not corporate management. The problem is the greedy shareholder. We have to focus on that. And that's been true from the beginning,' he told us.[4] He's not alone in his view that there needs to be a shift in the traditional investor mindset: Henderson argues that 'transforming the behavior of investors is just as important as transforming the behavior of firms'.

These days you can find the central ideas of stakeholder capitalism enlivening the lecture halls of the world's business schools, on the panels and podiums of business events and on the pages of the business media. The case for the new paradigm seems almost self-evident: ultimately, it doesn't work for business to have a narrow focus on short-term shareholder returns, at the expense of broader stakeholders and building the value of the company long term. That is a central thesis of this book, and the driving conviction of all our work with companies. But it's not without contention.

Many will argue that the critique of shareholder capitalism is all around us in environmental degradation and chronic socio-economic inequalities of many kinds. 'The system is broken!' seems an obvious conclusion. But how, exactly, is shareholder capitalism held to be the culprit? That can be distilled into three main arguments.

First, the charge is that shareholder capitalism creates an imbalance of risk among all the stakeholders of a company. We are told that shareholders must be rewarded for risking their capital, but that's only one type of risk. For example, as the *Financial Times* commentator Martin Wolf points out, employees cannot diversify their exposure to a company. Employee welfare – whether in terms of decent wages, working conditions, skills or, in Lipton's view, above all, security in retirement – has been a casualty of short-term shareholder capitalism. Mark Carney describes the imbalance like this:

There is an incentive for shareholders to take on greater risk since their downside is limited (they cannot lose more than all of their money under limited liability) but the upside is unlimited. This shifts risks to other claimants, notably employees and creditors. A similar dynamic holds true for externalities, such as pollution.[5]

Indeed, the second point in the critique of shareholder capitalism focuses on the scale and significance of those negative externalities, now perilously close to being out of control. Quarter by quarter, CEOs update investors on their results, marking their success in increased earnings – but with no regard to the company's external impacts. The expectation is that the tab for those is picked up by society at large. In the historic paradigm of short-term shareholder value, only financial performance counts – and that's become a very big drawback. Until the rules of the game change to incorporate other forms of value that are not financial, the risks to shareholders and to the wider world are not factored into the thinking. Henderson sums up the problem:

If you make your decisions by analysing financial statements, as most investors do, there's an enormous amount of information you just don't see. And if you don't see it, you're tempted to think it doesn't exist or doesn't matter.[6]

Third, a basic premise of shareholder capitalism is that the financial markets provide the best mechanism for distributing capital in the interests of social progress. It's hard to make that case today: equity markets have ceased to be a net source of investment capital for companies. Instead, they are sucking money out of them. The increasing popularity of share buybacks, for example, has become symbolic of a financial system feeding on itself. Buybacks offer a flexible way to get money into the hands of shareholders, they support the share price and, in the process, they enrich the corporate executives whose compensation these days is tied to the share price – with the result that wealth has been spiralling ever upwards, while the wages of employees have stagnated, or worse, in the same period. While company by company, case by case, the rationale for a buyback may be simple and sensible, stepping back to look at the bigger picture, you can see the problem.

According to the Harvard Business Review, among S&P 500 companies more than half of company earnings have gone into buybacks – 54 per cent, with a further 37 per cent paid out in dividends – leaving little to be invested in the future.[7] Research shows that 30 per cent of buybacks have been funded by corporate bonds; in other words, companies taking on debt to buy back stock.[8] Once held up as the most powerful engine of productive investment and innovation the world has ever seen, shareholder capitalism now looks to many like a vast value-extraction exercise, and the financial markets are primarily vehicles for speculative profits rather than long-term investment and growth. It's what Carney means when he talks about 'one of the biggest dilemmas of modern capitalism: restructuring business so that private profits are reinvested back into the economy rather than being used for short-term financialization purposes'.

Others have observed how there's an almost doctrinal air about the discussions. Kate Raworth, for example, writes, 'Our beliefs about economic growth are almost religious: personal in nature, political in consequence, privately held and little discussed.'[9] Judy Samuelson makes a similar comment about the nature of beliefs in this area:

Assumptions and incentives that underpin shareholder Primacy have developed a language and narrative of their own. Statements like 'pay for performance' and 'maximize shareholder value' are spoken as if they were handed down with the Ten Commandments.[10]

Yet, albeit with outliers at both extremes, in the mainstream the idea of stakeholder capitalism is gaining traction because it expresses the need to swing the pendulum back from shareholder primacy towards a multistakeholder perspective.

So it is that even as the stakeholder model of capitalism emerges as an answer to the reinvention of capitalism, it attracts a fair amount of scepticism from both ends of the political spectrum. On the left, it's all too easy to paint it as counter-revolutionary: giving the impression that things are changing while, in practice, taking the impetus out of more fundamental reforms. For example, while for many in the business world the BRT statement represented a sea change in corporate America, to many others it was so much hot air. Senator Elizabeth Warren, for instance, contrasted the rhetoric with the actions of the organisation. 'It's impossible to understand,' she said, 'how spending millions of dollars lobbying against worker protection is remotely consistent with the Business Roundtable commitments.' Among neoliberal free marketeers, on the other hand, stakeholder capitalism is decried as 'woke', while the Adam Smith Institute insists that 'profit is socially responsible' inherently.[11]

Among both investors and businesses, there are concerns about how multistakeholder capitalism will play out in practice. Perhaps the primary one is that it will lead to blurred accountability. People fear that the new paradigm requires business leaders to satisfy many masters – too many stakeholders with too many irreconcilable demands, inevitably leading to a diffusion of focus and accountability. Yet the capital markets are already moving fast towards bringing non-financial performance into the mainstream. Companies will have more consistent frameworks for reporting on material environmental and social issues, and data sets will become more robust with use. So, the key point is that taking account of multiple stakeholders (in this context, assuming the environment to be a stakeholder) and a broader set of issues will become part of what businesses will be held accountable for and be expected to report on – including to shareholders (see The New Realities of ESG, p. 239).

People are concerned, too, that stepping up to these societal issues will add significant additional cost for businesses. That may well be true, especially as regulation on ESG issues ramps up and externalities become internalised. However, it's becoming increasingly apparent that the business cost of ignoring the interests of a broader set of stakeholders and environmental realities will also impose major costs, maybe even greater costs.

And underlying all that is the worry that the pressure to attend to all these multiple priorities will insulate management teams from poor financial performance – it's a different expression of the same concern we noted about ESG that, for those who hold the view that the paramount responsibility of business is to deliver to shareholders, this whole question is a distraction. It's significant, then, to note that all the leading voices calling for stakeholder capitalism see this as the route to delivering long-term shareholder value – not just *a* route, but *the* route. They are not disbelievers in the market or in profit. On the contrary, they are unabashed capitalists: in the words of Ron O'Hanley, CEO of State Steet, one of the world's largest asset management institutions:

> My view is simple: we are not going to maximise shareholder value if we disregard the rest of the stakeholders.[12]

There's some myth busting to do about fiduciary duty as well. The purpose and function of a corporation isn't a matter of opinion, but of law; that's the fact of the matter, as we've been reminded often, usually by people aiming to avoid change. The primary responsibility of company directors is to their shareholders, goes the argument – they own the company, and the fiduciary duty of business executives is to protect their interests.

But the legal basis for shareholder primacy isn't as clear-cut as all that. For a start, it's not at all clear that shareholders actually 'own' the company in any meaningful sense. They may have contractual claims, but they're not really *owners*. In the UK this has even been ruled on by the Court of Appeal (in 1948 and reaffirmed in 2003): 'shareholders are not, in the eyes of the law, part-owners of the company.'[13] The economist John Kay, responding to the question 'who owns a company?' writes:

> The answer is no-one does, any more than anyone owns the River Thames, the National Gallery, the streets of London or the air we breathe. There are many different types of claims, contracts and obligations in modern economies, and only occasionally are these well described by the term ownership.[14]

Mark Carney suggests a better way of thinking about shareholders is as 'residual claimants': they get paid after everyone else – employees, creditors, suppliers and governments (through taxes).[15] So what kind of legal responsibility do company leaders have to these 'residual claimants'? The term 'fiduciary duty' simply refers to the relationship that exists when one person (or organisation) is entrusted to use their best judgement to act in the interests of another. According to the UN Principles for Responsible Investment (PRI), the most important of these duties are loyalty (particularly avoiding conflicts of interest) and prudence (acting with due skill, care and diligence).[16] When the

UN commissioned the law firm Freshfields to do a global study on whether fiduciary duties can allow environmental and social considerations to be part of decision-making, they concluded that this is 'clearly permissible and is arguably required in all jurisdictions'.[17]

That little phrase 'arguably required' here is radical: it means fiduciary duty not only permits business leaders to consider the interests of a broader range of stakeholders, it may be considered necessary to do so. The UN PRI quotes Paul Watchman, author of the Freshfields report and now a professor at the University of Glasgow:

> The concept of fiduciary duty is organic, not static. It will continue to evolve as society changes, not least in response to the urgent need for us to move towards an environmentally, economically and socially sustainable financial system.

When the Business Roundtable called for a move from 'shareholder primacy' towards 'stakeholderism', several prominent US law firms issued public advice notes supporting the legality of this position, referring to the 'business judgment rule' that courts will not review a board's business decisions as long as they were made 'on an informed basis, in good faith and in the honest belief that the action taken was in the best interests of the company'.[18]

So what does all that tell us? The law and the concept of fiduciary duty is not an inviolable truth but an evolving concept that can, and needs to, change with changing circumstances. And more than that: it tells us that even without a change to the laws, the choice to take an active role in tackling major societal issues is open to executives today, as stewards of long-term value creation.

That's why this comes down to leadership. For leaders,

whether they sit in the business world or the investment community, the question is where they choose to stand. Do you stick
with a traditional corporate mindset that sees in fiduciary duty
an alibi for why that can't be done? Or do you adopt an activist
mindset and help that shift to happen? As an activist leader,
you have the scope to use the levers, the resources and the sphere
of influence at your disposal to help 'reinvent capitalism', in
Henderson's language. For defenders of capitalism as the source
of prosperity, innovation and jobs in the world, as she says, it
is 'the world's most important conversation'. It's why you might
well meet it in a town hall meeting for employees or even at
the kitchen table with your family.

As CEO of Fortune Media, Alan Murray has had the opportunity over the years to listen to what's on the minds of the
people at the helm of many of the world's leading businesses.
In his book *Tomorrow's Capitalist: My Search for the Soul of
Business*, he recounts the shift he's witnessed:

> What became clear to me was that the frequency and inten-
> sity with which business leaders talked about purpose was
> increasing. More of them were putting it front and center.

What for him was remarkable was that 'the gathering forces
had propelled them to the front of the conversation, with a
force and conviction that I had not seen in my four decades as
a journalist'. He concludes that this new-found concern about
purpose directly links to a growing awareness among business
leaders that the interpretation of capitalism needs to evolve; to
be fit for the future there needs to be a broader, long-term view
of success:

> . . . it takes very little imagination to think of ways you can
> goose short-term profits at the expense of society. Despoil

the environment, slash research, take shortcuts in your product development that may cause problems years in the future, ignore long-term health effects. But over time, the interests of shareholders and stakeholders tend to converge.[19]

That's why shareholder capitalism *versus* stakeholder capitalism is a phony war. The proponents of stakeholder capitalism are not anti-capitalist, they're not anti-profit either. In fact, as Larry Fink writes, '*it is capitalism*, driven by mutually beneficial relationships between you and the employees, customers, suppliers and communities your company relies on to *prosper*. This is the power of capitalism.'[20] So when you cut through the noise, you hear a consensus taking hold around a core proposition.

In a nutshell, it is this: we need to shift away from a fixation on shareholder interests with a focus on the share price in the short term to the exclusion of everyone and everything else – to the exclusion of all other stakeholder interests, to the detriment of the natural systems we all depend on and at the expense of investing back into the business for innovation, resilience and growth. Achieving that is the pathway to delivering shareholder value more sustainably for the long term.

Except on the fringes, there's broad agreement about that core proposition. The phrase 'stakeholder capitalism' is trying to carry that whole argument and it's gained momentum because the need to break with the previous interpretation of capitalism is now so clear. Reinventing capitalism is about reshaping the rules to make it fit for purpose in the realities of today and the demands of tomorrow.

For the activists in business, this isn't a theoretical conversation: they're already out there in a multistakeholder world, working to a new definition of value creation that brings together financial and societal outcomes.

IV.

What Makes a Leader

What Makes a Leader

'If *I* can be the activist then nobody needs to say "you need to do more".' **Amanda Blanc**, CEO, Aviva

'In the long-term, social and environmental issues become financial issues. There really is no hocus-pocus about this.' **Lars Sørensen**, former CEO, Novo Nordisk

'Corporate America wants partial credit for showing their work but getting the wrong answer.' **Mellody Hobson**, Chair of Starbucks

'Industry has been part of the problem . . . But without industry there is no reinvention, and without reinvention there is no future.' **Ilham Kadri**, CEO, Solvay

'We aren't a corner shop; we're a multinational company, publicly quoted and a big part of society. Such status doesn't suit a narrow type of leader.' **Mark Schneider**, CEO, Nestlé

'I made the case that, long-term, our business model *necessitated* my taking on this issue.' **Ajay Banga**, Chair, Mastercard

'You've got to make it part of your normal schedule. When I commit to an initiative like this, the subject is on the management schedule, like any other thing we review.'

Jamie Dimon, CEO, JPMorgan Chase

'Corporations can bring a pragmatism that means they are probably the organizations that can drive most change in today's society.'   **Lars Jørgensen**, CEO, Novo Nordisk

'We have a purpose, but we know that 85% of the ballgame is developing granular pathways on how we achieve that purpose.'   **Sunny Verghese**, CEO, Olam

'The world will not return to "normal". But disruption gives us an opening – and opportunity to analyse, review and to reset everything we do. No matter who you are, the role you play matters. What will you do?'

Doug McMillon, CEO, Walmart

'The CEO today has to be a diplomat, a foreign policy expert, a sociologist, understand all the social trends, and has to be great at running the company.'

Indra Nooyi, former CEO, PepsiCo

'Business will be a big driver of social value in the future – because it makes sense for the business but also because they can and there's momentum in that direction.'

Michael Miebach, CEO, Mastercard

* * *

In this final chapter we want to look at what it takes, at a personal level, to be the kind of business leader that the world needs now. It's ten years since we published our first book together – *Everybody's Business: The Unlikely Story of How Business Can Fix the World*. Back then, this subject was mostly seen as peripheral to the real work of running a business. That's not the case any more: the urgency of societal challenges has forced it onto the agenda of business leaders. It's now clear for all to see that business leaders need a new way of engaging with the wider world.

The old model of leadership was formed in service of shareholder primacy, of the view that *the business of business is business*. Defenders of this model present themselves as tough-minded realists, and view fluffy concepts like 'purpose' and ESG as distractions from creating value for shareholders – or antithetical, even. But theirs is a waning worldview. And if you want a picture of the paradigm shift underway, just take a look at some of the titles on the list of all-time bestselling books on business leadership, among them *Crush It!*, *Only the Paranoid Survive*, *How to Castrate a Bull* and *Leadership Secrets of Attila the Hun*. To most of us, these titles look almost like a cartoon of how far things have already shifted – they sound dated and out of tune with the times we live in.

Yet there's an irony here: those leaders really getting to grips with societal challenges are some of the most 'tough-minded' people you're likely to meet in the corporate arena today. In *Everybody's Business* we quoted from an address given in 1953 at Harvard Business School by Professor Malcolm McNair, who was a pioneer of the school's famous method of teaching by looking at real-world case studies. It's worth looking at again:

William James, a great teacher of philosophy at Harvard during the early years of this century, made the useful distinction between people who are 'tough-minded' and people who are 'tender-minded'. . . . The tough-minded have a zest for tackling hard problems. They dare to grapple with the unfamiliar and wrest useful truth from stubborn new facts. They are not dismayed by change, for they know that change at an accelerated tempo is the pattern of living, the only pattern on which successful action can be based. Above all, the tough-minded do not wall themselves in with comfortable illusions. They do not rely on the easy precepts of tradition or on mere conformity to regulations. They know that the answers are not in the book.[1]

It takes this kind of tough-mindedness to be an activist in business. What's being described as *tough-minded* here isn't a sort of obstinacy: a kind of leadership that's stiff-necked, iron-willed, dead set on holding sway and having one's own way. The kind of tough-mindedness we're talking about is what McNair had in mind seventy years ago when he talked about people who 'wrest useful truth from stubborn new facts' and 'do not wall themselves in with comfortable illusions'. Leaders who can reinvent because they know there is no rule book here. In today's world it's also about having the confidence to be challenged, and the robustness to be agile and adaptable. It's the ability to ride out the storm – to keep your balance and hold your course.

These are the new qualities of leadership. Mellody Hobson, who, as chair of Starbucks and one of the most senior Black women in the US business world, has had to define her own style of leadership. Central to her philosophy is focusing attention fearlessly on what's not working, on what needs fixing. She asks the question, 'Can you be not threatened and nonthreatening?'[2] Hobson joined Ariel Investments as an intern and ended up as co-CEO. Aside from her role with Starbucks, she is on the board of JPMorgan Chase. Hobson describes herself as a Gen Xer, educated in a time when your maths teacher would give you partial credit for showing your workings even if the answer you came up with was wrong. She uses this as an analogy for the business world's attitude to societal issues:

> Corporate America wants partial credit for showing their work but getting the wrong answer. They want pats on the back for trying. The idea that trying is enough – that is not good enough in any other area of business. You don't get credit for trying to meet earnings expectations. You don't get credit for trying to deliver the product on time to your client. You either do or you do not. But in this area, we want credit for trying.

Treating societal issues with the same seriousness as core operational issues – setting targets, measuring outcomes, delivering on the plans – for us, that's the activist mindset and there are signs that it's becoming more prevalent in a new generation of business leaders. Wipro, the global IT family business that grew out of India, experienced a generational shift in 2020 when forty-four-year-old Rishad Premji took the reins from his father who had led Wipro for over half a century. The company became one of the first seven businesses in the world to get approval for their net zero targets from the science-based targets initiative: they plan to be what Premji calls 'true' net zero by 2030, with no offsets bolstering their progress: 'We are very serious, very sincere and very committed,' he explains. 'Energy and climate change is a hugely pressing issue: many people are talking about it; not enough people are acting fast enough on it.'[3] At the start of 2022, Wipro planned to hire 40,000 grad-

uates in the year ahead. In the offer letter they received were
the details of what they could expect the company to invest in
their personal development over the years ahead – and, tuning
into the sentiments of his young workforce, Premji declared
on Twitter:

> Millennials care deeply about issues like climate change, ineq-
> uity, racial injustice, gender inequality etc. and they want to
> know where the organisations they work for stand on these
> issues. The New Gen talent will make change happen. They
> are demanding it![4]

Leaders with these kinds of qualities will rise to the fore, not
just because the world needs it, but because business needs it.
Think of it like this: not so long ago, the primary task of a
CEO was to take the money you got from your customers and
give as much of it as possible to your shareholders – paying
some to employees and suppliers on the way. It was a simpler
time. We think of it as linear, 2D leadership – and it stayed like
this for decades. When you look back, you can see that the
corporate landscape was remarkably unchanged for decades:
when the Fortune 500 was first published in 1955, top of the
list was General Motors. At the turn of the millennium, General
Motors was still America's biggest company, and much of the
list was still there.[5]

In fact, the experience of running a large corporation in the
1950s remained more or less the same through to the 2000s.
Much would have changed, but the rules of the game were
basically the same. But just imagine you put a CEO from the
1950s at the helm of a global company today. It would be a bit
of a shock. Running a business has become a more complex
and unpredictable undertaking. 'We're living in a world of
perpetual technological change, social change, competitive

change . . .' one chairman, whose career had spanned several decades and as many sectors, told us. 'You have to continually re-justify your existence. That means ripping up the business model, restructuring your cost base, changing your technology stack, all at once, and all without missing your numbers – and that's before you get to an issue like climate change.'

When Indra Nooyi became CEO of PepsiCo in 2006, she helped break the 'bamboo ceiling' by becoming one of the first Asian-Americans to run a major American company. Looking back on her twelve years at the helm, she jokes, 'I'm glad I'm not a CEO today,' explaining: 'I had my share of challenges, but for CEOs now it's in spades.'[6] She reflects on what it takes to lead a company today:

> The CEO today has to be a diplomat, a foreign policy expert, a sociologist, understand all the social trends, has to be great at running the company, has to go from a world that was flat and global to a world that's got walls. Everything we had fifteen to twenty years ago is being turned on its head. So CEOs have to somehow straddle all this and figure out how do you bring action on big issues related to society?

Sunny Verghese is the co-founder and CEO of Olam, based in Singapore, and one of the world's largest agribusinesses. When the company celebrated its twenty-fifth anniversary in 2012, he announced his intention for it 'to be more activist in tackling global challenges'.[7] As we saw in A Shared Agenda with Government (p. 280), Olam has been working across the industry, with the express purpose to 'reimagine global food systems to operate within nature's boundaries'. But Verghese is clear that being 'more activist' is about more than having a snappy purpose statement:

> We have a purpose and a mission in terms of what we want
> to do as a firm, but we know that 85 per cent of the ballgame
> is really developing granular pathways and strategies on how
> we're going to achieve that purpose.[8]

In addition to his CEO role, Verghese spent three years as
chair of the World Business Council for Sustainable Development
(WBCSD), which gave him a broad view of how business leaders
are relating to the global crises. To be successful today, he says,
leaders need to be unafraid of 'taking on issues that are bigger
than themselves and their own sphere of influence'. His successor
as WBCSD chair is Ilham Kadri, the French-Moroccan CEO of
chemicals firm Solvay. 'All us of . . . need to wipe the slate clean
and bring forward the solutions that the world needs,' she says:

> So the real question becomes, how our industries can be part
> of the solution? How will we tear off that label that calls us
> the problem? Because yes, industry has been part of the
> problem . . . But without industry there is no reinvention,
> and without reinvention there is no future.[9]

It's clear that the days of 2D leadership are gone: today's
companies need multidimensional leaders, capable of juggling
demands from multiple stakeholders, taking on board constantly evolving environmental and social issues, managing
increasing levels of disruption and making difficult decisions
with incomplete information. More than once we've heard
leaders tell us that running a business is like changing an
aeroplane engine in flight – major transformations are taking
place, but the plane must stay in the air. Being a CEO has
always been a high-pressure job, but these days the pressure
seems to be coming from all directions. The big opportunity
is, as Kadri puts it, reinvention for a future where business

and industry play an active role in generating solutions that the world needs.

These perspectives are based on our experiences advising senior leaders – it's a practitioner view, not an academic view. But there's much to learn from the academic literature here – after all, the subject of business leadership has been extensively studied. And what better place to get a sense of this than by looking back through the archives of the Harvard Business Review. While happily admitting there may be some confirmation bias in our reading, nonetheless our experiences of how business leadership is changing are borne out by the management theory – stretching right back to Malcolm McNair's paper 'On the Importance of Being Tough Minded' (HBR, 1952), which we've discussed earlier.

One of the themes investigated is *motivation*: what motivates high-performing business leaders? In *What Makes a Leader?*,[10] from which we borrow the title of this chapter, the psychologist Daniel Goleman explored leadership potential and concluded that those with the greatest potential are motivated by more than 'external factors, such as a big salary or the status that comes from having an impressive title'. Instead, they are 'driven to achieve beyond expectations – their own or anyone else's' – and this, he says, means taking on hard creative challenges, not just administering business as usual. We've seen this in action: societal challenges are as tough as they come, and engaging with them through the business can unlock enormous leadership energy.

Reading the literature gives you a new view of what a leader is actually *for*. In a landmark paper, 'Creating Shared Value', Michael Porter and Mark Kramer set out their vision that leaders should aim to 'enhance the competitiveness of a company while simultaneously advancing the economic and social conditions in the communities in which it operates'.[11] This built on the work of Michael C. Jensen from a decade earlier, who proposed the concept of *Enlightened Value Maximization*.[12] Jensen was closely associated with the Chicago school view that *the business of business is business*, but thought that markets are inevitably ignorant of the many complex realities business leaders face. He saw the job of business leaders as, in part, 'to resist the temptation to conform to the pressures of equity and debt markets' when those markets don't grasp the issues at hand.

In *Accelerate!*, Harvard Business School's professor of leadership John Kotter describes the constant disruption and turbulence that business leaders must deal with – financial, social, environmental and political.[13] He argues that old hierarchical models of leadership can't handle this; instead, he says, business needs leaders who can 'mobilise voluntary energy and brainpower' in the company behind a 'shared purpose'. This was a relatively early mention of *purpose* in the literature, and in the previous chapter we discuss the latest thinking in more depth. The Harvard Business Review has now published dozens of articles on the subject. For example, in *From Purpose to Impact*, Scott Snook from the US Military Academy, together with Wharton Fellow Nick Craig, show how having a clear sense of purpose is 'the key to navigating the complex, volatile, ambiguous world we face today'.[14] They say that unless you're connected to a clear sense of what matters, and why, it's hard to go the distance.

In *Triple-Strength Leadership*, our former colleague Nick Lovegrove, together with Matthew Thomas, proposed that effective leadership requires a multiplicity of perspectives – particularly, across the three domains of business, government and civil society.[15] The ability to 'see it as the world sees it' is a critical step on the path to activism – stepping outside the corporate bubble and understanding how other stakeholders see the issues. Activist leaders instinctively seek out these perspectives – while not losing sight of what matters to them. And this is why activist leaders intuitively value diversity in their businesses, and work to create cultures that are inclusive of a wide range of backgrounds and identities. Recent years have seen many articles in HBR and elsewhere that discuss why a focus on diversity is an essential part of modern business leadership.

More recently, HBR published a piece by the Indian-American scholar Ranjay Gulati called *The Messy but Essential Pursuit of Purpose*, exploring what it takes to run a successful business that's purpose-driven.[16] He says:

> Deep purpose organizations are deeply committed to both positive commercial and positive social outcomes. Their leaders adopt a mindset of practical idealism.

Unsurprisingly, we love the notion of 'a mindset of practical idealism' – it's a good shorthand description of what we're calling 'the activist mindset' in business. Talking about purpose can often drift into feelgood, mushy sentiments – but Gulati captures the combination of clear-sighted ambition and hands-on delivery that is needed to make it meaningful.

We're not academics, and this isn't an academic text – but it's interesting to see how the management literature shows new dimensions of what it means to be a leader. It strengthens our picture of activist leadership. As we've been describing throughout this book, the activist leader is someone with a powerful sense of purpose, an ambition to make an impact which keeps them going through the inevitable challenges and bumps on the road; someone who knows how to mobilise others and harness the resources around them. Someone who knows what matters to them, and why – and this imbues their leadership with a strong sense of authenticity. When we admire someone for their leadership, in any walk of life, it's qualities such as these that we're usually admiring.

We spoke to the leaders of a few companies we think are doing pioneering work in this space, and whose businesses we've featured in this book, to ask them directly: what does activist leadership mean to you?

When Amanda Blanc became CEO of Aviva PLC in 2020, Bloomberg described it as 'one of the toughest jobs in European finance'.[17] Investors were complaining that Aviva, one of the world's biggest insurers and pension providers, had become an 'incoherent global empire' with a hotch-potch of different insurance businesses and asset management operations. It wasn't performing, and the shares had roughly halved in value over the preceding five years. So all eyes were on Blanc when she took up the role. She told the media at the time:

> I'm not a business-as-usual person and I haven't come here to do a business-as-usual job.[18]

And she lived up to that promise, acting swiftly to streamline the business, collecting £7.5 billion in disposal proceeds and transforming performance in its core markets. The company began to grow, and grow profitably.[19] Her focus on financial value was accompanied by an equally energetic focus on societal value. In particular, taking action on climate change – through its role as insurer and as a large investor, as well as through its own supply chain and operations. She announced the company would be the first major insurer to reach net zero carbon by 2040,[20] and became an outspoken advocate for climate action – warning her own industry to stop speaking with a 'forked tongue' on the subject.[21]

'Both of my grandparents were coal miners,' Blanc reflected, as we talked about her work on climate. 'So I feel the irony of this stance that coal is now very, very bad, yet it's only because of coal that I'm sitting where I sit today – but recognising that the world is changing.' We asked her how it came about that she had taken such an active position on climate. 'We had a meeting that I remember really well,' she told us: she reviewed the company's proposed sustainability targets as they stood, but they didn't seem right to her, so she decided to seek out external views from two very different perspectives. 'We went to an Australian NGO, run by a guy who had grown up in the Aboriginal bush. We gave him the report that we were going to publish and he said, basically, this is rubbish; it's absolutely not good enough.' At the same time, they gave it to one of the big auditors who said it was all fine: 'If you tick all these boxes, everything will be good – it'll be uncontroversial,' Blanc recalls them saying. 'So we had two absolutely different opinions.' There was a decision to make, and she went with the spirit of the NGO perspective. Looking at the business-as-usual option, she said, 'We must be able to do more. I believed that we could do more.'

She talks about this as if it were just good leadership, but most leaders in most businesses don't ask the question she asked: they're not questioning whether it's possible to do more on these big societal issues, and they rarely step outside the corporate worldview to get different perspectives. Most leaders would be happy to settle for the answer from the auditors. The choice she made is born of an activist spirit, pushing beyond mere compliance, driven by a conviction that more can be done – and needs to be done. But Blanc, like many leaders we meet with this kind of mindset, wouldn't describe herself as an activist. She laughs when we suggest this:

I just don't want to be the person on whose watch the decision was made to take a laissez-faire approach to climate and say, 'Well, we'll just do what everybody else does; we'll sit back and we'll hope for the best.' If *I* can be the activist then nobody needs to say 'you need to do more'. I don't want anybody to say I could have done more.

For Ajay Banga, executive chairman and former CEO of Mastercard, 'active leadership is the only form of leadership'. And if anyone knows what good business leadership looks like, it's Ajay Banga. Over a decade as CEO, he vastly expanded the company's reach: revenues roughly tripled and profits quadrupled. According to the *New York Times*, Mastercard's stock soared by more than 1,000 per cent during his tenure – outperforming competitors.[22] Alongside this impressive financial value creation, Banga is also recognised as a leader in creating social value. For him, the two go hand-in-hand. As we've written about earlier, under his leadership Mastercard became well known for its pioneering work on financial inclusion – and, talking to him, it's clear how this happened because it was designed to be not just a philanthropic strategy but a commercial strategy. When he arrived, the company's business model focused on winning market share for electronic payments – but this represented only 15 per cent of all payments in the world; the other 85 per cent of payments are in cash:

> It made more sense to me to broaden the aperture of our vision from focusing on the 15 per cent of existing electronic payments exclusively to focusing *also* on the 85 per cent of payments that remained in cash. We found that the cash economy was very connected to people being left out of the financial system, and in many markets financial exclusion is an enormous societal challenge. So working backwards, if we want to grow, we've got to solve for that.

Lots of banks have initiatives focused on financial inclusion; not everyone has the vision to shape the future growth of their business around an issue like this. It's a great example of how financial and social value can come into alignment, while determinedly building a business model that sustains both. Banga had long been interested in social development before joining Mastercard: born in Maharashtra, India, he gained a close-up perspective on the challenges of economic exclusion; and, during his time at Citi he led their global microfinance strategy. You get the sense that having the vision was the easy part for Banga; making it happen would be where the hard work began. The first big challenge was getting investors on board, and this is something he's clearly proud of achieving:

> I went to the investor community and made the case for why putting our shoulder to the wheel in the space of financial inclusion is worth it and why it's money well spent. We helped investors understand that financial inclusion would pay back my business over time – maybe not in my tenure as a CEO, maybe for my successor. But if you don't start now, you won't get there in five years.

He wasn't simply talking about another initiative for the company, but a new vision for the future growth of the business: 'I made the case that, long-term, our business model *necessitated* my taking on this issue.' When the issue is not 'an artificial thing for the business, then you have the right to play' so taking it to your investors as an opportunity can work, he insists:

> The wrong way to think about this is that by spending this money you're doing something investors don't want. There's no investor who wakes up in the morning saying, 'I really don't care what you do in the wider world, I only care about

my returns today'; they actually don't say that. It's when the CEO doesn't make the case adequately for why what they're doing is an important part of making the company better that it's a problem.

Lars Jørgensen, the CEO of Novo Nordisk, also sees aligning social value and financial value as part of leadership today: 'For me, that's one of the things that a CEO needs to do: to redefine how we provide value to society. It's legitimacy for our company, and redefining our business model for the future.' For Jørgensen, the key to that is thinking about partnerships in a new way. When we spoke with him, he had just come from chairing a cross-sector session in Copenhagen on the ever-increasing health challenge of obesity. 'We had everybody there who has an ability to drive change on this issue,' he told us – including mayors, health system leaders, academics and charities, alongside ministers and businesses. 'We ended up united around something that was much bigger than any of us could achieve individually.'

It's a snapshot of Jørgensen's philosophy in action: deliberately engaging with the broad cast of characters across the entire health ecosystem to find common cause on the big issues. And it's more than just showing up as a good systems player; it's also the groundwork for an evolution of the business model:

You could say that, in our sector today, we are all trying to push broken healthcare systems to pay for our medicines. When I meet heads of healthcare systems, I know that their first thought is that I'm a problem for them; a cost problem. But when I talk about this type of collaborative relationship with all the players in the system, I see people starting to think opportunities.

Jørgensen is asking: what if there were a new commercial model based on new partnerships across the health sector, aiming at both treating and preventing conditions? 'If you establish these types of relationships, you can drive a completely different set of discussions,' he explains. 'It goes from selling individual products to individual physicians who take it to individual patients into a new model – that's about population health, where we partner to bring products to populations.'

Novo Nordisk is experiencing what one analyst recently called 'insanely strong' growth:[23] it sells half the world's insulin, has new treatments for diabetes and is launching new drugs to tackle obesity. Yet among the over 400 million people worldwide who have Type 2 diabetes, many are left undiagnosed or untreated – and the company is at the heart of that challenge. You can hear more than a hint of pragmatic activism in the way he talks about this: 'I want us to go further,' he says simply. 'If you just look at the challenge out there, there's a huge unmet need. Today we reach only thirty-five million people with our diabetes treatments. Great though that is, it tells me that – even after a hundred years in the business – there's still room for improvement. We need to get to many more patients.' His perspective echoes Banga's approach when he first took on financial inclusion for Mastercard; he's at the start of a journey, working with governments and civil society to broaden access and, over time, evolve the model to expand commercial and social value in tandem.

Chronic illness is a huge and unsustainable burden on health systems all over the world. Jørgensen is not alone in thinking a radically different approach is needed – one that both answers the societal need and creates long-term opportunity for the business:

When I talk to our shareholders, I talk to this and explain
that partnership is the way of the future – certainly, for how
we do our innovation but also for how we take our products
out to the market. If we can help health systems by working
with them to prevent diseases and get to many more patients
but potentially also at a lower price point, then you enable
the healthcare care system to transact with you on a basis
that's much better. The future selling model will need to be
a function of this.

Jørgensen's predecessor, Lars Sørensen, was named Best
Performing CEO by the Harvard Business Review two years
running, in part because of the company's strategic approach
to societal issues. He told the HBR: 'In the long-term, social
and environmental issues become financial issues. There really
is no hocus-pocus about this.' Shaping the business to meet the
interests of society at large, he says, 'is nothing but maximising
the value of your company over long periods of time'.[24]

Mark Schneider, CEO of Nestlé, doesn't immediately strike
you as an activist. He has the perfect pedigree to run the giant
Swiss-based multinational, the largest food company in the
world: born in Germany, MBA at Harvard Business School, a
PhD from the University of St Gallen, multilingual, and with
impressive CFO credentials. We were keen to speak to Schneider
because Nestlé has a track record of taking on issues like human
rights, water use and deforestation. So, we asked him: when it
comes to issues like this, are you an activist? He told us:

Activist; yes. A zealot; no. It's important to make it an active
part of your agenda, but you need to know where to draw
the line. We're not a charity. We're not an NGO. This is not
philanthropy. If you're leading an organisation that has a vast
footprint, you can be a part of either blocking or moving

trends in your industry – and with that comes a responsibility to society.

The key point for him is how you decide to leverage the scale of the business to drive change: 'We aren't a corner shop; we're a multinational company, publicly quoted and a big part of society. Such status doesn't suit a narrow type of leader,' explains Schneider. That sensibility is built into the qualities he looks for in the individuals in his leadership team:

If you choose to be an executive at a company our size, one of the criteria we insist on is the ability to helicopter up and down: someone who can give you context but is also very willing to drill down into the details with you. If you're just sky-high at the 10,000-foot level, you don't get traction on the details. But if you're not able to rise above and see how that all links to the wider ecosystem around you in the world, then you're also not in the right place as a leader of this organisation.

Nestlé works across a wide range of societal issues, but they've made climate change and regeneration their first priority. For Schneider and his entire executive team, that's where the scale of the company and the scale of the issue intersect:

Climate change to me is the biggest and most defining issue of our time. It's getting awfully warm on this planet. If we don't address that, many of our lesser problems may not actually count that much. That's where I, personally, and my colleagues are on this: we all feel that given the impact of agriculture and food on the climate, we have to make a contribution. Our industry stands for a quarter of all emissions – and we are the largest food company – so this is our calling.

That for him is the big picture, the perspective from the helicopter at 50,000 feet of the climate challenge. Drilling down into the detail, he took himself out into the fields to meet the farmers. What he saw gave him conviction that this is doable. 'Not much happens fast in agriculture,' he laughed, 'but when you compare these fields side by side, one traditionally farmed, the other with regenerative methods, after a few years, you already see a difference.' However, the revelation for him was what making this transition asks of the farmers themselves:

> On a personal note, the part that really blew me away was that the farmers I met all had a similar story to tell. It took three or four years of increased investment and reduced yield before finally these new methods got traction; they had almost had to give up. So, there's a valley of tears.

It was a big insight for Schneider: these were farmers in Switzerland, one of the richest countries in the world; if they were experiencing such challenges, how much tougher it must be for farmers in many other places. And yet Nestlé's ambitions on climate depend on farmers adopting these new techniques:

> What became clear to me is: we as the buyer from these farmers, we have to actively help them because, otherwise, these people will not be able to make this transition. They're the most exposed in this supply chain. It's not enough for us just to insist that this has to be done. We have to help them with technical assistance, the premiums that we pay and sometimes financial assistance, to make it through that valley of tears.

At their AGM in 2021, Schneider won shareholder approval for a €3.6 billion investment over five years to tackle climate change and regenerative farming. 'Nestlé is really showing us a glimpse of how future business is going to be approached,' commented a GlobalData analyst: 'Other companies should take note.'[25] The message coming from Schneider is if you're serious that you want this to happen, you need to get serious about what it takes to deliver on it.

Organising to deliver is a big theme of Jamie Dimon as well. For almost twenty years he has been CEO of JPMorgan Chase, an astonishingly big bank, with total assets approaching \$4 trillion[26] (to give a sense of scale, that's roughly the combined assets of the Bank of England, the Bank of Italy and the Reserve Bank of India).[27] Described by the *New York Times Magazine* as 'America's least-hated banker',[28] Dimon was the chair of the US Business Roundtable when they made their momentous about-turn on the purpose of the corporation. JPMorgan Chase's social-facing initiatives are among the boldest and most mature that we've featured in this book, and Dimon has made them a hallmark of his leadership of the bank. So we asked him what advice he would have. 'It needs to be part of your mindset,' he begins, and then describes what this looks like for him:

> You've got to make it part of your normal schedule – it's just part of what you do. If it's not that, you'll skip meetings, you'll delegate – and if you delegate too far away, people see that and then to them it becomes like you're only paying lip service. Whenever I commit to an initiative like this, I get someone on the management team to be responsible for it, and put it on the management schedule every week and every month, like any other thing we review. Once you gear up for it in an organised manner you start accomplishing great things.

Dimon turns to JPMorgan's Advancing Black Pathways programme to describe how that works at the bank. The initiative was set up to tackle the question of the under-representation of Black talent in the financial services sector. 'We set up a dedicated group – because this is real work,' he explains. 'If you want to be better at this, you need to get the right people on it and tell them this is your only job.' That core group generates the data and understanding of the issue, sets the strategy and has access to networks right across the bank – and beyond – to get it done. The initiative is a multifaceted, multi-year programme that encompasses Black home ownership, black-owned enterprises and educational and career opportunities.

Key to JPMorgan's approach is that, on one hand, the initiative has the attention of Dimon and the leadership team at the centre and, on the other, it's delivered at a local level in the communities most directly affected. For example, when it was expanded in 2019 specifically to bring more Black talent into the wealth management industry, the bank partnered with Historically Black Colleges and Universities (HBCUs), establishing a network of nineteen academic institutions around the US connected into the programme.[29] 'And all of sudden, you know what?' Dimon says, 'you're recruiting better, you're understanding it better, you're talking about it better, you're making progress.'

Listening to Dimon, you hear a simple but vivid illustration of what we mean by the activist mindset brought to bear on an issue: from the outset, the intention has been not just to improve the bank's performance on the question but to tackle the issue itself. He's clear what they were aiming to achieve:

> If our objective were just to hire a few more experienced Black financial advisers into JPMorgan, we'd be hiring them from another bank and we wouldn't be adding to the number

of Black financial advisers. So what did our people do? They
started a devoted programme to hire and *train* a net 300 new
Black financial advisers in Wall Street. And we always measure
the results of everything we do. I want this to be successful.
I don't want to brag we hired Black advisers and then they're
failing. So, we track the people we're training; we follow how
they're doing in their communities. I want to know: how
many *successful* Black financial advisers do we have now
because of this work?

You get a sense of enormous practicality from talking to
these leaders – a definite hallmark of activist leadership.
Jørgensen at Novo Nordisk takes the view that 'pragmatic
activism', as he calls it, in the business world is made up of the
combination of the ambition to make a difference with having
the capability to get stuff done:

> Big corporations have both a passion and vision but also the
> ability to find the pragmatic way. When you look at those who
> can move agendas today – perhaps big cities can – but for
> sure large companies can. In business, we are always asking:
> how can we get things done, what do we need to do next?

A common barrier to taking action on societal issues is the
need many companies feel to have watertight plans before they
make any commitments. But these are messy, complex issues:
there are no well-trodden pathways and often it isn't realistic
to have everything mapped out at the start. Michael Miebach,
who has followed Ajay Banga as CEO at Mastercard, has experienced that first-hand. He was there at the very beginning
of the company's financial inclusion journey – indeed, 'from
the first hour', as he told us. 'But when it started, we didn't
know how it was going to play out.'

At the time Miebach was tasked with building Mastercard's business in Africa. 'We could see governments across the continent struggling to bring huge proportions of their populations into the formal economy and online,' he remembers, and the team took that as their strategic cue:

> We said maybe there's not a conventional business case, but seeing how governments are trying to shape where their economies need to go is a good leading indicator. I recall the board meeting where someone commented that this was probably the worst business case they'd seen in a long while – but that the idea made perfect sense! If we'd done a plan at that point, it would have been wrong the moment we'd finished it – there was no way we could know enough. So we said, 'Okay, let's be clear on the building blocks we can all agree on and that's a reasonable starting point.'

They did build the plan, of course, figuring out what was possible and then adapting and adapting again as they learned more. From the outset, the work has been rooted on two beliefs: that success for Mastercard was building a business that would be relevant to all – 'everybody could participate', not only the affluent few – and that they would need to work together with 'like-minded people' across the ecosystem to achieve the vision. 'Today we have commercial sustainability in our financial inclusion work. It's a long cycle but the fact that it's profitable allows us to stay with it and evolve it. It allows us to create truly lasting social impact through the business – in a way we couldn't if we treated financial inclusion as a purely philanthropic effort,' explains Miebach.

Amanda Blanc experienced a similar moment of decision at Aviva as they set out their ambitions on net zero. The vital thing, she explained, is to *get going*:

You've got to put to one side the actuarial hat, the *'you've got to have everything signed in blood'* mindset. You need to say, directionally, this is where we're going and we believe that we can get 80 per cent of the way there. And by the way, the whole world is going to be doing it so together we'll find a way.

When the board asked her how the measurement of carbon would work, she explained how much could be measured today and what would need to be developed along the way – and was able to assure them that nobody else was more advanced. 'They said we should just go for it – so that's what we did.'

Even leading a business where the reputation for delivering social value is acknowledged globally, Miebach recognises that the impetus to do it can seem counter-intuitive at the outset:

When you're in a business, it's not immediately obvious to people that social value is important to economic value. The starting point is often that this is an economic enterprise and so you choose one over the other. But what we've found over the last twelve years is that, in the end, economic value will increase if you provide social value. They depend on each other; they inform each other – and that's not initially intuitive.

Looking ahead, Miebach believes, 'Business will be a big driver of social value in the future – because it makes sense for the business but also because they can and there's momentum in that direction.'

Aviva, JPMorgan Chase, Mastercard, Nestlé, Novo Nordisk – the leaders of these businesses are some of the most high-profile leaders of the corporate world today. Their businesses are at the heart of the corporate establishment and yet it seems they're all engaging in a new way with societal challenges. And they're doing so in the interests of future-proofing their businesses. It remains to be seen whether they are able to create change at the speed and scale the world requires, but the existence of leaders like this should give us an optimism that we might not have thought possible a decade ago.

They have in common a restlessness, a desire to challenge assumptions about what's possible and a strong instinct that value creation involves both financial value and societal value. They are the antithesis of a narrow focus on shareholder value – so we asked them about that, too. 'Most CEOs of companies like this are going to be of my generation, more or less,' says Schneider. 'We all got a business education in the 1980s or thereabouts, and at that time, we were trained very much within the shareholder mantra.' He tells us that his favourite Harvard Business School professor was Michael Jensen, whose concept of Enlightened Value Maximization we discussed earlier. Jensen had 'a wider angle' perspective that's influenced Schneider's own thinking about running a business:

It's about long-term value. No business can be separate from society. It's part of society and it's serving us as people.

Ajay Banga agrees: 'Some time ago, you were told that you had to provide great returns to your shareholders. Legions of CEOs and leaders were trained to care about that – and only that.' But, as he sees it, it's different today: 'Now their stakeholders – particularly young employees in their own company – are saying "I need more than that. To follow you, I need to know that you care about more than that." I think that leaders who understand that and feel it in their heart, if they can, they adapt and show that form of leadership.'

Miebach has come only recently to the role of CEO, so we

asked him whether he thinks the expectation on business leaders to step up on societal issues is greater now than it was when his predecessor Banga took the role over a decade ago. 'Absolutely!' he agrees emphatically:

> Just take the topic of innovation in tech, as an example. The expectation now is that if your AI solution is going to create access issues; if you're likely to create externalities that are not fully understood yet, you damn well should think about these things. That was not even a conversation five years ago, but now the fact that we get that and act on it sets us apart, it gives us commercial edge and also it's simply the right thing to do.

We asked the same question of Jamie Dimon, and he told us that the pressure on companies to respond on societal issues has quadrupled in just the past few years. What's most challenging for CEOs today is not just the volume of these demands, but the politicised atmosphere that surrounds them.

You're expected to speak up in support of one policy one day and speak out against another the next – and whatever you do or don't say is almost guaranteed to upset significant constituencies. You're damned if you do and damned if you don't. This is the new jeopardy facing business leaders today. Dimon and his team have had to become agile at determining when to engage and when not to. To start with, you need to avoid becoming a 'pawn' in a polarised debate, he tells us: 'Don't let them jazz you up.' For JPMorgan Chase, the starting point is to anchor themselves in what matters to them as a business, he tells us:

> We ask ourselves: is this an issue we believe in and is it something we *do* something about? Then we describe what we do and why.

Always it comes back to speaking up where there are actions to back words. Their guiding principle is to engage on issues that are built into the 'values, systems and structures' of the business. When the Supreme Court's vote overturned Roe vs Wade, for example, JPMorgan quickly stepped out to state publicly that they would pay for employees to travel to states that allow abortion – on the basis that they were expanding established practice of covering abortion, and also travel costs for health when needed, in their employee benefits. LGBTQ+ rights is an area where the business has long been active. When in 2020 the Trump administration rolled back LGBTQ+ rights, the bank's executive spoke up – rooting their response in the equity policies of the company. Though the company deliberately steers away from discussing details of policy, Dimon is emphatic that 'it doesn't mean you cannot show your support on the issue'. The bank followed up, making new grants for non-profits working on the front line of LGBTQ+ rights[30] and expanding funding for the StartOut Pride Economic Inclusion Index to highlight policies that can support LGBTQ+ entrepreneurs.[31]

On a trip to Brazil, Dimon showed up in support of the Out & Equal Forum[32] – in itself significant given the strong opposition to LGBTQ+ rights in parts of Brazilian society and high levels of hate crime against the community there. Relaxed in answering questions on any aspect of LGBTQ+ rights around the world, telling the audience that businesses can be supportive even in countries with anti-LGBTQ+ policies, he said to the audience there: 'A company should stand up for what it believes in. I think you should be forceful.' Once the bank has made the decision to get behind an issue like this, Dimon makes it intrinsic to his leadership – ready to go straight to the heart of it, to be visible in demonstration of his personal commitment.

If I go to any city, anywhere in the world, these issues are on my list. I visit a community centre. I spend time with the politicians and regulators, talk to them about these issues; learn what they're doing about equity, about education – and bring something back here. It's just part of what I do.

It's such a deep-rooted and personal response that most of the activist leaders we meet hardly recognise themselves as 'activists' – they are simply doing what they see needs to be done. In Banga's view, leadership is 'not uni-dimensional' and he talks about 'the fullness of leadership': engaging on critical issues is simply what good leadership is and a spirit of activism is intrinsic to leadership. As he puts it:

If you're a social thinker, a human being in society – and you're lucky enough to have a position that you can speak from because you're a leader of some type, you should make people realise that we're on a burning platform. That the platform is on fire! That the issue of inequity, the issue of climate change, and the challenges of taking the long-term versus the short-term view; these are a burning platform. We don't have the luxury of a hundred years to fix it. We just don't. That's the issue: we don't have time on our side.

Mark Schneider has a similar view:

We, as executives, are supposed to make decisions. When everything is said and done, we're supposed to make decisions when things are still shaping up, and when you have a chance to be ahead of the curve. And I think it has become clearer and clearer to people that now's the time to act.

What sets these leaders apart is that they have stepped beyond the 'business-as-usual' model of yesterday's paradigm as not adequate for today's task. As Amanda Blanc did, they look at what the business was geared up to do in the normal run of things and ask: 'is that enough?' A sense of urgency infuses the way they inhabit their role. *Now's the time to act.*

∗ ∗ ∗

The beginning of any activist's journey is fascinating. Most don't start out with a burning desire to be an activist; they find themselves in a situation where they see something needs to change and they become part of making that happen. The story of Václav Havel is an extraordinary illustration of this. An author and playwright in his home country of Czechoslovakia, he felt compelled to use his plays as a commentary on the Soviet occupation of his country. For years labelled a dissident, Havel was eventually elected president of Czechoslovakia, and subsequently the Czech Republic. Reflecting on his journey he wrote:

> It begins as an attempt to do your work well. You do not become a dissident just because you decide one day to take up this most unusual career. You are thrown into it by your personal sense of responsibility, combined with a complex set of external circumstances.[33]

We've met, and have been honoured to work alongside, many people in business with an activist spirit. People who are, as Havel says, trying to do their work well, with a strong sense of personal responsibility and today faced with an extraordinarily complex set of external circumstances. Just as there are many types of activist, so there are many types of leaders and many leadership roles in business.

We've encountered the activist mindset in the general counsel who's looking hard at the new kinds of risk now facing the world and his business; in the packaging engineer who is excited by bringing her expertise to bear on new materials solutions that weren't possible even a few years ago; the director of marketing who is tuned into the new concerns of consumers and the corporate affairs leader who tries to channel the external world into the business. We've met it in the R&D director who can envisage a whole new way of designing sustainability into innovation, and the supply chain lead who pulls every lever at their disposal to raise the game in hundreds of other businesses on regenerative farming. We've met the chair of the board who sees it as their responsibility – and opportunity – to appoint a CEO who is up to dealing with this new imperative. Wherever they are in the business and whatever they do, they ask: 'What can I do to help?'

In this book we've looked at all kinds of businesses, in all kinds of sectors – tech companies, pharma companies, retailers, banks, leaders in fashion and world-class engineering firms; some are famous consumer brands, others are systemically important companies that most people have never heard of. We've looked at companies that grow, that dig and that make. They deliver goods and services that our modern lifestyles depend upon. And between them, they are massive producers of carbon emissions, they are filling the oceans with plastics, they are burning through Earth's finite resources. They are integral players in a global system that is fundamentally unsustainable – and one which is exacerbating deep structural inequalities in society. If you're a leader in business today, you're part of this picture.

So, it's of enormous significance to see that there are people in business engaging with this great conundrum – not in a grudging, half-hearted way but with energy, imagination and ambition to be part of the solution. There's not enough of them yet. But they are the future of leadership in business – the activist leaders. They are taking a clear-eyed look at the situation, they see what needs to change and they ask of themselves and of their business: what do we need to do to be part of the solution?

Endnotes

The Activist Mindset

1   Joseph Schumpeter, 'Activist investors are both greening and greying', *The Economist*, 10 June 2021.
2   Amanda Fortini, 'Erin Brockovich Wants to Know What You're Drinking', *The Atlantic*, September 2020.
3   Christopher Vogler, *The Writer's Journey*, Michael Wiese Production, 1988.
4   How Greenpeace creates change, Greenpeace, retrieved 19 August 2022.
5   Aaron K. Chatterji and Michael W. Toffel, 'The New CEO Activists', Harvard Business Review, February 2018.
6   Dr Carol S. Dweck, *Mindset: The New Psychology of Success*, Generic, 2017.
7   Michael E. Mann, *The New Climate War*, Scribe Publications, 2021.
8   Climate change: consequences of inaction, OECD, retrieved 25 July 2022.

A Time of Multiple Crises

1   Barbara Ortutay, Twitter unveils version of site that can bypass Russia block, AP News, 10 March 2022.
2   Hilton, Hilton Statement on Ukraine, 9 March 2022.
3   World of Change: Global Temperatures, NASA Earth Observatory, retrieved 25 July 2022.
4   Rain at the summit of Greenland, NSIDC, 18 August 2021.
5   Climatebrief.org, retrieved 30 September 2022.
6   The IUCN Red List of Threatened Species, retrieved 14 July 2022.

7   Dave Davies, 'The world's insect population is in decline – and that's
     bad news for humans', NPR, 24 February 2022.
8   Global Biodiversity Outlook 2, Convention on Biological Diversity,
     March 2009.
9   Joe Brock, Plastic pollution flowing into oceans to triple by 2040:
     study, Reuters, 23 July 2020.
10   The New Plastics Economy, Ellen MacArthur Foundation, 2016.
11   XiaoZhi Lim, 'Microplastics are everywhere – but are they harmful?',
     Nature, 4 May 2021.
12   The State of Fashion 2020, McKinsey & Company, 2020.
13   Ravi Naidu et al., 'Chemical pollution: A growing peril and potential
     catastrophic risk to humanity', *Environment International*, Volume
     156, November 2021.
14   Water Scarcity, UN Water, retrieved 14 July 2022.
15   'Climate change leading to water shortage in Andes, Himalayas',
     Science Daily, 17 December 2018.
16   Mariama Sow, Figure of the week: The shrinking Lake Chad,
     Brookings, 9 February 2017.
17   Closing the water gap, World Economic Forum, 18 June 2021.
18   The State of Food Security and Nutrition in the World 2021, UN:
     FAO, 2021.
19   What the Olympics could look like in 2048 if we continue destroying
     our planet, WWF, August 2021.
20   Hannah Ritchie, 'How much of the world's food production is
     dependent on pollinators?, Our World in Data', 2 August 2021.
21   Samantha Watters, US beekeepers continue to report high colony
     loss rates, no clear improvement, University of Maryland, 23
     June 2021.
22   UN report: Pandemic year marked by spike in world hunger, WHO,
     12 July 2021.
23   Obesity and overweight, WHO, 9 June 2021.
24   Saloni Dattani, Hannah Ritchie, and Max Roser, 'Mental Health,
     Our World in Data', August 2021.
25   Leila Abboud and Sarah Neville, 'Covid lays bare staffing crisis in
     Europe's hospitals', *Financial Times*, 23 December 2021.
26   Katja Ridderbusch, 'Can America's Healthcare Crisis Be Solved?',
     Georgia State University Research Magazine, November 2021.
27   Karn Vohra et al., 'Global mortality from outdoor fine particle
     pollution generated by fossil fuel combustion: Results from GEOS-
     Chem', *Environmental Research*, Volume 195, April 2021.
28   Antibiotic resistance, WHO, 31 July 2020.

29   World Inequality Report 2022, Executive Summary, World Inequality Lab, 2022.

30   World's billionaires have more wealth than 4.6 billion people, Oxfam International, 20 January 2020.

31   Chuck Collins and Josh Hoxie, 'Billionaire Bonanza', Inequality.org, November 2017.

32   Phillip Inman, 'Number of people in poverty in working families hits record high', *Guardian*, 7 February 2020.

33   How many working families are dependent on food banks in the US?, Oxfam America, 18 November 2014.

34   Inequality, OECD, retrieved 14 July 2022.

35   'Russia's 500 Super Rich Wealthier Than Poorest 99.8%', *Moscow Times*, 10 June 2021.

36   H. W. Rittel and M. M. Webber, 'Dilemmas in a General Theory of Planning', *Policy Sciences*, Stony Brook University, 1973.

A New Business Imperative

1   Ben Butler, Lorena Allam and Calla Wahlquist, 'Rio Tinto CEO and senior executives resign from company after Juukan Gorge debacle', *Guardian*, 11 September 2020.

2   Edward Helmore, 'Carl Icahn pressuring McDonald's to improve welfare of pigs raised for meat', *Guardian*, 22 February 2022.

3   Monica Nickelsburg, 'Activists, Amazon employees and climate scientists hold virtual protest over worker firings', GeekWire, 24 April 2020.

4   Emily Stewart and Alexia Fernández Campbell', '8,000 Amazon employees asked the company to do more on climate change', Vox, 22 May 2019.

5   Henry Timms and Jeremy Heimans, *New Power*, Picador, 2019.

6   Mary Baker, 'Why Engaging with Social and Political Issues Is a Non-Negotiable for your employee value proposition, Gartner, 23 February 2022.

7   Jordan Bryan, 'Corporate Advocacy of Social Issues Can Drive Employee Engagement', Gartner, 5 November 2019.

8   Perceptions on the EY Future Consumer, EY, July 2021.

9   2021 Global Reptrak 100, The Reptrak Company, 2021.

10   Swetha Venkataramani, 'The ESG Imperative: 7 Factors for Finance Leaders to Consider', Gartner, 10 June 2021.

11   Ashish Lodh, 'ESG and the cost of capital', MSCI, 25 February 2020.

12   Witold Henisz, Tim Koller, and Robin Nuttall, 'Five ways the ESG Creates Value', *McKinsey Quarterly*, November 2019.

13   Ibid., p. 9.

14   Rebecca Henderson, *Reimagining Capitalism*, Penguin Random House, 2020.

15   Alan Murray and *Fortune* Editors, 'Fortune 500 CEO Survey', *Fortune*, 24 May 2022.

16   Joseph Fuller and William Kerr, 'The Great Resignation Didn't Start with the Pandemic', Harvard Business Review, 23 March 2022.

17   Ryan Pendell, 'The World's $8.7 Trillion Workplace Problem', Gallup, 14 June 2022.

18   Judy Samuelson, *The Six New Rules of Business, Creating Real Value in a Changing World*, Berrett-Koehler Publishers Inc., 2021.

19   Increased corporate concentration and the influence of market power, Barclays, 2019.

20   Tim Wu, *The Curse of Bigness: How Corporate Giants Came to Rule the World*, Atlantic Books, 2020.

21   Fernando Belinchón and Qayyah Moynihan, '25 giant companies that are bigger than entire countries', Business Insider, 25 July 2018.

22   Tom Orlik, Justin Jimenez and Cedric Sam, 'World-Dominating Superstar Firms Get Bigger, Techier, and More Chinese', Bloomberg, 21 May 2021.

23   GDP (current US$), World Bank, retrieved 14 July 2022.

24   List of largest corporate profits and losses, Wikipedia, retrieved 14 July 2022.

25   Annual Report 2022, Walmart, 2022.

26   Walmart's brand value worldwide from 2016 to 2022, Statista, 25 March 2022.

27   Rest of the World, Rolls-Royce, retrieved 14 July 2022.

28   Supply Chain Management, Rolls-Royce, 2010.

29   Novo Nordisk History, Novo Nordisk, 2011.

30   Who we are, Novo Nordisk, retrieved 14 July 2022.

31   Wipro, Wipro Technology, retrieved 14 July 2022.

32   The Carbon Majors Database, CDP, 2017.

33   Plastic Waste Makers Index: Executive Summary, Minderoo, 22 November 2021.

34   Hannah Ritchie, 'Cutting down forests: what are the drivers of deforestations, Our World in Data', 23 February 2021.

35   Kate Raworth, *Doughnut Economics: Seven Ways to Think Like a 21st-Century Economist*, Random House Business, 2017.

36   Michael Penke, 'Toxic and radioactive: The damage from mining rare elements', Deutsche Welle, 13 April 2021.

37 Dustin Mulvaney and Morgan D. Bazilian, 'The Downside of Solar Energy', *Scientific American*, 1 December 2019.

38 Clara Guibourg and Helen Briggs, 'Climate change: Which vegan milk is best?', BBC News, 22 February 2019.

39 Tony Naylor, 'Ditch the almond milk: why everything you know about sustainable eating is probably wrong', *Guardian*, 5 September 2014.

40 Annette McGivney, 'Like sending bees to war', *Guardian*, 8 January 2020.

41 Tom Philpott, 'Lay Off the Almond Milk, You Ignorant Hipsters', Mother Jones, 16 July 2014.

42 Ian Randall, 'More than 780 million contact lenses are discarded in Britain every year . . .', Mail Online, 26 September 2019.

43 Bernice Lee, Jonathan Hepburn, Christophe Bellmann, and Isadora Ferreira, 'The Global Food Value Chain: A Snapshot', Chatham House, 20 September 2019.

44 Charli Shield, 'Seed monopolies: Who controls the world's food supply?', Deutsche Welle, 8 April 2021.

45 Professor Jennifer Clapp, 'The Rise of Mega-companies in the Global Food System', Alberta Institute of Agrologists, 3 March 2019.

46 Kate Taylor, 'These 10 companies control everything you buy', *Business Insider*, 28 September 2016.

FOCUS: be clear what matters and why

1 Walter Isaacson, *Steve Jobs*, Simon & Schuster, 2011.

2 How does PepsiCo conserve and protect water?, PepsiCo, retrieved 14 July 2022.

3 Brian Krzanich, CES 2014 Show Keynote Speech Transcript, transcribed by S. Pangambam, *Singju Post*.

4 Accenture and Microsoft plan digital IDs for millions of refugees, BBC News, 20 June 2017.

5 VW, Daimler, Porsche embrace refugees, see fix to future labor shortages, Automotive News Europe, 19 September 2015.

6 Watch the award-winning better shelter refugee tent being assembled, designboom, 31 January 2017.

7 Join us for a conversation about our transition to net zero carbon, Rolls-Royce, 17 June 2021, retrieved 18 July 2022.

8 Global Leadership: Rolls-Royce and the path to Net Zero, CogX, 15 June 2021.

9 Kate Birch, Meet the CEO: Tufan Erginbilgic is named the CEO Rolls-Royce, Business Chief, 1 August 2022

PERSPECTIVE: see it as the world sees it

1   Mark Carney, *Value(s): Building a Better World for All*, William Collins, 2021.
2   Howard Chase, *Issue Management: Origins of the Future*, Issue Action Publishers, 1985.
3   Matthew Syed, *Rebel Ideas: The Power of Thinking Differently*, John Murray Publishers, 2021.
4   8 Things to Know About Palm Oil, WWF, January 2022.
5   Mikaela Weisse and Elizabeth Goldman, 'We Lost a Football Pitch of Primary Rainforest Every 6 Seconds in 2019', World Resources Institute, 2 June 2020.
6   4 vital steps to protect the world's remaining rainforests, World Economic Forum, 4 December 2020.
7   Rhett A. Butler, '10 Rainforest Facts for 2021', Mongabay, 12 September 2021.
8   Forests, WWF, retrieved 18 July 2022.
9   Frances Seymour, '2021 Must Be a Turning Point for Forests. 2020 Data Tells Us Why', World Resources Institute, 31 March 2021.
10 David Gibbs, Nancy Harris, and Frances Seymour, 'By the Numbers: The Value of Tropical Forests in the Climate Change Equation', Global Forest Watch, 5 October 2018.
11 Hannah Ritchie and Max Roser, 'Palm Oil, Our World in Data', June 2021.
12 Palm-oil market in 2021, M. P. Evans Group, retrieved 22 July 2022.
13 Chart 1: Redrawn from Hannah Ritchie and Max Roser, 'Palm Oil, Our World in Data', December 2020. Chart 2: Redrawn from Mikaela Weisse and Liz Goldman, 'Primary Rainforest Destruction Increased 12% from 2019 to 2020', Global Forest Watch, 31 March 2021.
14 Economic Well-Being of US Households in 2020, The Federal Reserve Board, May 2021.
15 The unequal impact of COVID-19: A Spotlight on frontline workers, migrants and racial/ethnic minorities, OECD, 17 March 2022.
16 Emily Stewart, 'Why stocks soared while America struggled', Vox, 10 May 2021.
17 Molly Kinder, Katie Bach, and Laura Stateler, 'Profits and the pandemic . . .', Brookings Metro, April 2022.
18 Urban Diabetes: Understanding the challenges and opportunities, Cities Changing Diabetes, January 2016.
19 The Challenge, Cities Changing Diabetes, retrieved 15 August 2022.

20   Vaidehi Shah, 'How do palm oil and paper giants fare on transparency?', Eco-Business, 15 October 2015.

21   Lyndsey Dowell, Anne Rosenbarger and Sarah Lake, 'Palm Oil Mill Data: A Step Towards Transparency', World Resources Institute, 17 December 2015.

22   Moment of Truth, Greenpeace, 19 March 2018.

23   Sime Darby Plantation Launches Crosscheck, Sime Darby Plantation, 23 May 2019.

24   Palm Oil Industry Invests in Radar Monitoring to Detect Deforestation, GIM International, 1 November 2019.

25   New Radar Alerts Monitor Forests Through the Clouds, Global Forest Watch, 2 March 2021.

26   5 facts about food waste and hunger, World Food Programme, 2 June 2020.

27   Tristram Stuart, The Global Food Waste Scandal, TEDSalon, Spring 2012.

28   Food loss and waste 'an ethical outrage', UN chief says on International Day, United Nations, 29 September 2020.

29   Esben Hegnsholt et al., 'Tackling the 1.6-Billion-Ton Food Loss and Waste Crisis', Boston Consulting Group, 20 August 2018.

30   Matthew Syed, Rebel Ideas: The Power of Thinking Differently, John Murray, 2020.

PIVOT: adopt the activist mindset

1   Lilian Gikandi, '10% of all greenhouse gas emissions come from food we throw in the bin', WWF, 21 July 2021.

2   Lucy Parker, Interview with Tesco CEO Dave Lewis, Brunswick Social Value Review, September 2020.

3   Annual Report 2021, Standard Chartered.

4   Standard Chartered Bank Admits to Illegally Processing Transactions in Violation of Iranian Sanctions and Agrees to Pay More than $1 Billion, The United States Department of Justice, 9 April 2019.

5   Standard Chartered Hosts Regional Correspondent Banking Academy in collaboration with the African Development Bank, African Development Bank Group, 11 July 2019.

6   David Fein, 'To Fight the Illegal Wildlife Trade, Disrupt its Business Model', Financial Times, 7 October, 2018.

7   Bill Winters, Our Commitment, Standard Chartered, retrieved 18 July 2017.

8   Lester R. Brown, 'The Rise and Fall of the Global Climate Coalition', Earth Policy Institute, 25 July 2000.

9   Elsa Wenzel, '10 climate NGOs companies should know', GreenBiz, 22 April 2022.

10   Bernard Looney, Reimagining energy, reinventing BP, bp, 12 February 2020.

11   bp and Equinor form strategic partnership to develop offshore wind energy in US, bp, 10 September 2020.

12   bp and Ørsted to create renewable hydrogen partnership in Germany, bp, 10 November 2020.

13   bp acquires majority stake in largest US forest carbon offset developer Finite Carbon, bp, 16 December 2020.

14   Jeff Hogue, We Need To Talk About Conscious Consumption, Levi Strauss & Co., 2 June 2021.

15   Danielle Samaniego, Levi's Wellthread – A Laboratory for Progress, Levi Strauss & Co., 17 March 2021.

16   Kendra Clark, Levi's enlists Jaden Smith & top Gen Z influencers in first global campaign in three years, The Drum, 19 April 2021.

17   Levi's 'Buy Better, Wear Longer', Levi Strauss & Co., 22 April 2021.

18   Elizabeth Segran, 'Levi's wants you to stop buying so many jeans', *Fast Company*, 21 April 2021.

19   Levi Strauss CEO Chip Bergh on sustainability, new demin cycle, CNBC Squawk on the Street, 9 July 2021.

20   Sustainable Development: New goals for a sustainable future, H&M, 2017.

21   Vision and strategy, H&M, retrieved 18 July 2022.

22   The Rana Plaza Accident and its aftermath, International Labour Organization, retrieved 18 July 2022.

23   Meeting between the CEO of H&M Karl-Johan Persson and the prime minister of Bangladesh, H&M, 5 September 2021.

24   What Fashion Brands Should Do with Wages, Copenhagen Fashion Summit 2019, Global Fashion Agenda, 26 May 2019.

25   H&M Group Sustainability Performance Report 201.

26   Responsible purchasing practices, H&M Group, retrieved 15 August 2022.

AMBITION: aim to make a real impact

1   Hannah Bae, 'Bill Gates' 40th anniversary email', CNN Business, 6 April 2015.

2   Adam Morgan, *Eating the Big Fish: How Challenger Brands Can Compete Against Brand Leaders*, Wiley, 1999.

3   Douglas Bell, 'Volvo's Gift to the World, Modern Seatbelts Have Saved Millions of Lives', *Forbes*, 13 August 2019.

4   Volvo, A Million More, retrieved 18 July 2022.

5   Coca-Cola Surpasses 5by20 Women's Economic Empowerment Goal, The Coca-Cola Co., 8 March 2021.

6   Edward Bickham, 'The Conflict-Free Standard: Building an Industry Coalition to address the challenges of conflict gold', Doughty School for Corporate Responsibility, Cranfield School of Management, and the CSR Initiative at the Harvard Kennedy School, November 2017.

7   Progress Report 2021, Science Based Targets Initiative, June 2022.

8   Brad Smith, President and Vice Chair Microsoft, Microsoft will be carbon negative by 2030, Microsoft, 16 January 2020.

9   Diana Bass, Inside Microsoft's Mission to go Carbon Negative, Bloomberg, 4 June 2020.

10 Brad Smith, President and Vice Chair, Microsoft launches initiative to help 25 million people worldwide acquire the digital skills they need in a COVID-19 economy, Microsoft, 30 June 2020.

11 TEALS Program, Microsoft, retrieved 18 July 2022.

12 What is the TEALS Program, Microsoft, retrieved 18 July 2022.

13 A Letter from Satya Nadella: 2020 Microsoft Corporate Social Responsibility Report, Microsoft, 2020.

14 Peter Horst, 'Brand Leaders: Here's How to Avoid the Purpose Trap', *Forbes*, 26 June 2017.

15 About us, Mastercard, retrieved 30 September 2022.

16 Leaders On Purpose, The CEO Study 2018.

17 Mastercard Commits to Connect 1 Billion People to the Digital Economy by 2025, Mastercard Center for Inclusive Growth, 28 April 2020.

18 Anand Giridharadas, *Winners Take All: The Elite Charade of Changing the World*, Penguin Books, 2019.

19 One Million Black Women, Goldman Sachs, 12 January 2022.

20 Unilever Sustainable Living Plan, Unilever, 2010.

21 How are we doing against our Sustainable Living Plan targets?, Unilever, 10 May 2018.

DISRUPTION: do something different

1   Apple Environmental Responsibility Report, Apple, 2019.

2   Walter Isaacson, *Steve Jobs*, Simon & Schuster, 2011.

3   Lisa Jackson, Apple Insider, retrieved 8 August 2022.

4   Augusta Pownall, 'Apple designs "greenest Mac ever"', Dezeen, 21 October 2018.

5   Stephen Cousins, 'The 75 per cent problem: aluminium's carbon footprint', RICS, 17 August 2021.

6   Apple Environmental Responsibility Report, Apple, 2019.

7   Ibid.

8   Augusta Pownall, 'Apple designs "greenest Mac ever"', Dezeen, 21 October 2018.

9   Apple Environmental Responsibility Report, Apple, 2019.

10   Apple paves the way for breakthrough carbon-free aluminium smelting method, Apple, 10 May 2018.

11   Apple Environmental Responsibility Report, Apple, 2019.

12   Rio Tinto and Alcoa announce world's first carbon-free aluminum smelting process, Rio Tinto, 10 May 2018.

13   Stephen Nellis, 'Apple buys first-ever carbon-free aluminum from Alcoa-Rio Tinto venture', Reuters, 5 December 2019.

14   Apple Environmental Responsibility Report, Apple, 2019.

15   Clayton M. Christensen, Michael E. Raynor and Rory McDonald 'What Is Disruptive Innovation?', December 2015.

16   Disruptive technology/innovation, *The Economist*, 11 May 2009 (updated 3 September 2009).

17   Clayton M. Christensen, *The Innovator's Dilemma*, Harvard Business Review, 1997.

18   Toward a Circular Economy, Philips CEO Frans van Houten, McKinsey Sustainability, 1 February 2014.

19   Ibid.

20   Philips increases Green Revenues . . ., Philips, 20 February 2017.

21   Philips Warehouse Managed Services, Philips, retrieved 18 July 2022.

22   Lauren Phipps, How Philips Became a Pioneer of Circularity-as-a-Service, GreenBiz, 22 August 2018.

23   Toward a Circular Economy, Philips CEO Frans van Houten, McKinsey Sustainability, 1 February 2014.

24   About Us, Philips, retrieved 18 July 2022.

25   Toward a Circular Economy, Philips CEO Frans van Houten, McKinsey Sustainability, 1 February 2014.

26   Nicole Lotz, Necessity is the Mother of Invention, Design Comment, Open University, 26 October 2020.

27   Bernard Looney, Purpose, collaboration and imagination, LinkedIn blog, 3 April 2020.

28   BSR Conference 2014, Maersk CEO Nils Andersen, November 2014.

29   New Maersk Triple-E ships world's largest and most efficient . . ., Green Car Congress, 21 February 2011.

30 'The Triple-E Maersk container ship will be the world's largest ship and the most efficient', New Atlas, 12 February 2011.

31 Eoghan Macguire, 'Maersk "Triple E": Introducing the World's Biggest Ship', CNN, 26 June 2013.

32 Infographic: Maersk Triple-E Class, AP Moeller-Maersk.

33 BSR Conference 2014, Maersk CEO Nils Andersen, November 2014.

34 Maersk Cradle to Cradle Passport, Maersk, 21 February 2011.

35 Using Product Passports to improve the recovery and reuse of shipping steel: Maersk Line, Ellen MacArthur Foundation.

36 Ibid.

37 About the SRTI, Ship Recycling Transparency Initiative, retrieved 19 July 2022.

38 Frédéric Simon, Maersk eyes 'leap frog' to carbon neutral fuels in shipping, Euractiv, 29 June 2021.

39 A. P. Moller-Maersk accelerates fleet decarbonisation . . ., Maersk, 24 August 2021.

CORE: take action in the business

1 'Shifting the System', Summit 2021, interview with James Quincey and Mariana Mazzucato, Ellen MacArthur Foundation, 10 June 2021.

2 Jena McGregor, 'With protests, silence is "not an option" for Corporate America', Washington Post, 1 June 2020.

3 Anthony Applewhaite, Certifiably Equitable, Brunswick Social Value Review, 17 February 2021.

4 About, MTN Group, retrieved 19 July 2022.

5 Metromile, retrieved 19 July 2022.

6 By Miles, retrieved 19 July 2022.

7 Would You Drive Less If You Paid for Insurance by the Mile?, Metromile and Jackson Institute for Global Affairs, 19 August 2015.

8 Erik Kirschbaum, 'German car makers who once laughed off Elon Musk are now starting to worry', Los Angeles Times, 19 April 2016.

9 Bob Woods, 'GM, Ford are all-in on EVs . . .', CNBC, 13 June 2021.

10 Maita Schade, The Bottom Line of Electric Cars, Agora Verkehrswende, March 2022.

11 Statement by BYD President: Stella Li, BYD, 24 May 2018.

12 Water Saving Toilets, The Green Age, retrieved 19 July 2022.

13 Laurie Clarke, 'The climate crisis is forcing us to drastically rethink our toilets', Wired, 23 November 2019.

14 Jed Alegado, 'Coca-Cola, PepsiCo, and Nestlé found to be worst

plastic polluters worldwide in global cleanups and brand audits',
Break Free From Plastic, 9 October 2018.

15 Beat Plastic Pollution, UN Environment, retrieved 19 July 2022.

16 The Great Pacific Garbage Patch, The Ocean Clean Up, retrieved
August 2022.

17 World Without Waste Report, Coca-Cola, January 2018.

18 World Without Waste Report, Coca-Cola, January 2019.

19 World Without Waste Report, Coca-Cola, January 2020.

20 Ibid.

21 Introducing a world first: a Coca-Cola bottle made with plastic
from the sea, The Coca-Cola Co., 3 October 2019.

22 Coca-Cola collaborates with tech partners to create bottle prototype
made from 100% plant based sources, The Coca-Cola Co., 21
October 2021.

23 World Without Waste Report, The Coca-Cola Co., January 2019.

24 FutureSmart Mining, Anglo America, retrieved 19 July 2022.

25 At Nike, CR = Sustainable Business + Innovation, Nike, 1 June 2009.

26 Sustainable Business Performance Summary FY10/11, Nike.

27 Carly Fink, 'Nike: Sustainability and Innovation through Flyknit
Technology', NYU Stern Center for Sustainable Business, August
2016.

28 Tim Spears, 'NIKE flyknit technology patent once again legally
challenged by adidas', designboom, 1 December 2017.

29 Space Hippie: These Nike Sneakers are Trash, Nike, 5 February 2020.

30 Hannah Jones, interview with Joel Makower, 'Embedding sustainability into design', GreenBiz, 15 October 2011.

31 'Shifting the System', Summit 2021, interview with James Quincey
and Mariana Mazzucato, Ellen MacArthur Foundation, 10 June 2021.

32 Race To Zero Campaign, United Nations Climate Change, retrieved
19 July 2020.

33 Greta Thunberg, Twitter post, 25 April 2021.

34 About Climate Action 100+, Climate Action 100+, retrieved 19 July
2022.

35 Climate Action 100+ Net Zero Company Benchmark . . ., Climate
Action 100+, 30 March 2022.

36 Andrew Edgecliffe-Johnson, 'Climate plans of big companies need
substance', Financial Times, 14 March 2021.

37 Jennifer Morgan, 'Why carbon offsetting doesn't cut it', World
Economic Forum, 22 September 2021.

38 'Tightening the Net: Net Zero Climate Targets and the implications
for land and food equity', Oxfam International, August 2021.

39 Larry Fink, The Power of Capitalism, Annual Letter to CEOs, BlackRock Inc., 2022.
40 Playing Offense to Create Value in the Net-Zero Transition, McKinsey Sustainability, 13 April 2022.
41 Case Study – Kellogg, Science Based Targets, retrieved 19 July 2022.
42 Case Study – Thalys, Science Based Targets, retrieved 19 July 2022.
43 Case Study – Sony, Science Based Targets, retrieved 19 July 2022.
44 What is 'nature positive' and why is it the key to our future?, World Economic Forum, 23 June 2021.
45 Bill Gates, *How to Avoid a Climate Disaster*, Penguin Random House, 2021

SYSTEM: drive for systemwide change

1 Christopher L. Avery, 'Business and Human Rights at a time of Change', Amnesty International, November 1999.
2 John H. Cushman Jr, 'Nike Pledges to End Child Labor and Apply US Rules Abroad', *New York Times*, 13 May 1998.
3 Lauren Debter, 'The World's Largest Retailers 2022', *Forbes*, 12 May 2022.
4 Walmart's Efforts Toward Sourcing Seafood, Walmart Sustainability Hub, 8 June 2020.
5 Waste: circular economy, Walmart, 28 June 2022.
6 Madeline Farber, 'This is Walmart's Plan To Do More Business with Female Entrepreneurs', *Fortune*, 30 March 2017.
7 Project Gigaton, Walmart Sustainability Hub, retrieved 19 July 2022.
8 Biodiversity loss brings ecological systems closer to a tipping point, UN News, 22 May 2010.
9 Farming With Biodiversity, WWF, 2021.
10 Walmart Produce Sustainability Summit, Walmart, 13 April 2021.
11 'Loss of biodiversity poses as great a risk to humanity as climate change', *The Economist*, 15 June 2021.
12 Walmart Produce Sustainability Summit, Walmart, 13 April 2021.
13 Ibid.
14 Our History, Brambles, retrieved 18 July 2022.
15 Ibid.
16 Less resources, more value, together, Brambles CEO Graham Chipchase, Brambles, retrieved 18 July 2022.
17 Our 2025 sustainability vision is to Pioneer Regenerative Supply Chains, Brambles, retrieved 18 July 2022.

18   Letter from the Chair & CEO: Towards a Regenerative Supply Chain, Brambles, 2021.

19   Brambles takes the top spot as the most sustainable company globally, Brambles, 11 March 2020.

20   Extended Producer Responsibility, OECD, retrieved 19 July 2022.

21   Sustainability report 2021, Tetra Pak, 2021.

22   Alag Karo, Source segregation of waste, Tetra Pak, 16 August 2021.

23   Jacqueline Decon, 'Tetra Pak and Eco Friendly Thai in recycling drive', ScandAsia, 12 July 2022.

24   4 Partnerships Advance Carton Recycling, Tetra Pak, retrieved 19 July 2022.

25   Tetra Pak and Stora Enso join forces to triple recycling capacity of beverage cartons in Poland, Tetra Pak, 21 July 2021.

26   A second life for carton packages, Tetra Pak, retrieved 19 July 2022.

27   Voices of Innovation: A History of Innovation, Tetra Pak, 25 January 2021.

28   Emilie Filou, 'How green are tetrapak food cartons?', *The Ecologist*, 19 January 2010.

29   Polymers, Tetra Pak, retrieved 19 July 2022.

30   Voices of Innovation: A History of Innovation, Tetra Pak, 25 January 2021.

31   Sustainability report 2021, Tetra Pak, 2021.

32   Clean Skies for Tomorrow: Sustainable Aviation Fuels as a Pathway to Net-Zero Aviation, World Economic Forum & McKinsey & Company, November 2020.

33   Ibid.

34   Charitable Giving Statistics, National Philanthropic Trust, 2021 – retrieved 15 August 2022.

35   'Rs. 1 trillion Spent on CSR in Seven Years by India Inc', CSR Journal, 10 March 2022.

36   Sue Kelsey, EVP Global Prepaid and Financial Inclusion, When invisibility isn't a super power, Mastercard, 28 April 2020.

37   One billion and beyond, Mastercard, retrieved 13 August 2022.

38   Mastercard Impact Fund, Mastercard Center for Inclusive Growth, retrieved 15 August 2022.

39   Empowering small businesses for a digital future, Mastercard Center for Financial Inclusive Growth, September 2021.

40   Mastercard Strive Community awards $1m to digital and data-first projects to strengthen small businesses, Mastercard, 14 July 2022.

41   Helping women entrepreneurs survive and thrive in the digital economy, Mastercard Center for Inclusive Growth, 14 October 2020.

42   Mastercard and Rockefeller Announce Data.org, Mastercard Center for Inclusive Growth, 22 January 2022.

43   Making Cash Ancient History in Egypt, Mastercard News, 27 September 2016.

44   Shamina Singh, Founder and President, Mastercard Center for Inclusive Growth, retrieved 13 August 2022.

45   The 7 Traits of Advancing Cities: Engage Anchor Institutions, JPMorgan Chase, retrieved 15 August 2022.

46   Investing in Opportunity, Detroit, JPMorgan Chase Corporate Responsibility Report, 2018.

47   Joseph L. Bower and Michael Norris, JPMorgan Chase: Invested in Detroit (A), Harvard Business School, March 2018.

48   Ibid.

49   The 7 Traits of Advancing Cities, JPMorgan Chase, retrieved 15 August 2022.

50   Investing in Opportunity: Chicago, JPMorgan Chase, 2018.

51   Investing in Teams Saving our Home Planet, Tin shed Ventures retrieved 13 August 2022.

52   Ryan Macpherson, Claudine Emeott, Ken Gustavsen, and Moses Choi, Corporate Impact Investing in Innovation, The Stanford Social Innovation Review, 24 February 2021.

ADVOCACY: find your voice on the issue

1   Camilla Hodgson, 'Manufacturers lobby to weaken UN global plastics treaty proposal', *Financial Times*, 25 February 2022.

2   Natasha Lomas, Report reveals Big Tech's last minute lobbying to weaken EU rules, TechCrunch, 22 April 2022.

3   Kenny Torrella, 'The difference you make when you eat less meat', Vox, 22 April 2022.

4   Lobbying 'Blind Spot' Undermining Progress on Climate, Influence Map, 14 April 2021.

5   'Søren Skou Calls on IMO to Set 'End Date for Fossil-Fueled Shipping', The Maritime Executive, 10 September 2021.

6   Brad Smith, President and Vice Chair Microsoft, Microsoft will be carbon negative by 2030, 16 January 2020.

7   Bernard Looney, CEO bp, Reimagining Energy, Embracing Opportunity, IP Week, 27 February 2020.

8   CEO Alliance pledges support to EU net-zero goal, Renews.Biz, 2 October 2020.

9 Using our Voice for a Zero Carbon Future, Unilever, retrieved 13 August 2022.

10 Pepsi Announces Bold New Climate Ambition, PepsiCo, 14 January 2021.

11 Amanda Blanc, Net Zero by 2040: A message from our Group CEO, Aviva, 1 March 2021.

12 Our Coalition Partners, Open For Business, retrieved 13 August 2022.

13 Gender Equality: #WeSeeEqual, Procter & Gamble, retrieved 13 August 2022.

14 UN Women and Procter & Gamble announce newest commitment to gender equality across the Indian subcontinent, Middle East and Africa region at the #WeSeeEqual Summit, UN Women Arab States, 19 February 2019.

15 Gender Equality #WeSeeEqual, Procter & Gamble, retrieved 13 August 2022.

16 UN Women and Procter & Gamble announce newest commitment to gender equality across the Indian subcontinent, Middle East and Africa region at the #WeSeeEqual Summit, UN Women Arab States, 19 February 2019.

17 Act 2 Unstereotype makes end-to-end inclusive marketing a priority, Unilever, 15 June 2021.

18 Behind the selfie: reversing the damage of digital distortion, Unilever, 21 April 2021.

19 Marc Gunther, 'Free Processors: will the Industry Follow Suit?', *Guardian*, 13 January 2014.

20 Intel's Efforts to Achieve a 'Conflict Free Supply Chain', Intel, May 2014.

21 How Intel is working with YouTubers to 'unbox' their use of conflict-free resources for processors, Natan Edelsburg, The Drum, 1 August 2016.

22 Alexander C. Kaufman, 'How Intel Eliminated War from Its Supply Chain', Huffington Post, 21 January 2016.

23 Sandra Laville, 'Coca-Cola Admits it Produces 3m tonnes of plastic waste a year', *Guardian*, 14 March 2019.

24 Lorna Thorpe, 'Tesco sparked debate on food waste', *Guardian*, 15 May 2014.

25 Dave Lewis, CEO Tesco, 'Publishing food waste data can sting – but we must all do so', The Grocer, 27 September 2018.

26 UK named 'exemplar' as Food Waste Reduction Roadmap Membership passes 210, Wrap, September 2020.

27 Nike Materials Sustainability Index, July 2012.
28 Leslie Kaufman, 'Google Wants to Save the Planet With Satellite Images', Bloomberg, 11 November 2021.
29 Ibid.
30 Racial Gaps in Financial Outcomes: Big Data Evidence, JPMorgan Chase & Co. Institute, April 2020.
31 JPMorgan Chase Expands Second Chance Hiring Efforts in Columbus, JPMorgan Chase, 26 April 2020.
32 Matthew Heimer, 'Why JPMorgan Chase Wants to Give More Former Criminal a Second Chance', Fortune, 21 October 2019.
33 Giving people with Criminal Backgrounds a Second Chance, JPMorgan Chase & Co. PolicyCenter, retrieved 15 August 2022.
34 Urban Diabetes: Understanding the Challenges and Opportunities, Cities Changing Diabetes, January 2016.
35 How dirty is your data? A look at the energy choices the power cloud computing, Greenpeace, April 2011.
36 Kumi Naidoo, Apples New Green Manifesto: Renewable Energy is Ready to Become Mainstream, Greenpeace, 29 April 2014.
37 Steven Levy, 'Apple Aims to Shrink its Carbon Footprint With New Data Centers', Wired, 21 April 2014.
38 Olam CEO and Co-Founder speaks at UN on Achieving the SDGs, 25 April 2016.
39 AtSource, Olam International, retrieved September 2022.
40 Cocoa Compass, Olam International, 24 October 2019.
41 Christine Tan, moderating panel with Sunny Verghese, Co-Founder and CEO of Olam ..., CNBC, 12 April 2019.

MOMENTUM: get going, keep going

1 Matthew Harper, 'Kicking the Habit: CVS to stop selling tobacco', Forbes, 5 February 2014.
2 Jennifer M. Polinski et al, 'Impact of CVS Pharmacy's Discontinuance of Tobacco Sales on Cigarette Purchasing (2012–2014), American Public Health Association, April 2017.
3 Bernard Looney, CEO bp, LinkedIn, retrieved 15 August 2022.
4 BP releases trade association report, bp, 26 February 2020.
5 LEGO Group to Invest 1 billion DKK boosting search for sustainable materials, LEGO, 16 June 2015.
6 LEGO Group to invest up to US$400 million over three years to accelerate sustainability efforts, LEGO, 15 September 2020.

7   The LEGO Group reveals first prototype LEGO brick made from recycled plastic, LEGO, 23 June 2021.

8   Oscar Schwartz, 'Could Microsoft's climate crisis "moonshot" plan really work?' *Guardian*, 23 April 2020.

9   It Takes Two – Attitude Gap Behavior Report, Zalondo, 2021.

10   Heather Clancy, 'PepsiCo CSO on embedding sustainability into 'day to day business', GreenBiz, 1 February 2021.

11   LEGO Group reveals the first prototype LEGO brick made from recycled plastic, 23 June 2021, retrieved 20 August 2022.

12   Brad Smith, President and Vice Chair Microsoft, Microsoft will be carbon negative by 2030, 16 January 2020.

13   Brad Smith, President and Vice Chair Microsoft, One year later: The path to carbon negative – a progress report on our climate 'moonshot', 28 January 2021.

14   The Building Blocks for Net Zero Transformation: A practical guide to embedding net zero aspirations and actions across your business, Microsoft and PWC, September 2020.

15   Brad Smith, President and Vice Chair Microsoft, One year later: The path to carbon negative – a progress report on our climate 'moonshot', 28 January 2021.

16   Ibid.

17   Richard Wachman, 'The business of fighting Aids', *Guardian*, 3 November 2011.

18   HIV is everybody's business, UNAIDS and Anglo American, 15 November 2016.

19   Anglo American HIV/AIDS employee testing programme reaches highest ever participation rate of 90%, Anglo American, 3 December 2012.

20   Anglo American maintains HIV/AIDs leadership with commitment to extend treatment to dependants of employees, Anglo American, 1 December 2008.

21   Anglo American's coal division in South Africa wins global business coalition award for top international workplace HIV and AIDS programme, Anglo American, 23 June 2009.

22   Two Major Anti-AIDS Initiatives Launched at WEF Davis to Eradicate New HIV Infection in Children in Four Years, Cision PR Newswire, 27 January 2012.

23   Working in partnership to achieve an AIDs-free generation, Anglo American, 1 December 2014.

24   Globe and Mail Examines Mining Company's HIV/AIDS Management Program, KHN Morning Briefing, 11 June 2009.

25 World AIDS Day 2020: Global Solidarity, Shared Responsibility, Anglo American 1 December 2020.

26 The fight against HIV/AIDS is everyone's business, Anglo American, 10 June 2021.

27 Veebs Sabharwal, 'Unilever becomes 2000th accredited living wage employee', Retail Gazette, 2 November 2015.

28 New National Minimum Wage offenders named and shamed, Department for Business, Innovation and Skills, UK Government, 5 February 2016.

29 Our Mission, Resolution Foundation, retrieved 15 August 2022.

30 Unilever: accredited as global living wage employer in 2022, Fair Wage Network, retrieved 15 August 2022.

31 Unilever commits to help build a more inclusive society, Unilever, 21 January 2021.

32 Alan Jope, CEO Unilever, We're ensuring that every worker in our supply chain earns a living wage and this is why, World Economic Forum, 21 January 2021.

33 Christopher Walker, 'The global Living Wage – Unilever's master-class for ESG professionals', Christopher Walker, Responsible Investor, 5 February 2021.

34 Business Roundtable Redefines the Purpose of a Corporation to Promote 'An Economy That Serves All Americans', Business Roundtable, 19 August 2019.

35 Alan Jope, CEO Unilever, We're ensuring that every worker in our supply chain earns a living wage. This is why, World Economic Forum, 21 January 2021.

36 What to make of Unilever's commitment to living wage and diversity in its supply chain, Oliver Morrison, Food Navigator, 21 January 2021.

37 Hanna Ziady, 'Owner of Ben and Jerry's: We'll ensure every worker in our supply chain gets a living wage, CNN Business, 21 January 2021.

38 Jessica Lyons Hardcastle, 'Pepsi Beats Safe Water Access Goal, Doubles Commitment', Environmental Leader, 29 March 2013.

39 PepsiCo achieves safe water access goal to reach 25 million people five years early, PepsiCo India, 15 June 2020.

40 PepsiCo plans to invest US$5.4 million in Latin America over the next three years in access to clean water and resupply to help communities during the pandemic, BNAmericas, 22 March 2021.

41 The PepsiCo Foundation announces R6m investment to bring water access and sanitation projects to South Africa, PepsiCo, 25 November 2020.

42   PepsiCo Announces 'Net Water Positive' Commitment, PepsiCo, 17
     August 2021.
43   PepsiCo's innovative Net Water Positive projects, PepsiCo, 22 March
     2022.
44   Striving for Positive Water Impact, PepsiCo and The Nature
     Conservancy, 2011.

The Activist's Guide to the Conversation
about the Role of Business in Society

1   Chart 1: Redrawn from Janet Du Chenne, 'ESG investing: roots to
     return', Deutsche Bank, 26 November 2020
     Chart 2: Redrawn from Enhance our global footprint, Annual
     Report, PRI, 2021.
     Chart 3: Redrawn from 'Major-Supported E&S Resolutions, The
     2021 Proxy Voting Season in 7 charts', *Morning Star*, 5 August
     2021.
     Chart 4: Redrawn from Cumulative number of policy interventions
     worldwide per year, Regulation database update . . ., PRI Blog, 17
     March 2021.
     Chart 5: Redrawn from Searches for 'ESG' globally, Outlook 2022:
     Sustainable investment, Schroders, 11 January 2022.
     Chart 6: Redrawn from Google searches for sustainable products in
     the 'shopping' category, An Eco-wakening . . ., The Economist
     Intelligence Unit, 2021.
     Chart 7: Redrawn from Peter Willets et al., Number of NGOs in
     Consultative Status with the UN Economic and Social Council for
     each Year from 1945, The Conscience of the World, 1 January 1996.
     Chart 8: Redrawn from Google Searches for 'Cancel Culture' and
     'Woke,' 2016–21, The Politics of the Culture Wars in Contemporary
     America, Manhattan Institute, 25 January 2022.

The New Realities of ESG

1   Bloomberg Intelligence, February 23 2021.
2   UN Principles for Responsible Investment, retrieved September 2022.
3   UN Principles for Responsible Investment, Blog post, Lorenzo
     Saa, Chief Signatory Relations Officer, June 14 2021.
4   Commissioner Allison Herren Lee, 'A Climate for Change: Meeting
     Investor Demand for Climate and ESG Information at the SEC', US
     Securities and Exchange Commission, 15 March 2021.

5   Larry Fink, A Sense of Purpose, based on Annual Letter to CEOs 2018, Harvard Law School Forum on Corporate Governance, 17 January 2018.

6   Mark Hall, 'The greatest wealth transfer in history', *Forbes*, 11 November 2019.

7   Cheryl Arcibal, 'Wealthy Asians likely to bequeath US$2.54 trillion to their heirs by 2030', *South China Morning Post*, 1 December 2021.

8   Capgemini Research Institute, World Wealth Report 2020.

9   Sustainable Signals, Institute for Sustainable Investing, Morgan Stanley, September 12 2019.

10 Swipe to Invest: the story behind millennials and ESG investing, MSCI, March 2020.

11 ESG and Its Alphabet Soup of Acronyms, ESG Foundation, January 27 2022.

12 Hester M. Peirce, Commissioner US Securities and Exchange Commission, Statement on Environment, Social and Governance Disclosures for Investment Advisors and Investment Companies, 25 May 2022.

13 Andrew Edgecliffe-Johnson, 'Business can stop the ESG backlash by proving it's making a difference', *Financial Times*, 23 August 2021.

14 IFRS, Path to Global Baseline – ISSB outlines actions required to deliver global baseline of sustainability disclosures, May 18 2022.

15 The Rise of Intangibles in an Increasingly Complex Business Environment, Ipsos in Reuters, 2 September 2019.

16 Robert Eccles, video interview with Tariq Qureishy, A Tesla in Finance, MAD Talks, 5 February 2017.

17 Michael O'Dwyer and Andrew Edgecliffe-Johnson, 'Big Four Accounting Firms Rush to Join the ESG Bandwagon, *Financial Times*, 30 August 2021.

18 Gillian Tett, 'The new front for green revolution rests on warrior accountants', *Financial Times*, December 4 2018.

19 Celia Huber, McKinsey, Our Insights, 'Ron O'Hanley of State Street on corporate resilience and ESG', McKinsey, July 13 2021.

20 Larry Fink, The Power of Capitalism, Annual Letter to CEOs 2022, BlackRock Inc., 2022.

21 Larry Fink, The Power of Capitalism, Annual Letter to CEOs 2022, BlackRock Inc., 2022.

22 Tariq Fancy, 'The Secret Diary of a 'Sustainable Investor' – Part 3', August 20 2021.

23 Budha Bhattacharya and Kin Yu, 'Putting Big Data at the Heart of ESG', Pulse of Fintech H1 21, KPMG, retrieved 20 August 2022.

24 How impact seeks to enhance the risk-return equation, BlackRock, Fundamental Equities, August 9 2021.
25 Moody's, ESG Solutions, retrieved September 2022.
26 EU Commission Corporate Sustainability Reporting Directive Proposal, Questions and Answers, April 21 2021.

The Power and Problem of Purpose

1   Aaron Hurst et al., 2016 Global Report Purpose at Work, LinkedIn, 2016.
2   Rachel Barton et al., Affinity and beyond: from me to we, the rise of the purpose-led brand, Accenture, 2018.
3   Larry Fink, Profit and Purpose, Annual Letter to CEOs 2019, BlackRock Inc., 2019.
4   Indra Nooyi and Ajay Banga, Perspectives, Brunswick Review, 15 March 2022.
5   Grant Freeland, 'Indra Nooyi's Passions: People, Performance & Purpose', Forbes, 24 February 2020.
6   Indra Nooyi, Leading with Purpose: Changing the Way We Make Money to Change the World, LinkedIn, 11 July 2028.
7   Indra Nooyi and Ajay Banga, Perspectives, Brunswick Review, 15 March 2022.
8   Larry Fink, Profit and Purpose, Annual Letter to CEOs 2019, BlackRock Inc., 2019.
9   Mark Carney, Value(s): Building a Better World for All, William Collins, 2021.
10 Statement on Corporate Governance, Business Roundtable, September 1997.
11 Business Roundtable Redefines the Purpose of a Corporation to Promote 'An Economy that Serves All Americans', Business Roundtable, 19 August 2019.
12 Lucy Parker, interview with Professor Colin Mayer, 'A Framework for Purposeful Business', Brunswick Social Value Review, 15 March 2022.
13 Simon Sinek, Start With Why, Penguin Books, 2019.
14 Peter Horst, 'Brand Leaders: Here's how to avoid the purpose trap', Forbes, 26 July 2017.
15 Rachel Barnes, 'Is purpose-washing damaging the industry?', Campaign, 12 February 2018.
16 John Browne and Robin Nuttall, 'Beyond corporate social responsibility: Integrated external engagement', McKinsey & Company, 1 March 2013.

17 Lucy Parker, interview with Professor Colin Mayer, 'A Framework for Purposeful Business,' Brunswick Social Value Review, 15 March 2022.

Systems and Circular Transformation

1   John Elkington, Gresham College, retrieved 15 August 2022.
2   John Elkington, *Green Swans*, Fast Company, 2020.
3   Donella H. Meadows, *Thinking in Systems: A Primer*, edited by Diana Wright, Sustainability Institute, Chelsea Green Publishing, 2008.
4   EV100 Projects, Climate Group, retrieved 19 July 2022.
5   Race to Zero Campaign, United Nations Climate Change, retrieved 19 July 2022.
6   Growing Better: 10 Critical Transitions to Transform Food and Land Use, The Food and Land Use Coalition, September 2019.
7   Guido Schmidt-Traub, 'Five lessons for taking your system change global', Systemiq, 4 March 2021.
8   Oliver Balch, 'The disruptors: How Jeremy Oppenheim is leading the charge for systems change', Reuters, 14 November 2018.
9   Sunny Verghese, Building a Better Sustainable Future Together, TEDxTiESG, 2 February 2021.
10 Donella H. Meadows, *Thinking in Systems: A Primer*, edited by Diana Wright, Sustainability Institute, Chelsea Green Publishing, 2008.
11 Circular economy action plan, Environment, European Commission, retrieved 18 August 2022.
12 Alexander Chipman Koty, 'China's Circular Economy, Understanding the New Five Year Plan', China Briefing, 16 July 2021.
13 G7 Berlin Roadmap on resource efficiency and circular economy (2022-2025), G7 Germany 2022.
    Pre-Summit Y20 2022: Circular economy to save the planet, 22 May 2022, G20 Indonesia,– retrieved 18 August 2022.
14 Matt Mace, 'Banking and finance giants issue support for circular economy investment', edie, 10 September 2020.
15 What is a circular economy?, Ellen MacArthur Foundation, retrieved 19 July 2022.
16 A New Circular Economy Action Plan, European Commission, 11 March 2020.
17 Caroline Daniel, Building a Circular Economy, Brunswick Social Value Review, 22 January 2020.
18 The New Plastics Economy, Ellen MacArthur Foundation, 2016.

19   Transforming into a circular business, IKEA, retrieved 19 July 2022.
20   Developing Regenerative Chemistry, Ellen MacArthur Foundation, retrieved 19 July 2022.
21   Bruno Oberle et al., 'Global Resources Outlook 2019: Natural Resources for the Future We Want. . .', United Nations Environment Programme, 2019.
22   Heather Clancy, 'Nestlé digs deeper into regenerative ag, puts $3.6B behind net-zero plan', GreenBiz, 7 December 2020.
23   Professor Christopher Barrett, 'Nestlé's carbon cutting investment to have big impact on food system', Cornell University, 3 December 2020.
24   A journey to becoming 100% circular and climate positive: H&M Group, Ellen MacArthur Foundation, retrieved 19 July 2022.
25   'Why the circular economy is all about retaining value', McKinsey Sustainability, 18 October 2016.
26   Patrick Schroder and Jan Raes, 'Financing an inclusive circular economy', Chatham House, July 2021.
27   Ibid.
28   Global Plastics Outlook, OECD, 22 February 2022.
29   Ibid.
30   Open Data Platform, Global Footprint Network, retrieved 19 July 2022.

A Shared Agenda with Government

1   Thomson Reuters Regulatory Intelligence Feeds.
2   Regulation database, PRI, retrieved 19 July 2022.
3   Nations agree to end plastic pollution, United Nations, retrieved 19 July 2022.
4   Donella Meadows, *Thinking in Systems: A Primer*, edited by Diana Wright, Sustainability Institute, Chelsea Green Publishing, 2008.
5   What is the inevitable policy response?, Principles for Responsible Investment, retrieved 18 August 2022.
6   Emmet Ralph, 'The State of Sugar and Health Taxes in 2021', Kerry Group, 8 February 2021.
7   Jack Blundell, 'Gender pay gap closes by one fifth after reporting introduced', London School of Economics, 26 March 2021.
8   About Us, Sustainable Food Policy Alliance, retrieved 19 August 2022.
9   Mariana Mazzucato, *The Mission Economy: A Moonshot Guide to Changing Capitalism*, Allen Lane, 2021.
10   Apple paves the way for breakthrough carbon-free aluminum smelting method, Apple, 10 May 2018.

11   Charles Redell, 'Pepsi Steps Up Water Commitment with Focus on Chinese Farms', Greenbiz, 19 September 2011.

12   ADB, Olam to support smallholder farmers livelihoods disrupted by Covid-19, Asia Development Bank, 9 December 2020.

13   Kristen Scheyder and Elizabeth Reynoso, City Accelerator Initiative Earns National Recognition for Public-Private Partnership, Citi Blog, 13 July 2021.

14   Our approach, Cities Changing Diabetes, retrieved 18 August 2022.

15   Praveer Sinha, 'The power of Public-Private Partnerships to turn around dysfunctional utilities: The case of Tata Power in Delhi', World Bank Blogs, 10 November 2015.

16   CSR Annual Report 2020 – 2021, TataPower-DDL, 2021.

17   Fred Kaplan, 'The Pentagon's Innovation Experiment', MIT Technology Review, 19 December 2016.

18   Brad Smith, President and Vice Chair Microsoft, Microsoft will be carbon negative by 2030, Microsoft Blog, 16 January 2016.

19   Bill Gates, *How to Avoid a Climate Disaster*, Penguin Random House, 2021.

Politics and the Corporate Voice

1   Ian Bremmer and Cliff Kupchan, 'Risk 9: Corporates losing the culture wars', Eurasia Group, 3 January 2022.

2   Thomas Carothers and Andrew O'Donohue, 'How to understand the Global Spread of Political Polarization', Carnegie Endowment for International Peace, 1 October 2019.

3   Michael Kenny and Davide Luca, 'The urban-rural polarization of political disenchantment', LSE, November 2020.

4   Jessica Chasmar and Kelly Laco, 'DeSantis slams 'woke' Disney after CEO condemns parents' rights bill', Fox News, 10 March 2022.

5   Colin Lodewick, 'The war between Disney and Florida keeps escalating', *Fortune*, 20 April 2022.

6   Rick Clough and Christopher Palmeri, 'Walmart and Disney Join Companies Halting Donations After Riot', Bloomberg, 13 January 2021.

7   Ted Johnson, 'Disney, Marvel to Boycott Georgia if Religious Liberty Bill Is Passed', *Variety*, 23 March 2016.

8   Hannah Miao, 'Georgia voting rights activists pressure big corporations to oppose GOP-backed ballot restrictions', CNBC, 14 March 2021.

9   David Gelles, 'Inside Corporate America's Frantic Response to the Georgia Voting Law', *New York Times*, 5 April 2021.

10 'CEO activism in America is risky business', *The Economist*, 14 April 2021.

11 The economic and business case for LGB&T inclusion, Open for Business, September 2015.

12 Alan Murray and Catherine Whitney, *Tomorrow's Capitalist: My Search for the Soul of Business*, PublicAffairs, 2022.

13 The Hidden Common Ground Initiative, Public Agenda, 11 July 2022.

14 Building an Equal Opportunity Workforce, IBM, retrieved 19 July 2022.

15 Ibid.

16 Corporate Political Responsibility Taskforce, Erb Institute, University of Michigan, 18 February 2021.

17 Judd Legum and Tesnim Zekeria, 'These 25 rainbow flag-waving corporations donated more than $10 million to anti-gay politicians in the last two years', *Popular Information*, 14 June 2021.

18 Sarah Murray, 'When Should Business Take a Stand?', *Financial Times*, 9 March 2022.

19 Sarah Murray, 'When should business take a stand?', *Financial Times*, 9 March 2022.

20 Judith Evans and Harriet Agnew, 'Mayonnaise with "purpose" rebuke shows discontent Unilever is facing', *Financial Times*, 12 January 2022.

21 Harriet Agnew, 'Unilever has "lost the plot" by fixating on sustainability, says Terry Smith', *Financial Times*, 12 January 2022.

22 Judith Evans and Harriet Agnew, 'Mayonnaise with "purpose" rebuke shows discontent Unilever is facing', *Financial Times*, 12 January 2022.

23 Daniel Pryor, 'Disaster corporatism will make use poorer', Adam Smith Institute, 26 January 2022.

The Big Debate about Capitalism

1 Rebecca Henderson, *Reimagining Capitalism*, Penguin Random House, 2020.

2 Klaus Schwab, Davos Manifesto 2020, World Economic Forum, 2 December 2019.

3 Lucy Parker, interview with Marty Lipton, The Long View, Brunswick Social Value Review, 21 December 2020.

4 Ibid.

5 Mark Carney, *Value(s): Building a Better World for All*, William Collins, 2021.

6   Rebecca Henderson, *Reimagining Capitalism*, Penguin Random House, 2020.
7   William Lazonick, *Profits Without Prosperity*, Harvard Business Review, September 2014.
8   Gregory Calderone, 'Debt-Financed Share Buybacks Dwindle to Lowest Level Since 2009', Bloomberg, 27 January 2019.
9   Kate Raworth, *Doughnut Economics: Seven Ways to Think Like a 21st-Century Economist*, Random House Business, 2017.
10 Judy Samuelson, *The Six New Rules of Business: Creating Real Value in a Changing World*, Berrett-Koehler Publishers Inc., 2021.
11 Daniel Pryor, 'Capitalism after covid: the case against disaster corporatism', Adam Smith Institute, 26 January 2022.
12 Celia Huber, 'Ron O'Hanley of State Street on corporate resilience and ESG', McKinsey & Company, 13 July 2021.
13 Mark Carney, *Value(s): Building a Better World for All*, William Collins, 2021.
14 John Kay, 'Shareholders think they own the company – they are wrong', *Financial Times*, 10 November 2015.
15 Mark Carney, *Value(s): Building a Better World for All*, William Collins, 2021.
16 What is fiduciary duty and why is it important?, PRI, 8 September 2015.
17 Ibid.
18 Aronson v. Lewis, 473 A.2d 805, 812 (Delaware 1984).
19 Larry Fink, The Power of Capitalism, Annual Letter to CEOs 2022, BlackRock Inc., 2022.
20 Alan Murray and Catherine Whitney, *Tomorrow's Capitalist: My Search for the Soul of Business*, PublicAffairs, 2022.

What Makes a Leader

1   Professor Malcolm P. McNair, 'On the Importance of Being Tough Minded', Baker Library Special Collections, Harvard Business School, 1952.
2   A happy warrior: Mellody Hobson on mentorship, diversity, and feedback, McKinsey Global Institute, 18 June 2020.
3   Davos 2022: In Conversation with Rishad Premji, CNBC, 25 May 2022.
4   @RishadPremji, Twitter, 23 February 2022.
5   50 years of *Fortune*'s list of America's largest corporations, Fortune 500, retrieved 19 July 2019.
6   Indra Nooyi and Ajay Banga, Perspectives, Brunswick Social Value Review, 15 March 2022.

7   Aaron Lowe, 'Singapore's Olam "to be more activist in tackling global challenges"', *Straits Times*, 2 July 2014.

8   Sunny Verghese, Chairman, Olam International, COP26 – Will it Make a Difference?, 7th Inconvenient Questions International (IQi), World Business Council for Sustainable Development, 24 November 2021.

9   Ilham Kadri, CEO Solvay, Chemistry – can it serve as a catalyst for a green and circular rebound, Euractive Debates, 1 December 2020.

10   Daniel Goleman, *What Makes a Leader?*, Harvard Business Review, January 2004.

11   Michael E. Porter and Mark R. Kramer, *Creating Shared Value*, Harvard Business Review, January–February 2011.

12   Michael C. Jensen, *Value Maximisation and Stakeholder Theory*, Harvard Business School, 24 July 2000.

13   John P. Kotter, *Accelerate!*, Harvard Business Review, November 2012.

14   Nick Craig and Scott A. Snook, *From Purpose to Impact*, Harvard Business Review, May 2014.

15   Nicholas C. Lovegrove and Matthew Thomas, *Triple-Strength Leadership*, Harvard Business Review, September 2013.

16   Ranjay Gulati, *The Messy but Essential Pursuit of Purpose*, Harvard Business Review, March–April 2022.

17   Chris Hughes, 'Aviva's new Boss Has One of the Toughest Jobs in European Finance: Opinion', *Insurance Journal*, 8 July 2020.

18   Katie Scott, 'Amanda Blanc says Aviva needs "to be the leader in our industry again"', *Insurance Times*, 6 July 2020.

19   Aviva Annual Report and Accounts 2021.

20   Aviva becomes the first major insurer worldwide to target Net Zero carbon by 2040, Aviva Newsroom, 1 March 2021.

21   Oliver Ralph, 'Aviva chief warns insurers on "forked tongue" over climate change', *Financial Times*, 1 March 2021.

22   David Gelles, 'The CEO Who Promised There Would Be No Layoffs', *New York Times*, 6 November 2020.

23   Stine Jacobsen and Nilolaj Skydsgaard, 'Novo Nordisk lifts 2022 outlook after strong quarter, shares jump', Reuters, 29 April 2022.

24   Adi Ignatius and Daniel McGinn, 'Novo Nordisk CEO Lars Sørensen on What Propelled Him to the Top', Harvard Business Review, November 2015.

25   Ryan Whittaker, 'Nestlé's €3.58bn plan to halve carbon emissions by 2030 suggest overall industry shift', GlobalData, 3 December 2020.

26   Top 100 Largest Central Bank Rankings by Total Assets, Sovereign Wealth Fund Institute, retrieved 25 July 2022.

27 Ibid.
28 Roger Lowenstein, 'Jamie Dimon: America's Least-Hated Banker', *New York Times Magazine*, 1 December 2010.
29 JPMorgan Chase Commits $30 Million to Support Historically Black Colleges and Universities and Students, JPMorgan Chase, 16 June 2022.
30 Anagha Srikanth, JPMorgan Chase is donating $5 million to these LGBT+ causes, The Hill, 14 January 2021.
31 StartOut Announces Collaboration with JPMorgan Chase to Expand their Economics Insights Work Around LGBTQ+ Communities . . ., Business Wire, 29 June 2021.
32 Jamie Dimon interview, Out & Equal, LGBT Forum, 2017.
33 Václav Havel, *The Power of the Powerless*, October 1978, edited by John Keane and published in English by M. E. Sharp, 1985.

Acknowledgements

As we get ready to publish this book, we've been working together for twelve years. In that time, our subject – the role of business in society – has gone from the margins into the mainstream. This book is only possible thanks to the growing number of people who have played their part in making that happen.

First and foremost are the leaders in business who are working in practice to change the paradigm – those at the top of companies, as well as those deep in the operations. We've been lucky to work with many of them, and we've followed closely the journeys of many others. They are showing that it's possible to shape new ways of doing business, and in this book we share what we've learnt with and from them.

The urgent need for business to do things differently has also drawn the attention of some powerful thinkers – challenging the purpose of the corporation, rethinking the nature of capitalism, and understanding the systemic role of business in the world today. We're hugely grateful for these dialogues, which have enriched and informed much of our own work and this writing. We've especially valued our discussions with Andrew Morlet on creating systems change; with Colin Mayer, who is re-framing the debate on corporate purpose; and with Paul Polman, who has paved the way for so many other leaders.

Distilling such vast and unruly subject matter into a practical read requires the steady guidance of an experienced publishing team, and we've been fortunate to work with the best. Arabella Pike's great clarity set us off with the confidence we needed to get going, and the HarperCollins team have made every step along the way a pleasure, Alex Gingell, Jo Thompson, Martin Brown, Nicola Webb, Niriksha Bharadia, Rebecca Fortuin and Sam Harding.

This is a book about activism, so we want to acknowledge those on the front-line of creating social change. Particularly, the many campaigning organisations who play a critical role in pushing the global crises up the corporate agenda. We've worked with some of them, and we've helped companies engage constructively with the campaigns of others. They are essential agitators, and we appreciate the challenges they bring.

We're enormously grateful to have a professional home with the Brunswick Group, which has enthusiastically championed this work for more than a decade. So many friends and colleagues in the firm have helped to shape this thinking over the years; too many to name them all. We have much to thank the firm's leadership for – Alan Parker, Helen James and Neal Wolin, who have given us a unique platform. There are so many others we've been privileged to work alongside, and we're especially thankful to Agnès Catineau, Benoit Grange, Bill Pendergast, Caroline Daniels, Charis Gresser, Courtney Chiang Dorman, Dan Lambeth, Dan Roberts, Ian Roe, Jayne Rosefield, Laura Buchanan, Maria Figueroa Kupcu, Matt Levine, Nik Deogun, Pru Bennett, Quinn Wikeley, Rob Pinker, Simon Sporborg, Susan Gilchrist, Tim Payne, Tom Burns, Will Carnwath and William Medvei

Finally, and with heartfelt thanks, we want to acknowledge our colleagues in the global Business & Society team – Alex Burnett, Alexandra Worth-Moynihan, Alastair Morton, Anna Middendorf, Anna Richter, Anushah Khan, Brian Potskowski,

Chloe Hawkins, Cressida Curtis, Diana Walker, Ellie Fallon, Elizabeth Thomas, George McFarlane, Giacomo Hurst, Ira Hersh, Jack Stewart, Joseph Doyle, Joseph Roberts, Jordan Bickerton, Justine Harris, Kirsty Good , Liz Dahan, Meaghan Ramsey, Natasha Burroughs, Nora Coghlan, Phil Drew, Raff Marioni, Robert de Jongh, Robin Knight, Ruairidh Macintosh, Sarah Miscampbell, Robert de Jongh, Stacey Chow, Tarini Kumar, Tom McGivan, Wolfgang Blau and Zamzam Osman. Their work is to help businesses rethink the role they play and take meaningful action on the crises facing the world. This book is dedicated to them.

Index